anzacs

anzacs

stories from new zealanders at war

tony williams

Hodder Moa Beckett

Dedication

I dedicate this book to all those who have had the unwanted calamity of war thrust upon them and who went through hell but did their duty.

ISBN 1-86958-809-6

© 2000 Original text – Tony Williams
The moral rights of the authors have been asserted.

© 2000 Design and format – Hodder Moa Beckett Publishers Limited
Published in 2000 by Hodder Moa Beckett Publishers Limited [a member of the Hodder Headline Group]
4 Whetu Place, Mairangi Bay, Auckland, New Zealand

Produced and designed by Hodder Moa Beckett Publishers Ltd
Colour separations by Microdot, Auckland, New Zealand
Printed by Publishing Press, Auckland
All rights reserved. No part of this publication may be reproduced or transmitted in any form or by any means, electronic or mechanical, including photocopying, recording, or any information storage and retrieval system, without permission in writing from the publisher.

Acknowledgements

Thanks to all the people I interviewed for the book who were so generous with their time and their knowledge and who supplied photos from their private collections.

My thanks also to the wives of many for their hospitality in providing tea, often accompanied by other goodies such as biscuits and cakes.

A special thanks to Bob Russell, president of the New Zealand Ex-Prisoners of War Association, who introduced me to many of the people I spoke to. My thanks also to Steve Matheson, Alan Anderson, George Oldfield, Laurie Stack and Baz Nissen for their assistance.

My thanks to Mrs Elaine Turner, wife of John Turner, who arranged permission for me to use the diaries of Bert May and the unpublished war memoirs of Michael Hanan.

A special thanks to Belinda Heaslip, who assisted with this book, transcribing most of the interviews. She also typed and did the initial edit of written material. Her help throughout was invaluable.

My gratitude also to the staff of Hodder Moa Beckett for their advice, assistance and patience, and to Graham Adams, my editor.

All photographs kindly supplied from the family collections of those interviewed for this book. The quotations on page 9 are from *The End in Africa* by Alan Moorehead, published by Hamish Hamilton, and *Winged Dagger: Adventures on Special Service* by Roy Farran, published by Collins.

Contents

Introduction: The Black Beast of War	9
A Man of Courage – Michael Hanan	13
Protected by the Waters of the Nile – Jim Henderson	39
The Vow – Frank Hitchcock	45
You'll Never Know How Lucky You Are – Hansi Keating (née Silberstein)	67
At Death's Door – Murray McColl	77
The Cretan Shepherd – Murray McLagan	93
More Interested in Escaping – Stan Martin	101
War Diary – Bert May	109
Inhumane Treatment Prevailed – Cyril Miles	123
You Do It Because You've Got To – Pat Moncur	131
Mad as Maggots – Ian Newlands	137
The Glamour Boys – Maurice O'Connor	153
He's Alive, He's Alive – Bob Russell	161
Unforgettable Arch – Arch Scott	175
A Man of Integrity – Allan Smith	195
Tears and Laughter – Frank Snelgar	213
Grantie – Irene Stembridge (née Grant)	219
Navy Jack – Jack Tomlinson	225
Bullets among the Buttercups – John Turner	253
The Last Rites – Cecil Wright	259
Got to Be a Kiwi – Frank Gibbison	265
On the Hook – Jack Spiers	273
Grey Ghosts – Baz Nissen	279
A Man with Guts – Hini (Jim) Komene	287
Epilogue: Journey's End	293
Appendix	295

Introduction
The Black Beast of War

"We met the New Zealand Division coming head on towards us, in a way the enemy would see it coming. They rolled by in their tanks, trucks, guns and armoured cars. The finest troops of their kind in the world, the out-flanking experts, the men who had fought the Germans in the desert for two years, the victors of half a dozen pitched battles. If ever you wanted to see the most resilient and practised fighter of the Anglo-Saxon races, this was 'he'."

From the book *The End in Africa* by the distinguished war correspondent Alan Moorehead.

"We passed several New Zealand positions, where the troops stood up and gave us the 'thumbs up' sign with a grin. Just to look at their confident, smiling faces was good for the spirit. They had been beaten out of Greece by overwhelming odds, they were ill-equipped and underfed, but it takes more than that to daunt the finest fighting troops in the world."

From the book *Winged Dagger: Adventures on Special Service* by much-decorated soldier Roy Farran.

Though the preceding quotations are true in a general sense, different individuals have different experiences and perceptions and the stories that follow are very varied, very personal and very real.

This book does not contain a sanitised version of tactics, medals and bravery. There is courage, nobility and humanity on these pages, often humour, but there is also death, blood, sweat, faeces, broken bodies and crushed spirits.

The stories have been edited for the sake of fluency, but they are essentially told in the words of the individuals who lived these moments. Many of them came from taped interviews, but time and time again I was surprised to have crinkled notebooks thrust into my hands. Inside was page after page of handwriting addressed to their families. Some of these private memoirs were typed. One was also bound.

None of them was a mere one-page letter. They ran from thousands to tens of thousands of words. Often they had come about in response to a family member's curiosity about what had happened in the war. As I read them, I found them very personal and intensely moving. The pen had become an instrument by which the writer could purge himself of his worst experiences.

I have censored nothing in this book, but it has been censored by the men themselves. When the savageries they had been forced to commit on "the enemy" became too terrible to mention, the words would dry up and their eyes would look away to the floor with shame and guilt.

Technically, an ANZAC is a soldier who fought in the Australian and New Zealand Army Corps in the First World War and thereafter in joint Australian/New Zealand forces, but the term has been used colloquially to mean any New Zealand soldier in the same way that ANZAC Day has come to commemorate all New Zealand war veterans. I have also included stories in this book from two men who have been New Zealanders for the last half a century but who fought with the Royal Navy during the war and one woman who was born in Germany. Their stories were far too good to leave out.

Introduction

War is essentially man's inhumanity to man. Any war can be averted by the skilful diplomacy of politicians. When they fail, they inevitably pass the buck to generals and when they fail, the buck (which in this case means the bullet and the shell and the shrapnel) gets passed on to the "ordinary blokes".

They are people who until that moment have been living their lives among family and friends. War does not just tear apart bodies and buildings. It also tears apart these relationships. War tears apart everything. But people are resilient and resourceful and, if they survive, they can put everything back together again.

This book mainly contains stories from the Second World War. One of the reasons it was written was because the old soldiers, sailors and airmen are starting to drop away now.

I had the rare privilege of looking into the eyes and listening to the voices of those I interviewed. I hope that in these pages I have been able to convey the intense levels of emotion that often accompanied their words, personal and real, which deserve to be heard. These are their stories....

# A Man of Courage
Michael Hanan

The following extracts are taken from a detailed account Michael Hanan wrote for the benefit of his family. He fought through almost the entire war, finally attaining the rank of lieutenant.

Greece

As Easter 1941 drew near, it was on those wind-swept hills in the north of Greece, amid the fears and the uncertainty of war, in those first few days, we all found our inner selves.

We realised we knew each other better than we knew our own brothers, such was the strength of the "bond of comradeship" that existed between us. We learned that not far below the surface in every man is that animal instinct to kill to survive. We "grew up" in those wind-swept hills, we "grew up" in those first few days.

Even after a few days with the only railway line and the narrow winding roads being blitzed by the German Air Force, causing supply problems, and the collapse of the Greek Army and the Yugoslav Army, it was becoming obvious that the withdrawal of Mackay Force was to take place.

I could write much on that withdrawal from the north of Greece, of that long road back, bombed and strafed by enemy planes that came and went without any opposition. A road that led us back through Sotir, Vevi, Grevena, Kalabaka, Trikkala, Ventikas, the east to Larissa, where we met the main traffic of the retreat. Then on to Pharsala, Lamia, Braillos to Atlandi, where we rejoined the New Zealand Division.

After nearly a month's absence, it was good to be back. We had withdrawn 250 miles. As I think back to that withdrawal and the rearguard positions we held, three incidents are very clear in my mind. The first was at Sotir, where we fought the first rear guard, covering the retreat, and inflicted heavy casualties on the German infantry.

We moved back and dug in on a rise covering the road on our left and a flat open plain in front with a stream winding through the flat ground below us. In support were Australian Infantry and the Rangers [an English battalion] and artillery in the rear.

As evening closed in, Mackay Force moved back along the road. Guns, tanks, and trucks filled with troops streamed back across the bridge beside us. At first, in an endless convoy and as darkness closed in, small batches of trucks carrying troops who had covered the withdrawal up front raced past with a shout of "good luck", as they saw us digging in. Finally, the last truck passed. Engineers blew the bridge and, in the darkness and bitter cold, we settled down to wait for the enemy. Our orders were "to hold until midday the following day".

The position was precarious and isolated. The platoon commander had his headquarters almost half a mile away behind the other section, which meant we would be fighting our own independent battle without any contact with him. Also when the time came to withdraw, it meant moving across a forward slope for half a mile without a vestige of cover, in full view of the enemy and it was my place to be the last man to leave.

The night temperature fell well below zero, with an icy wind blowing off the snow. We were without greatcoats as we would be travelling light, except for our weapons, when we ran the gauntlet in the morning to withdraw. We spent the night trying to keep warm the best way we could. It was too cold to sleep and bully beef and biscuits washed down with water didn't do much to help. Many thoughts go through your mind during that period of waiting.

I was to experience it many times in the years that followed. The thought of what the dawn would bring: "Will I still be alive this time tomorrow?" I felt a little homesick as my thoughts strayed to home and what a lonely place to die in this country, so far away, if die I must. Perhaps a feeling of uncertainty, perhaps a twinge of fear, and yet a feeling of excitement in the gamble you would be taking with your life when you put it on the line, a gamble that could only be experienced in war.

Morning, and at first light, a few hundred yards in front, the enemy infantry, pouring down the road and spreading out on each side. Gone were any doubts, uncertainties, and fears of waiting, and a strange feeling almost of elation as the machine-guns opened up and we were committed to destroying those figures out in front. It was a feeling of hate that had built up with the period of waiting, or perhaps propaganda, or perhaps fear, or revenge.

I gave much thought to the strange feeling of elation as I aimed, squeezed the trigger, and saw the result and deep down felt it was the animal instinct to survive. Those figures with their distinctive uniforms and tin hats were no longer human beings, but something evil that threatened your very existence.

Under increasing enemy pressure, which built up all morning, we held, until at midday we began to withdraw. Luckily, the German tanks and artillery had not appeared in any strength.

The rear guard was a tribute to Bill Hakaria, a great friend and soldier whose friendship and loyalty meant a great deal to me that morning. We were the last guns to withdraw. We covered the infantry and the rest of the platoon, then it was our turn. The enemy began to move in with increased fire as they realised we were pulling out. I sent the section out in ones and twos as we covered them with rifle fire. Bill and I were the last two left in the position. He could have gone earlier but seemed reluctant to move out.

I turned and said, "On your way, Bill. I'll cover you until you are well on the way and be behind you if anything goes wrong."

No one else had stopped to think of the plight of the last man to leave, which was my job as corporal.

So together we began our run across that half-mile of open ground, like a couple of rabbits zigzagging from one side to the other, diving into any small depression when the fire became too accurate, then up and away again. Yet I think we both knew that if either one of us had gone down the other would have dragged him to safety. Finally, we dived down the bank into the old river bed, where the trucks were waiting.

Bill and I clambered aboard and we were off to the next rear guard position, and other positions along that road that would take us back to Athens. But that rear guard at Sotir in the north of Greece, with its little village, its muddy road, its wind-swept hills and the bitter cold and the loneliness would always be imprinted in my memory with thoughts of Bill Hakaria. He was to be killed in action two years later at Alamein. I was with No. 3 Platoon at the time and Dave Taylor, the other section sergeant, brought me the news. I felt not only a great loss but a hatred for the enemy out in front.

The second incident I write of in Greece was the withdrawal over a narrow, tortuous road that wound through the Venetikos Forest and across the Venetikos Mountains. The Greek Army had been caught and obliterated on this road three days earlier by German planes. Trucks, guns, wagons and bodies littered the area. Bomb craters caused detours and trucks blocking the road had to be manhandled into ravines. Our trucks, at times bogged down in the mud and slush, had to be pushed out.

In 24 hours we covered only six miles! It was a scene of desolation and destruction. A once-proud army completely destroyed because of the lack of air cover. We picked up a Greek colonel, who stayed with us for the next few days on my truck. He seldom spoke, seeming dazed and shocked by the fury of the attack and loss of his unit. He looked as if he had been pulled out of a desk job and given a command.

For three days we crawled along, averaging six or seven miles each day. We would have suffered the same fate as the Greek Army, except that heavy rain clouds and thick mist covered the hills, hiding us from the searching enemy aircraft. It was a strange turn of fate and became known as the "Miracle of the Mists", staying above us as we moved at a snail's pace towards the main road.

The other incident I record that shows the odd happenings in war was in the final days of the Greek campaign. The platoon had been dispatched with four Bren carriers, some of 19th Battalion, plus two anti-tank guns, to hold the road open at Megara at all costs, covering the withdrawal.

We took a real pasting as we moved back along the road, bombed and strafed all day. We were either diving into drains or climbing out and going like blazes until the next lot attacked. We were the last truck in the convoy and were racing down the road during a lull in raids, when out of the blue a lone German fighter swept in and attacked. We were caught unawares as he came down the road behind us.

I watched as his machine-guns ripped up pieces of tarseal from the road. I remember bracing myself for the pain that was to come and thinking, in that brief second as I watched, "Was this to be death?" We were sitting ducks, caught in the open with nowhere to go. About six feet from the truck he stopped firing and turned away. I often wondered if he ran out of ammunition, or whether at the last minute he saw those figures crouching on the truck and let us live. Maybe his guns jammed. I will always wonder as one more burst from those eight machine-guns would have destroyed the truck and all on board.

We reached Megara at dark and dug in, covering the road and railway line. The brigade withdrew at 9pm. I think we would have been left there if it had not been for Colonel Kippenberger coming up in his staff car and telling us to tack onto the end of the 4th Brigade at 2am. We passed through a sleeping Athens at 4am, only a few miles ahead of the German spearhead.

We laagered a few miles out of Athens, and destroyed all but one truck, which was to take the machine-guns and ammunition to where we would make our last stand in Greece, the beach at Porto Rafti, about 12 miles away.

Trucks were drained of oil and run until they seized up. Tyres were slashed, radiators holed, etc. Rory Wellington, the other Maori boy in the section and my driver, almost wept as his pride and joy was wrecked. Blankets and any rations were given to the Greeks. Then as a clear day dawned, we moved out in small groups to march those last 12 miles to the beach. It was to be a long 12 miles and a long day.

[The New Zealand Division withdrew to Crete where the battle soon resumed.]

Crete

During the morning we moved to a position between Platanias and the Tavronitis River, not far from the town of Pirgos. We were attached to 5th Brigade. We dug our positions with spades and tools borrowed from the locals, bayonets or whatever we could scrounge. We were quite weather-proof except for heavy rain. Luckily this summer was hot and dry.

The position was on a ridge among the olive trees and vineyards, covering the Maleme Airfield and the beach. Our four machine-guns were the original guns we had carted from Egypt to the north of Greece and back, and had refused to jettison when ordered to by the Embarkation Officer.

The next two weeks we spent in preparation and recreation. I will always remember the beauty of the island, its olive trees and vineyards, its mountain ranges, its little villages with their wine shops and the friendly people but, above all, the deep blue sea that lapped its shores.

Air attacks were a daily occurrence. A Hurricane squadron on the drome took off to do battle against impossible odds and was slowly whittled down. From 13 May, the Maleme area was blitzed daily, at times for hours on end.

They came and went as regularly as a bus service. We were told that a paratroop attack plus a sea invasion was expected about 19 May. We were very short of all equipment, ammunition and rations. Late on the afternoon of 18 May, the last three Hurricanes and a Gladiator took off from the drome, swept low over the area in a final salute, then headed out to sea, bound for Egypt. It seemed to leave a strange feeling of foreboding and loneliness as we watched them go and darkness closed in on the island.

At first light on the morning of 19 May, the bombers and fighters returned and throughout the day kept up a ceaseless bombardment. Smoke and dust hung in a cloud over the whole area.

The paratroop attack didn't come that day, but that night we knew we were being softened up and, as we checked our machine-guns and weapons, we knew that we had entered that final phase before an attack.

At 6am, on 20 May, the bombers and fighters were back and for two hours they tore the area apart. They literally "dug" 45 ack-ack guns off the hill above the drome. It was continuous bombing. As one wave of Stukas pulled out of their dive, another wave began their screaming descent. The fighters were back and forth, raking the area with machine-gun and cannon fire. Again a cloud of smoke and dust darkened the island and the air was heavy with the acrid smell of explosives and destruction.

At 8am, amid the confusion, smoke and noise, there was suddenly an uncanny silence as the bombing stopped and an eerie sound like a great swarm of bees began and out to sea was a sight that was hard to believe. The entire horizon was black with planes, many towing gliders, tier upon tier. It was the biggest mass of aircraft assembled together that I ever saw during the war, or since.

We pulled the belts into the machine-guns and stared as the armada of planes moved steadily towards us. A paratroop attack had never been used in the war and this was on a scale beyond our wildest imagination.

As the planes swept overhead, the sky was suddenly filled with multi-coloured parachutes. There were hundreds in the air at once. For a couple of seconds we stood watching, amazed, then all hell broke loose. This was the moment we had been waiting for. We were committed. The waiting and wondering were over!

They fell on top of us, beside us and in front. At times a few yards in front of the guns. Gliders skidded to a halt only yards away and on the beach in front of us. The volume of fire was such that many died before they landed or when they attempted to leave the gliders, and all the time above us, the planes still spewed out those multi-coloured 'chutes. There seemed to be no end to them.

It was a day of not only fierce, but also vicious fighting. These were chosen troops, fighting for a foothold, which we were just as determined to deny them. Prisoners would be a hindrance to either side. This was survival, "destroy or be destroyed". I think many men were amazed at the bitterness and hate with which they killed that day in Crete.

As darkness came, only a handful of the enemy was still alive in our immediate area. Hundreds of parachutes and bodies littered the ground, or hung grotesquely from the olive trees in their parachutes, or were scattered about beside the gliders that carried them.

That night there was no sleep, even though there were only pockets of resistance left. A burst of fire would start a "miniature war" in return. We put out "listening patrols" in the vineyard below us, to stop any infiltration. It didn't pay to move too far afield in the dark as any noise brought a burst of fire. You were just as likely to be shot by your own troops as by the enemy, as there were some pretty itchy fingers on triggers that night and, in the dark, with no means of communication, nobody was sure who was who.

During the night, we saw the flashes of the naval guns as the Navy destroyed an attempt at a seaborne invasion. Not one single craft got through.

On the morning of 21 May, the bombing and strafing began again at first light with renewed severity and out to sea were dozens of troop carriers. But as the planes neared the island, they turned and flew up a valley hidden behind a hill, about two to three miles away in an undefended area, where they landed without opposition and moved forward as ordinary infantry.

All day the planes ran a shuttle service, dropping fresh troops and equipment without interference, but our machine-guns and mortars still denied them the use of the drome, which was vital to them to bring in heavy equipment. We came under increased machine-gun and mortar fire, in an attempt to dislodge us from the ridge.

That night was a long one without any sleep or rations, as the enemy, reinforced with fresh troops, stepped up the attack, pushing into the hills behind us.

There was no contact with the rear or between units and to make matters worse, we were beginning to run out of ammunition for the Vickers guns. During the day, we again came under heavy mortar and machine-gun fire and two of our own ack-ack guns that had been captured were used to shell the ridge. Our own casualties were beginning to mount and, during the late afternoon, a party going back in search of rations and ammunition failed to return. Yet as darkness came again, we still felt confident, but realised how confused the battle had become with the enemy infiltrating along the hills to our rear.

For a fourth night we went without sleep or rations. We had to wake each other up during the night as when there was a lull you dropped off without realising it. About mid-afternoon, with ammunition for the machine-guns running out and no sign of getting any more, we were pulled back onto the reverse slope of the ridge, which gave us some protection. Being the forward gun, we had quite a distance to go to the cover of the ridge top. We got plenty of "hurry up" as we made our dash uphill, diving and ducking through the olive trees.

I dragged Eric Kay with me, who was shocked and dazed after being shot in the nose. We stayed on the reverse slope with the 21st Battalion throughout the night. We had no sleep and were kept busy during the night as the enemy pushed forward on two sides.

On 24 May, planes began crash landing on the drome and beaches. A state of confusion through lack of any communication from brigade level down began to show in the battle. The front cried out for leadership, decisions and a combined effort together.

Our own platoon commander, for some reason that I could

never understand, split the platoon up, sending half to 21st Battalion and 10 of us to 20th Battalion, and then he took off with friends in the 28th Battalion and was captured. This action was the cause of a number of the platoon being left on Crete. The company commander lacked the leadership to come forward, bind the remains of the company, hold them together, and, above all, lead them.

These two officers, who had previously been almost arrogant with their new-found authority the Army had bestowed on them with men at their beck and call, and who considered themselves in a class above the private soldier, forgot one thing – that when the real test comes it is the common soldiers who sit in judgement of the officers. They are the judge and jury and the judgement those men pass down always stands.

On the 24th and 25th, as the lines became more settled, we were again subjected to heavy bombing and strafing. Again, the air was thick with dust and smoke and the stench of death. An air of doom seemed to be settling over the area.

This was the turning-point in the battle. Many factors caused us to give ground: the bombardment from the air, the lack of communication between units, the lack of ammunition, arms, armour and lack of fresh troops to retake the airfield at Maleme (where the enemy was pouring in fresh troops). But above all, it was that continuous bombing and strafing all day and into the night. It is difficult to fight an enemy on the ground when being pounded from the air.

So with 20th Battalion we drew back to a new position on the hills above Galatas, tired, hungry and with a feeling of sadness and bitterness that we had been forced back – wondering if the day would ever come when we would have air cover to equal that of the enemy. As records showed after the war, the enemy, with the heavy casualties they had suffered, and the fierce resistance they had encountered, were at the same time considering withdrawal and evacuation. But now the battle swung in their favour.

On the evening of the 25th, we were ordered to rejoin the

company. We were heavily bombed as we made our way through a vineyard. A couple of bombs fell among us and I remember, as the dirt and dust cleared, noticing that several grapevines a few inches in front of my head had been sliced off just above ground level.

Five of our 10 men were killed or wounded, some very badly – one with both legs and an arm off. We carried the wounded to a field dressing station, which was a small shed. The doctors and orderlies worked with makeshift lights and equipment trying to cope with the wounded pouring in. It was a pitiful sight to see dozens of badly wounded men lying on stretchers or under olive trees, patiently waiting and hoping they would be next to be treated. All the doctors and orderlies could do was to give an injection to ease the pain. Somebody once wrote, "The wounded don't cry!" How true those words were. We made our wounded as comfortable as possible and moved back to make contact with the company late that night.

On 26 May, we were withdrawn to a position near the wireless station, south-east of Canea. We were caught in the town for several hours, when the enemy planes razed Canea to the ground after they spotted two Bren carriers. We were sheltering under a small bridge when they reduced the town to heaps of rubble. We took up our positions again in the vicinity of the wireless station. There was severe fighting on all sides with heavy machine-gun and mortar fire. The lack of sleep and shortage of rations were beginning to tell, as the enemy, with fresh troops, kept up the pressure, realising we were withdrawing.

The following morning we withdrew with 4th Brigade to a position 12 miles south-east of Suda Bay, where we were bombed and strafed from daylight till dark with a vengeance. I ran into my friend Bill Alley. It was great to see him in one piece.

On the night of the 27th, the remains of the company joined the 20th Battalion, and Colonel Kippenberger, a fine leader and soldier, gave us the news: we were to march through the night across the White Mountains. Anyone who fell out for any reason would be left behind. An evacuation was to be attempted from the small inlet of Sfakia.

It was a cruel test on men, tired after a week of fighting, a week without sleep. The only food was what we picked up here and there. Men were almost at the point of exhaustion, footsore and thirsty, as water was almost non-existent in the hills. The narrow metal road wound and climbed several thousand feet into the mountains.

I will always remember that road, jammed with marching men, walking wounded, men who had lost their units, trucks with the badly wounded, a seething mass. We marched for 10 hours during the night and found ourselves dropping off to sleep standing up when we stopped for short periods.

Just before daylight, we were halted, told to disperse in the scrub each side of the road and wait for orders. Orders that never came! In seconds we were asleep where we sat. Someone woke me to say the company had moved off. It was a strange feeling. The road that had been packed with troops was without a sign of life. How we were left behind is a mystery. Had we moved with the others, we would have been pushed into a transit area at Sfakia and captured.

As the enemy planes were bombing any movement on the road, we moved down the side of the valley where there was some cover. We had only moved a couple of miles when we were almost shot up by the Australian infantry, who were taking up the next rear guard position. I spoke to the officer and at his suggestion decided to stay and give them a hand. Water was rationed by the spoonful and if I dozed off my dreams were always of the water pouring over a dam we had built across the creek at home.

The next day was one of the longest days I remember. The pressure increased, and my only thoughts were of survival. At 9pm, under cover of darkness, we slipped quietly back in small groups and formed up to march those last long miles to the beach. At times, parachute flares hung in the sky above, as the enemy planes searched for a target, but nobody broke ranks.

As the minutes turned into hours, without any sign of the sea, I think many of us wondered if the Navy would be able to wait. There were only a few hours of darkness remaining to allow the ships to get well clear before the enemy planes found them. All of a sudden, the road dropped steeply towards a small stony beach. Navy boys with loud-speakers were shouting orders to "hurry". Then we were running towards the waiting landing craft, boarded and then out to the destroyers waiting in the inlet.

It was almost 3am when we clambered aboard and found a place on deck. I had hardly sat down when the destroyer began moving out to sea. The sailors moved among the clutter of troops with hot cocoa. One of the crew filled my tin hat with the steaming hot liquid and, despite the sweat and grime, it was nectar from the gods. I watched as the silhouette of Crete faded into darkness.

Libya

We moved to Sidi Aziz with a company of infantry to strengthen the perimeter defence around 5th Brigade HQ, as several mobile enemy columns were on the rampage.

We dug in as best we could in the rocky ground, only managing to get down about a foot. Just on dusk, a German column made the mistake of thinking that we were a German position and came straight in towards us.

Strange! That feeling of exultation that I felt as I watched them come closer and closer. No compassion that they were human beings like ourselves, just that overriding urge to destroy them. Hatred or fear? I didn't know. As I watched through glasses the results of my machine-gun fire, I found myself cheering and shouting encouragement.

The 18-pounder beside us joined in, leaving a line of trucks, including a couple of ambulances, burning. The acting colonel of the battalion asked me if I had given the order to open fire. I said I had and he mumbled something about the Geneva Convention and the burning ambulances. He said, "All you are doing, corporal, is antagonising the enemy."

I argued that they shouldn't have been with an armoured column. He apologised the next morning.

As darkness closed in, I walked over to the remains of the half-track that had been towing an 88mm field gun at the head of the column. It was a sight that stayed with me for a long time. The officer and driver still sat in the front. In the rear sat the gun crew of eight or 10 men. They had died without moving when we opened fire. They still sat bolt upright, the burnt and charred skin hanging from their cheekbones. I turned and walked slowly back to the gun line, wondering, "Why man's inhumanity to man?" We were pawns in a life where you destroyed or were destroyed.

Throughout the night, there was a lot of movement and tanks and transport out in front. Nobody was sure who was who. Then, at first light, a salvo of shells crashed into the area, sending everyone diving for cover. Then followed a barrage for several hours which was, I think, the heaviest shelling I was to experience. It literally ploughed the area up. Brigadier Hargest, the 5th Brigade Commander, who was a First World War man, wrote later that "because of the small area shelled, it was heavier than I had experienced in World War One".

Bill Hakaria yelled out to me in the middle of all the confusion, "I think old Perce was right, you made those bastards angry, Hanan."

Out to the right, and almost behind us, sat 40 German tanks. Our anti-tank boys put up a brave effort, supported by two 18-pounders, but they were hopelessly out-gunned and out-ranged by the bigger guns of the enemy's tanks.

No sign of infantry or troops, just 40 dirty big tanks. A nightmare for any ground troops, a dismal sight. I remember thinking as we watched, "Where in the hell are our own tanks we had heard so much about? Where is our bloody Air Force that never shows up? Why haven't we got an anti-tank gun to match his 88mm that was destroying our anti-tank guns without even coming in range? Why didn't our tanks' armament equal the firepower of the enemy? Would we ever learn? Were we too proud to learn from the enemy?"

The private soldier lying in his slit trench being shelled knew the answers. Why not the men at the top? We needed our own tanks, not to have to call on attached armour, which never really seemed under brigade command. We needed the Air Force to drop its high and mighty attitude and to realise it was a close support group to the man on the ground. To take a leaf from the enemy's book and give close support when required.

The irony of the situation out there on the ridge was the very heart of the Africa Corps: Rommel himself with 50 tanks and guns, probably the pick of his Panzers, had raided the Egyptian border and was returning. Their destruction could have brought the campaign to a quick and more satisfactory end and perhaps saved the bitter fighting in future campaigns in the Western Desert.

What a prize! We had been warned they were coming. Why weren't our armoured brigades radioed? We had been told we had 300 more tanks than the enemy did. Why hadn't aerial reconnaissance seen such a large force moving towards the border? An aerial strike could have destroyed it.

We fired for a while then, realising the futility of the situation, watched as the tanks began moving slowly down the ridge, machine-gunning as they came. There was no sign of enemy infantry. The anti-tank guns were quiet, burning or blown to pieces. They had put up a gallant effort. The whole area was a shambles of burning trucks. Men were standing up as the tanks stopped and were ushered to the centre of the area. A couple of tanks had gone straight to Brigade Headquarters, where Hargest surrendered. It was all over. Forty men had died and many were wounded from the small force in that brief action at Sidi Aziz.

The tanks had come in almost from behind us so as German troops began to appear we just had to move to the centre area, where everyone was gathering. One or two of the Germans became very agitated about the soft-nosed ammunition in the Tommy guns and revolvers. They got quite hostile and I had a fair idea what they were getting at but made out I didn't understand.

We moved to where everyone was congregating. It was a sad day but we were glad to be alive. It was to be a hard, long day before it ended. We were told to march to Bardia, almost 26 miles away. Rommel and his tanks moved off, leaving us guarded by motorcyclists with machine-guns mounted on sidecars, plus a few infantry in trucks.

I still had a feeling that the division might return with their light tanks and free us, but it was not to be.

It was a hard march. They kept us moving at a fast pace to get near to their troops in Bardia. Several officers started off carrying sleeping bags but it wasn't long before they were discarded. I felt sorry for the Brigade Headquarters men who hadn't done a great deal of marching.

Nine o'clock that night, we marched into Bardia and once through the minefields and perimeter defences, all hope of being rescued was gone. We were moved into a compound and I was talking to the section and said out aloud, "Hell, I'm dry" when a hand touched my shoulder – a German standing behind me with a machine-gun handed me his water bottle.

I took a swig. It was cold coffee and tasted wonderful. I handed it around the section. It was empty when it came back to me. I handed it back to the German guard. Our eyes met as I said, "Thank you." He nodded and almost gave a faint smile of friendship.

For a few seconds we looked at each other, two men worlds apart, yet I felt a friendship towards that man. I hope he lived, that man who gave us his water bottle that night and I hope I didn't open fire on him in the days that followed with other campaigns. I remember thinking that night as I turned away, what a stupid, stupid, bloody war.

[In captivity, lots were drawn to see which prisoners would be shipped to Italy on a German hospital ship. Luckily, Hanan's name was not drawn. He was freed when the South Africans took Bardia and his captors fled. After leave in Alexandria, he was once more at the battlefront.]

Minqar Qaim

At about 8.30am, a huge column of transport, shimmering in the morning haze, and led by several tanks, was seen heading towards us. Our artillery opened up, which brought instant results and we were heavily shelled all day. Towards late afternoon, three enemy tanks broke through, shelling and machine-gunning as they approached our positions. The artillery just behind us opened up at point-blank range, firing at the tanks. For a while we were caught between the tanks firing (now only a hundred yards from our position) and our own artillery fire. It was a very nasty situation, reminiscent of that morning at Sidi Aziz.

The tanks retreated after failing to break through. We all breathed a sigh of relief when they left. The artillery had done a grand job in turning them. As darkness fell, the shelling died down but it was apparent that the division was almost completely surrounded and might risk annihilation when daylight came from air-raid attacks. We were told that we were to "break out" during darkness at about 1am. The infantry would attack with two battalions, causing a diversion in another sector and then we were to smash through the enemy positions.

Nearly 1000 trucks, carriers, anti-tank porters and quads towing artillery guns, all loaded with as many men as they could carry, were to break through. My section, plus some of the infantry, were on a three-tonner, with all our guns and ammunition, etc. For a mile and a half in the darkness, we approached the enemy lines, then suddenly all hell let loose. Flares, multi-coloured tracers and machine-gun fire ripped into the convoy. A couple of trucks burst into flames. Men were dragged onto other already overladen trucks. An ambulance beside us exploded in a sheet of flame, lighting up the mass of trucks.

We had run into the 21st Panzer Division's tanks. The convoy faltered, almost coming to a standstill, under the heavy fire. It looked a very grim situation as the mass of transport began to bunch up. It was John Grey, Colonel of the 18th Battalion, to whom we were attached, who got the convoy moving. He came through the transport, standing in his staff car with a megaphone, shouting so that he could be heard above the confusion and firing, "Smash through them and keep going east!" It was all that was needed, there was only one way out. Once we were among the enemy's tanks, they would be firing at their own troops.

The entire convoy slowly gathered speed and charged down the wadi, straight at the enemy tanks, spewing out their multi-coloured tracers. Then in the darkness and clouds of dust in what was to become a stampede of transport, we crashed into the enemy lines – over slit trenches, holes, troops, supplies and anything that lay in the way of our dash for freedom!

It was an extraordinary sight. There we were, yelling and shouting to urge the drivers on, and hanging on to the trucks to stop us being thrown off, as we bounced, bucked and pig-jumped our way through. I remember a 25-pounder artillery gun racing beside us with some character astride the barrel whooping like a rodeo rider.

By a strange quirk of fate, the firing from the tanks and enemy infantry was just clearing the convoy by a foot or so, or hitting at ground level.

The drivers drove like men possessed. Doc Parkinson, who was our driver, went through the gears as if driving a high-class racing car. I don't thing he ever drove before, or afterwards, like he drove that night at Minqar Qaim.

[Hanan's cool nerves and authority in action were recognised and he was put through an Officer Training Course.]

Leadership

I spent many hours in the tents of the platoon, getting to know each man individually by his first name or by his nickname. I insisted they call me by my first name. There was to be no "Sir", except in front of senior officers. Never once did they let me down. I cancelled red tape wherever possible.

One instance was when they brought their mail to me for censoring. Knowing how personal those letters were and the embarrassment of supposedly having to read them, I just said, "Is there anything in here that shouldn't be? If not, then seal it and I will sign the envelope. Your word is good enough for me."

Maybe this was only a small thing, but it all went to building a trust between men and officer and it wasn't long before that trust was returned.

I was aware how much my every move would mean to the morale and confidence of these men and to their performance as a team and how much they depended on me.

As we filed through the darkness towards our position one night, I looked skywards and offered a simple prayer, "Let me die before I ever falter or fail in any way the faith these men have in me." In the months ahead, I would become their confidant and mentor; they would come to me with their fears and doubts.

On one occasion after we had taken a battering, three men came to me almost in tears to ask if they could go back, as they were at breaking point. I told them that with the casualties we had suffered I couldn't spare them and that even if I could I would be doing them a disservice because if they walked away from the situation they would always regret doing so. One of them replied that it was all right for me, that I didn't have a nervous bone in my body. I explained to him that we all had the same emotions and just because at times they showed them outwardly they were just as courageous – as long as they did their job – as any man who showed no outward emotions.

During one battle, the engineers had pushed a Bailey bridge across the river where the old bridge had been demolished. The approaches and the bridge were in view of the enemy and were under constant artillery, mortar and air attack. The bridge earned the name of "Heartbeat Bridge".

Any trucks attempting to use it were soon in flames and littered the roadside. Brian Pleasants, the company commander, and I left to recce the situation. We decided to run the gauntlet and cross by "Heartbeat Bridge". The approaches on both sides were deserted except for the wrecked vehicles. We waited until the enemy planes made their bombing and strafing attack then, ducking and diving like a couple of rabbits, we crossed the bridge to the shelter of the ridge.

We made our way along the ridge, littered with enemy dead, already with their pockets inside out and stripped of personal belongings and anything of value. It always seemed so distasteful, but war is war and men's actions and ideals change.

Brian returned to the other platoons and I to collect my platoon to rendezvous on the riverbank. To save casualties in getting the men across the bridge, the platoon was to have been taken by the battalion Intelligence Officer to well below the bridge, where he was to find a suitable place to ford, then he would take them across and wait for me to pick them up.

I found them well below the rendezvous spot, bitterly cold and huddled together like drowned rats, soaked from the shoulders down. It turned out that the officer had led them so far, then they had run into shell and mortar fire and he had panicked and taken himself back to the safety of Battalion Headquarters, after telling them to follow the track, which actually was the wrong track to the ford.

They had followed his orders, crossed in the wrong place and with guns, ammunition, personnel arms and equipment had found themselves in water up to their shoulders. One man almost drowned and one of the machine-guns was lost in the swift current. I told the officer concerned (despite his seniority) what I thought of him and that never again would I trust him and neither would any of my platoon.

I realised how much the men depended on me for assurance and the faith they had in any action or decision I made. Sometimes, when I was catching a few hours' sleep, they would wake me to go and look at something or listen to a sound, or seek advice on what action they should take. They seemed, at times, like children wanting assurance on what to do in a situation that had arisen and with faith in whatever action I took or words I spoke.

Italy

Finally our trucks caught up with us and we moved through the town of Castel Frentano, towards the town of Orsogna, which was to be the next objective before the weather deteriorated. Orsogna, with its snow, wet and cold, built like a fortress on a high hill with a steep, winding road the only access, would be a name that most of us would always remember as the Italian winter closed in.

On the front side was an almost sheer cliff that made it impossible to approach the town, let alone to mount an attack, as it overlooked every means of approach. It also gave a clear view of our line and any movements. The steep road into the town was easily covered by enemy tanks and machine-guns because of the narrow advance front up the only road. It was going to be a hard nut to crack.

Yet Freyberg, in his usual style, decided to make a frontal attack on 7 December. Two attacks had already been made. The first, an attempt to enter the town, had failed because of infantry meeting tanks and mobile guns covering the road. Then, when our tanks attempted to move up the narrow road to give support, they were soon immobilised or knocked out.

The second attack was made to cut the Orsogna road to Ortona, hoping to force the enemy to evacuate Orsogna. The road was cut and occupied, but, because there were no roads and steep, almost sheer escarpments, it was impossible to get tanks or anti-tank guns forward to hold the position. Enemy tanks again forced a withdrawal from the ground gained. To support the attack on 7 December, we dug in on the most forward slope of Brecciarola Ridge beside the road, and not very far from the town.

Jack Partridge had been allotted to me as an extra sergeant. He had been a major in the Army in New Zealand, but had to revert to sergeant until he had been in action. Then on my recommendation, he could regain his commission as second lieutenant. About nine years older than me, he was an ex-bank accountant, a good steady soldier whom I could gladly have recommended had he lived that day on Brecciarola Ridge.

I had dug a shallow slit trench just forward of the two sections between them, and was sitting on the edge surveying the town with binoculars. I left the trench to check everything, sort out any problems, and give assurance to the men. Within seconds of leaving the trench, a mortar bomb landed it in, blowing my rifle and haversack to pieces.

Jack Partridge couldn't believe what he had seen. He said he had heard of lucky escapes, but if he hadn't seen it, he would never have believed it. It was a sad and torrid day that 7th of December on Brecciarola Ridge. By evening, Jack Partridge would be dead, and five men – including myself and Brian Pleasants, the company commander – would be wounded.

An incident that I have often recalled occurred after coming back from prowling about. I was sitting on the edge of the slit trench which was half-full of water. Cold, wet and tired, I placed the Tommy gun between my knees with the muzzle a few inches from my face. I went through the unloading procedure, taking off the magazine, etc, as we were trained to do and had done on many occasions.

I remember thinking to myself as I looked at the muzzle deflector, "Now, if you have faith in your unloading procedure, just press the trigger and all you will hear is a faint 'click' as the firing pin comes forward."

I found I was almost daring myself to have faith in my unloading procedure. As I reached down to press the trigger, some instinct made me push the barrel slightly to one side, and a soft-nosed, .45-calibre slug screamed past my ear.

Some mud had prevented the extractors gripping the round in the breach, leaving one up the spout. Instinct, or maybe my guardian angel, gave me a nudge at the last minute.

Jack Collis, my sergeant, looked at me and asked if I had done it on purpose. I shook my head and said, "Like hell I did."

It was something I always remembered, "Never be too sure – the unexpected, the exception, can always happen."

There were many incidents at Cassino and some amazing escapes from death. At times I marvelled what we had lived through, that line between life and death was so very slender. I remember being caught in a mortar barrage in a street on the outskirts of Cassino. They landed in front and behind us and on the footpath right beside the cobblestone street where we lay.

We would have been wiped out and the only thing that saved us was that the cobblestone street we were hugging was about 15 inches below the sidewalk so, apart from the concussion, we were unscathed. As we moved forward, Ray Marshall (known as

"Hiawatha" because of his Maori-Indian extraction) came up beside me and then in his relief and frankness said, "Christ, Mick, I never prayed so hard in my life!" It was such a spontaneous remark from him, that I put a hand on his shoulder and said, "Hiawatha, it must have worked!"

On another occasion, I had a couple of wounded men. One of them, Ray Dowd, was wounded badly in the stomach and needed urgent treatment. I ignored an order from Battalion HQ that "Under no circumstances were trucks to be used forward of the rear echelon area." We got away with it, the men were back in the dressing station in no time and Ray Dowd lived.

Even the enemy was caught out. By the time they woke up to the fact that a 15cwt truck was a target and began shelling the area, the truck was well gone. I don't think he could believe his eyes or that anyone would be so stupid as to bring a truck into the forward positions. It had been a risk to take a truck so far forward and I could have lost both truck and driver and the wounded, but it was a gamble that saved a man's life and I got away with it. When the truck had gone, we were crouched in a trench, and as the enemy began shelling, the words of my old friend Jack Collis summed up the incident: "I hope for all our sakes, Mick, that your luck never runs out!"

Those words weighed heavily on my shoulders as in the platoon there was this feeling that I could drag them through situations almost unscathed and that my decisions were always the correct ones. Deep down, after more than four years, I wondered just how much longer my luck would last.

[Hanan's luck lasted until he was sent on leave back to New Zealand in September 1944.]

War's End

My leave was finishing and the return of officers overseas became optional as the war was fast coming to an end. One day I was summoned to report to Army Headquarters in Paeroa, where the major in charge showed me a cable from Italy, saying that the battalion had asked for my return.

When I seemed a little apprehensive in making a decision, he said, "It is an honour for your unit to ask for your return."

I replied that I realised that, but as I had given five years of my life to the battalion and the war, I would like 24 hours to consider the request. He agreed and again the turmoil returned as I agonised over making a decision during those 24 hours. I had given the battalion five years, yet I still felt a strong loyalty to return to my men and I knew the magnet was beginning to drag me back into its power.

But now another force, the love of my girl, was tugging against the magnet.

I reported back the next day with my decision (or maybe it was my compromise), in which I put the onus back on the battalion.

I asked that a cable be sent stating that I would return immediately if the battalion considered my return necessary, to which the major agreed. Then for the next two days I suffered the turmoil of how to break the news to my parents if the reply to the cable meant I had to return.

I was summoned back again to Paeroa and, sitting at the table, the major opened a folder and handed me the return cable. It read, "Lt. Hanan's return would now be on a voluntary basis." He then asked me for my answer.

I thought for a moment and then replied, "I think five years is enough. To go back might be pushing my luck too far. I am going to call it a day." I was posted to the Reserves to be called up if necessary.

As I walked away, I knew that the love for the dark-haired girl that I had met on leave had at last destroyed the power of the magnet that had held me in its grip for so long. I got a little "tight" with some old friends that night and arrived home in the early hours of the morning. My father met me in the kitchen, as in his wisdom he knew the turmoil I was going through.

I will always remember his words that morning; they have stayed with me always.

"Son, if you feel you must return, then mother and I accept your decision. All we ask is that you let us know as soon as possible so we have time to prepare ourselves for that day when it comes."

I had never realised the pain and hurt they had suffered, waiting for some indication of whether or not I was going back to war. Turning to this man, whom I admired so much for his honesty and courage, this man, in whose image I had built myself, I put a hand on his shoulder and simply said the words he had waited so patiently to hear: "Dad, I'm home. I'm not going back!"

The end of the war came a few months later and the dark-haired girl became my wife. Then followed a daughter and a son and it was the love and affection of these three that erased forever the turmoil of war, until it became only a distant memory.

Protected by the Waters of the Nile
Jim Henderson

"Can you please hang on, he has to get into his leg," was my first introduction to Jim Henderson. Jim is the author of several books and will be well known to many for his Open Country *radio programmes that ran for many years.*

I was born in Motueka, Nelson province. I grew up on the Takaka Hill on a sheep farm that my father had broken in. Our house was on the bare ridge at the mercy of the wind and the rain. As the years passed, the saplings grew into pine trees and the sound of the wind through the pine trees is something I will always remember.

I went to Nelson College for five years and learned nothing. Not a damn thing! Except I loved English and reading and writing. On the farm, my mother said, "If the sheep began talking in French, Jim would never look up from his book."

I went on to the local newspaper, the *Nelson Evening Mail*, as a proofreader, then to the *Freelance* newspaper in Wellington.

After two years at the *Freelance*, I joined up for the Army because at that stage you felt it was the natural thing to do. There was no patriotism, no great love of adventure or anything like that.

First of all I had six months in Fiji and from there we went to North Africa where I spent three months. I got taken prisoner of war at Sidi Rezegh, which means Saint Rezegh, who was a sort of Mohammedan saint. God knows what he did, but they named a patch of desert after him and there they had to have a battle.

I was in the artillery where I thought I'd be pretty safe. I thought I wouldn't have any guts for this fighting hand to hand. "Ninety-mile" snipers they called us.

Once the infantry and tanks had been driven off, we were helpless. We got really smashed up there. The artillery that time at Sidi Rezegh had the heaviest casualties of the artillery in World War Two. That was our bloodiest event. Most of them were from 29 Battery (2NZEF) and I'm the poor mug that joined the 29th Battery.

In the battle, the infantry had been driven off and then the artillery were left to the tanks and there was this sort of scurrying ... utter chaos, and we were chopped up as helpless as a crab without his claws.

The infantry was up the front. It was about 8 to 9am in the morning, not even a cup of tea and the infantry were driven off and we had to fight them off with the artillery. We had to shoot back with our 25-pounder guns, but it was too slow. It's not an anti-tank gun. The tanks waltzed in and wiped us out.

I stood up to lend a cobber a hand and, *voila*, I got shot through my leg.

I felt the bullet ... time seemed to slow up ... I felt it going through my leg and come out the other side. There was no feeling or pain whatsoever. Being shot was like a brace and bit boring into my foot, sort of a white-hot feeling boring through slowly as it went through my foot. I thought to myself, "I must remember this" ... blinking old journalism.

The one in my chest I didn't know about for three or four days. I hadn't felt it at all. Actually I was pain free with the other wounds as well for three or four days.

No one ever thinks they are going to be wounded. In war books, people are seldom wounded. The reality is that people cry out to their cobbers after being bashed. I got shot through the foot, I got shot through the thigh, I got shot across my chest, and there's some sort of scar from something I can't remember on the back of my neck.

Years later, I realised I had been shot all from the left-hand side. My right-hand side was unscathed.

I remembered that before I was shot I had gone down to the Nile with a nurse, Gertrude Henderson, of Christchurch, at 11pm one night. It was weird and eerie, this mighty river flowing through the centuries. We stood there in awe at the majesty of this river.

I suddenly remembered and told her of where I had read that if anyone had dipped part of his body in the sacred Nile, it would be preserved from the battle.

Then in three months' time into battle we went and I got shot up all on the left-hand side and years and years later I suddenly remembered this and I thought, "Which side was it now that I had dipped in the Nile? Was it the right or the left?"

I hunted through some old letters that I had sent home to Mum. I'd never bothered to check it before but by crikey … there it was in September 1941 and I said as I kicked off the letter: "Dear Mum, for those who are interested in the trivia of history, I dipped my right leg in the Nile.… "

That's eerie.

At the battle I was left for dead. One bloke, a New Zealander, started to pick me up and I let out a yell. But he didn't have time. He was pushed on as others were by the Germans who had broken through.

I was lying in a slit trench and I was shot through my leg and so forth and I couldn't get out of it. I had no fear of death but I was bloody thirsty.

The thirst was so terrible that at one stage I drank a bit of my own pee. I managed to crawl over towards a haversack and pull out a metal container and peed into that. I took a sip of it. It's the most vile, horrible bitter taste. I thought, "Oh gosh you can't live on that."

I managed to reach into the haversack and pull out a tube of McLean's toothpaste and ate half of that and that cleared out my mouth a bit and got rid of this raging thirst.

Then after at least a day I began to feel sleepy and away I went into a trance. It was the feeling like you're at the end of a bath and it was lovely, it was all going to end … the finish of pain and thirst and fighting, it would all be gone. Then I got a prick in the arm, and it was a German officer.

He said, "By gosh, you look as if you've been getting into trouble." I nearly passed out again at the shock of his perfect English.

I was a soldier no more. Not that I ever was a soldier – I was always an observer, a civilian in battle dress.

This German and another German made signs that the ambulance would be coming. Sure enough, a German came with an ambulance, picked me up and took me into a huge hospital where every nationality was lying there wounded. Other medical men of all nationalities had been swept in to help to look after the wounded.

A German came towards me while I was half in the rats [feeling dopey] and I saw a swastika on his shoulder and I said [with disgust], "Oh, German…."

It was my first contact with a German apart from the one I had met who had spoken perfect English. And this second German spoke in perfect English too and he said, "No, no, you've got it all wrong. For you, my friend, the war is over. We're friends now, we're friends."

He reached over and held me by the wrist and stroked my forehead with his other hand. With that I passed out a second time with the shock of the sympathy.

I thought the Germans were some sort of hairy, merciless ape, but now I realised they were human beings.

Gangrene set into my leg and they took me by ship to an Italian hospital in Bari. They told me my leg had to come off. At first they couldn't decide where to cut it and finally they left two inches below the knee. That enabled me to wiggle it out about, which is a great thing.

Before this, an Italian stole my wristwatch. I had offered my watch, which was the only thing that I had, to a German as I was being carried into the hospital. With Germanic accuracy and a sense of the dramatic (there was a sandstorm raging at that time), he shrugged his shoulder and waved the offer aside.

I told the Italian who stole my watch, "You dirty thief, you."

He laughed and said, "Tell it to Churchill."

I had two years as a prisoner of war in Bari. You certainly missed your comrades when you're a POW [Prisoner of War]. I never thought I would get shot, let alone be a prisoner of war.

There were some absurd stories that came out of it.

This little bedraggled Italian fella came to us and said: "Will the war end soon?"

We thought, "How ridiculous asking prisoners!"

So to cheer him up I said, "It will end fairly soon, I think."

He said, "Will it end in three months?"

"Three months! That's too tough. That's too much? Why?"

With a tearful sniff, he said "In three months they're sending me to the Russian front."

The poor little Iti, going there up against the Russians in the snow and ice.

Italian plans never seemed to work out. There was great bravado, and singing and arias and rejoicing, but it never seemed to work out in the end.

One day an Italian lieutenant came to our prisoner-of-war camp accompanied by a little fox terrier and he said, "Now, beware, we are going to fumigate this hut."

He put up signs and posters, saying, "Beware, deadly poison," and so on and he heaved us all out. He warned us against this dreadful poison and we all had to heed him and go off for the day.

Towards dusk, he flung open one of the doors of the barracks in triumph and shaking his head, but still intact, out trotted the little fox terrier.

After two years we were exchanged for "junk" – a boatload of wounded Italians and Germans. That was the end of the war for me in about August 1943.

When I got back to New Zealand I tried to write it down. The words were just cardboard, it was dreadful. What I tried to write was absolutely false. It just couldn't get going.

Then suddenly in Wellington Hospital these little attempts finally warmed me up and I got cracking and in 10 days wrote about going into action until the end of it when we were exchanged for the Italian wounded. It just all vomited out at once. The book, *Gunner Inglorious*, sold over 100,000 copies.

To have written it down was a wonderful thing. It ended all the nightmares and bad dreams of the war, and I've never had any since. Most people have had them. Most people don't talk of it. It cleared my mind away by writing about it. I always reckon that people who have been smashed up in war or in accidents or in hospital if they could only write their stuff down it would cure their mind a hell of a lot.

The Vow
Frank Hitchcock

When he went overseas, Frank Hitchcock had little appreciation of his native land. But war and suffering in the wastes of a European winter gave him a whole new perspective on New Zealand.

I was born in Hamilton East and lived there until the age of about two, then we moved to Auckland.

In 1936, prior to entry into training college, I had gone teaching at a school in the hinterland of the Coromandel Peninsula about 10 miles into the bush from Whitianga. I taught there for one year and I was paid £15 per pupil. There were only seven children to teach between two brothers who had been granted land in the region after the First World War.

I lived in a Maori hut with supersacks stretched between four tea-tree poles driven into the dirt floor as a bed. There was a table and a chair. We used to cook with a Primus stove and there was also a fireplace with a camp oven.

A couple of times I went out pig hunting with some mates that I played rugby with in the Whitianga team. We would put the pig in the camp oven which was a big iron pot. We would heap the ashes on top and it would come out beautifully.

I went through training college in 1937-1938 and after sitting a rigorous entrance examination I got my teaching certificate. In 1939, I did my probationary year teaching at Onehunga School in Auckland.

When the war broke out, I joined up on the first day. Life was pretty Spartan and dull during the Depression. We had no money and when I say no money, I mean no money. You'd walk as far as you could to save the tram fares. Life was incredibly dull.

There was a huge delay before anything happened after I signed up. The Air Force didn't call me up so I wrote to them a couple of times to see what was going on until finally I got a telegram from the Government asking me if I would leave New Zealand within a fortnight, as a Fleet Air Arm cadet.

I jumped at it. I hated teaching, I hated my dull life in New Zealand, there was nothing for me here.

We left New Zealand on Friday 13 September 1940, but our convoy was lucky. We had a very uneventful trip.

I remember the first payday we got. We lined up and took our caps off. We were given the princely sum of 28 shillings. Lofty Mabin, who came from quite a wealthy family in Nelson, said to the paymaster: "Is this all we get for a week's pay?"

The paymaster replied, "That's for a fortnight, mate."

There were about 20 of us on a ground training course at Gosport in Portsmouth and then we went to the flying course where I failed the pilot's course. We had sworn the oath of allegiance to the Navy in Wellington and what they had told us was if we failed the flying course we would be given a deck commission. I told them I wasn't interested in a deck commission.

By then, the courses were behind because of the bad weather and they sent us to the Isle of Wight, just to sit there. Sometimes I wished I had never got into the Fleet Air Arm, it was so slow.

Finally I got some leave and went to London and went to see Bill Jordan, who was the New Zealand High Commissioner, and I told him about my plight. I said, "They are not taking any notice of me, I'm just doing nothing."

"Unfortunately, Frank," he said, "there are no RNZAF training facilities here, and if you want to get out in the Air Force you're going to have to join the RAF and you'll have to start at the bottom again."

And I said, "All right, Bill, get me out."

So I started all over again. The new recruits stayed at these huge hotels in London before being sent to Devon to do initial training, squarebashing and God knows what else. Eventually I got to Canada to the Navigation School.

When I had finished the course there they sent me to Prince Edward Island to do an advanced course in sea navigation.

It was now 1943 and I still hadn't got onto operations after signing up in September 1940. It was unbelievable.

When I finally got my final flying-out test in sea navigation, I was dead lucky. The instructor, who was a squadron leader, gave me a flight plan to fly to a point in the Gulf of St Lawrence and we had to descend through cloud on the way back. As we came out of the clouds, there was the aerodrome right beneath us.

Then I went to all sorts of refresher courses. I remember one course we did in a swimming bath ... how to get in and out of rubber dinghies. Then we did a parachute jump, I don't know why. Then we went into compression chambers and I thought, "If I'm flying over the sea, I'm not going to be flying very high."

Eventually I was sent to an OTU (operational training unit) at East Fortune, which is in the south-east corner of Scotland on the railway line to Edinburgh. I remember the day we got there. It was snowing and the alarm was going off. When we asked what was happening, a fellow said. "There's a 'Kangaroo Red'."

I said, "What does that mean?"

He said, "One of the Beaufighters has just crashed in flames."

I teamed up with a chap called Clive Lyell. I was lucky to get him. Clive was a very experienced pilot, very careful.

After OTU, we were sent to Langham to 489 Squadron, which was a Beaufighter torpedo squadron. There was an Australian squadron there, 455 Squadron, which was armed with rockets. There was only me and Clive, and Chappie Chapman who were New Zealanders, and Chappie had an English navigator.

After we got there, we sat around for a while waiting to go on ops. On the third day, the squadron leader took us all up and showed us around Norfolk and the Wash, to familiarise our pilots with the approaches when they came in to land.

Unfortunately, the flight leader lost an engine and tried to glide over the boundary fence and the plane stalled and went straight down from 150 feet. That was the end of the squadron leader, Chappie and his navigator.

The squadron usually operated from Scotland, which was closer to the German shipping lanes. It was our job, when advised by the Norwegian underground, to attack the convoys from Sweden to the North German ports.

Early in 1944, they sent the squadron to Langham in Norfolk to be nearer the D-Day beaches. We continued to operate from there in the Norwegian waters and fjords, but we had a much longer haul. We had to carry more petrol and it was more dangerous.

On D-Day, we operated over the English Channel for shipping protection. When we woke up on the morning of D-Day, we were flabbergasted to find that every plane in the Allied Air Forces had been painted black and white. We could recognise an Allied plane but you couldn't guarantee that the Yanks could.

We were up before full light. We went up the channel towards Calais and we intercepted a flotilla of German torpedo boats [E boats]. We didn't carry torpedoes that day; we carried, for the only time I've ever been on ops, 500lb bombs.

Clive and I were positioned in the rear of the squadron. We could see the flak coming up from the E boats, so we turned round and came in again. We were last over by about 20 minutes. The navigator's seat was made of fairly substantial steel with a parachute underneath it. Apparently the flak had come right underneath the navigator's seat. It didn't hit me. I wouldn't have had any children if it had. Clive went down and dropped his bombs and fired his cannons. We were airborne all that day and we never saw a German plane once.

I was shot down on 29 August 1944. It was a beautiful autumn day. We were told that there was a large German convoy on its way to the northern German ports and we were warned that it was very well armed.

"'The Pen' Bardia 1941 – the hole we lived in for five weeks." – Michael Hanan.

Michael Hanan back in the hole one year later (1942).

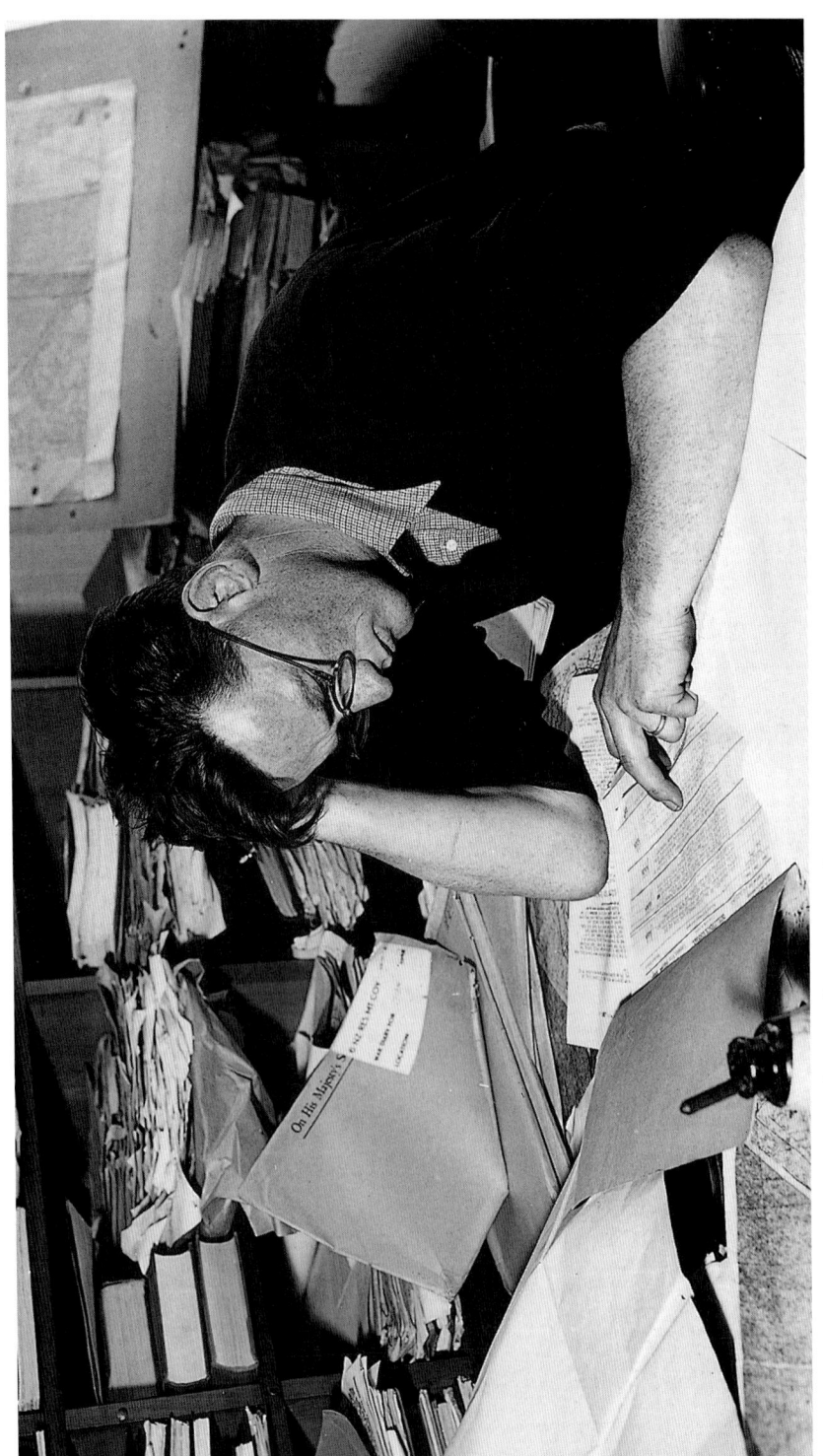

Jim Henderson after the war as a civilian working on war histories.

Frank Hitchcock in warrant officer's uniform, with friends in London, shortly after his release from a POW camp.

Hansi Keating (then Silberstein), a few months after being liberated from Belsen Concentration Camp.

Murray McColl at training camp early in the war.

Murray McColl (middle row, second from right) with other injured soldiers at Kloster Haini Hospital awaiting repatriation in 1943. In the front row at the left is Jim Blue – the man who crawled over Murray when he was wounded. Second from the right in the same row is Tom Woods. Tom was blinded by a bullet that went through both eyes and was going to be buried on the battlefield as he was believed dead.

At last light we were to fly in from the west with the sun behind us. The 445 Squadron had fired its rockets. The broadside of rockets for the Beaufighter is just about equivalent to the broadside of a light cruiser. We were last in, as usual.

To fire a torpedo from a plane, you have to fly straight, at a certain speed, not more than 150 knots, and you have to fly fairly low. The ship we were going to attack was still firing but there was only one gun going so we didn't worry too much.

Then there was this almighty bang in the port engine and the next thing we were on fire. Clive turned around and was going to try and fly home. I was sitting there not doing very much for about 30 seconds, then the flame was coming back on my Perspex cabin and it was starting to blister and I started to get very, very frightened.

I said to Clive, "Put it down. You are going to have to put it down now. If we get more holes in it and it goes down, we will go straight to the bottom."

Clive put the plane down in the sea and it was a magnificent landing. All I had to do was to unscrew my Perspex cover and release the dinghy which was on the port side.

We were told to screw our Morse code key down, so they could take a fix on us. I knew that wouldn't be any use, but I did that anyway. We got out and there was the rubber dinghy just gently rocking on a smooth sea, so I got into it.

There was no sign of Clive and I could see the plane was going to go down shortly.

I got back into the plane through my Perspex cabin and crawled over the cannon boxes, right through the flames, and grabbed Clive by the shoulders. He had gone forward and knocked himself out on something, it might have been the torpedo sight.

He came to and we stepped back onto the wings, and stepped into the dinghy without getting our feet wet. And just then, down the plane went.

We stayed there all night in the dinghy. There was nowhere to go. We were in the open sea. We could see the convoy we had just attacked. It was a beautiful night. I ate some of the chocolate that was in the emergency rations and went to sleep.

At first light, we were picked up by an armed German trawler. They threw a couple of ropes down to us and we climbed up. I'll never forget how the trawler "fished" the dinghy and pulled it up onto the deck.

We landed at Helgoland and there was an armed sentry on the jetty with a rifle with a fixed bayonet. As he signed a paper for us, the two sailors who had escorted us dropped the dinghy beside us and off they went.

The sentry told us to pick up the dinghy.

And I said to Clive, "If he wants the dinghy, he can bloody well carry it himself."

The sentry prodded me in the backside with his bayonet and I quickly picked up the dinghy.

We stayed there for a few days because of a huge storm and when it subsided we continued on to an interrogation camp in the Rhine Valley. About a fortnight later, we were sent to Poland.

We stayed there until the Russians made their big push at the beginning of 1945. On 17 January, the Germans told all prisoners that they were to be moved at one hour's notice. Two days later, early one bitterly cold evening, we were assembled and marched out of the gates into the gloom and falling snow on what was to become a trek of over 200 miles.

We found that this was to be the pattern of our lives as they forced us to march on what became known as the "Death March". In order to leave the roads free for the retreating German Army, we marched at night, and slept, if we were lucky, in a barn by day.

[Frank has a handwritten, day-by-day account of the march by an anonymous soldier. It came into the possession of Clive Lyell and then was passed on to his son, who passed it on to Frank in 1999.]

A Record of the Forced March Made by Occupants of Stalag Luft 7 Jan/Feb 1945

On January 17th 1945 at 1100 hours we received one hour's notice in which to pack our kit and make ready to leave camp by marching, at the same time we were informed by Ober-Feldwebel Funck that for every one man who fell out of the column on the march, five other men would be shot. (This order was given verbally but to my knowledge was never carried out.)

The start was postponed until 3.30am January 19th during which time 68 sick men were evacuated to the Civilian Ilag in Kreuzberg and, I later discovered, were being moved from there by road and rail to Stalag 344 (formerly Stalag VIII B) and from there to an Ilag in Lubeck.

Each man was issued with the German conception of two days' rations before leaving on the march, which was finally begun at 3.30am January 19th. No transport was provided for any sick who may have fallen out en route, whilst the only medical equipment carried was that carried by the MD and three sanitators on their backs.

Details of the March
19 January
Left Bankau and marched to Winterfelt, a distance of 28km. This was done under extremely trying conditions and severe cold, at times including a 40mph blizzard. The only accommodation at Winterfelt was numerous small barns.

20 January
Marched from Winterfelt to Karlsruhe arriving at 1000 hrs, having left Winterfelt at 0500 hours, the distance being only 12km. At Karlsruhe, we were housed in an abandoned brick factory. Here, for the first time we were supplied with two field kitchens with which to cook for 1500 men, each kitchen being actually capable of supplying 200 men.

The MD was provided with a horse and cart for transport

of the sick, it being big enough to hold six sitting cases. Coffee was provided. After a rest of 11 hours, we were again ordered to move. The camp leader and the MD both protested against further marching until the men were adequately fed and rested, the Germans replying that it was an order and as such must be complied with else reprisals would be enforced.

The same night, we left Karlsruhe and marched to Schonfeld, arriving at 0900 hours on 21 January, covering a distance of 42km. We found upon arrival here no accommodation available so after marching another 3km to a small state farm at Danwauld we were billeted there. The conditions during the night were extreme, the temperature being minus 13 degrees Celsius.

The hospital wagon was filled after the first 5km, and from then onwards men were being picked up on the roadside in a collapsed and frozen condition, it being only by sheer willpower that the majority were able to finish the march. This night march of such distance was in order to cross the River Oder before the bridge was destroyed.

21 January
At Danwauld we were billeted in the cowsheds and barns of a state farm while a room was provided for the sick who were taken there, at a village of Lossen (from here the sick were eventually removed to Stalag III at Luckenwalde). Rations issued here amounted to 100 grams of biscuits per man and half a cup of coffee.

22 January
At 0300 hours, orders were given by the Germans to prepare to move off at once but, being dark, there was some delay getting the men out of their sleeping quarters in the straw as they were unable to find their baggage. The guards thereupon marched into the barns and discharged firearms, no casualties. The column was marching again by 0500 hours, 23 men being

lost, their whereabouts being unknown. They may have been left behind asleep or may even have made good their escape.

Also, a further 31 sick men were evacuated (we believe) to Lansdorf, but at the time of writing no further news has come to our hands as to their fate. We marched on to Jenbwitz, a distance of 31km, and once again housed in the barns of a state farm. Here we were issued for 1470 odd men a total of 114kg of fat, 46 tins of meat, barley and peas, whilst ¼ litre of soup was issued each man.

23 January
Was an uneventful march of 20km from Jenbwitz to Wangen.

24 January
We rested the day at Wangen sleeping in barns, while the sleeping quarters was a cowshed. 31 sick were evacuated to Sagan; 400 loaves of bread were issued.

25 January
Left Wangen at 0400 hours for Heidersdorf and covered 30km.

26 January
Rested for full day at Heidersdorf where we were issued with 600 loaves of bread to last two days.

27 January
Left Heidersdorf and marched 18km to Pfeffendorf where we arrived at night.

28 January
Left Pfeffendorf for Standorf at 0500 hours and covered 31km. Issued with 24 cartons of knackerbrot, 150kg of oats, 45kg of margarine, 50kg of sugar. 22 sick were left at Schweidritz, en route, for transporting by train to Sagan.

29 January
We left Standorf at 1800 hours and marched to Peterwitz, a distance of 22km where we arrived at 0400 hours. This march was carried out in darkness and once again in extremely trying conditions, with a howling blizzard blowing almost the whole time. Four German refugees – one woman, one child and two men – were found dead and frozen on the wayside. The men arrived at Peterwitz in an utterly exhausted condition. Before leaving Standorf we had been promised that we would have to march no further as transport would be supplied from Peterwitz. 104kg of meat were issued, one sack of salt, 35kg of sugar and 100kg of barley.

30 January
At Peterwitz, 30 men from Stalag 344, who had been left without guards, joined our column. 296 loaves of bread were issued, 50kg of oats and 35.5kg of margarine.

1 February
Marched from Peterwitz to Pranswitz, a distance of 18km, where we remained until 5 February. On the first of February, we were issued with 680 loaves of bread and 37.5kg of margarine, 250 loaves of bread, 100kg sugar, 200kg of flour and 150kg of barley. On 4 February, the issue was 250 loaves. At night on 4 February, the Commandant visited the farm and read out an order from the DKW to the effect that five men were to be released and would be liberated at the first opportunity. The purpose of this, we were unable to understand.

5 February
Before leaving we were issued with 500 loaves of bread, 95kg of margarine and 530 tins of meat. We were marched from Pranswitz to Goldberg, a distance of 8km. On arrival at Goldberg we were put into cattle trucks, an average of

55 men to each truck. By this time there were numerous cases of dysentery and facilities for men to attend to personal hygiene were inadequate, in fact didn't exist. The majority had no water on the train journey for two days.

When permission was finally given for the men to leave the train to relieve themselves, humorous guards ordered them back inside again and we had to be continually obtaining permission for the men to be allowed out. Before commencing the train journey, we were issued with 1/15 loaf per person to last us the two-day train journey which ended at Luckenwalde, south of Berlin, on 8 February.

General Information

After the first two days, most of us managed to make, during the few spare hours at our disposal, crude but workable sleighs which served well, for the transport of kit, etc, while the roads remained frozen. Others, unable to make these sleighs, were obliged, owing to the weight and their rapidly weakening condition, to discard much of their personal kit, many even taking the drastic step of discarding their blankets.

After the River Oder had been crossed and the shortage of rations was being felt, keen bartering was the order of the day although the prices seem, in retrospect, rather distorted e.g: my wristlet watch fetched from a French POW whom I was able to contact at one of our longer stops, one 500g loaf bread, 5 French pain d'épice, one packet of dried onions and one small packet of biscuits.

Other watches, many more expensive than mine, were sold for as little as one loaf. Others of course were luckier and managed better. Along with the general shortage of rations, the shortage of cigarettes was keenly felt. Oh, the joy of a draw from a scrounged "butt" of a cigarette rolled from mint tea!

Summary

As a result of the march and the deplorable conditions, the morale of the men was extremely low. They were suffering from extreme degrees of malnutrition and at the time of writing suffering practically to a man of an outbreak of particularly violent dysentery. They were quite unfit for further movement, good, ample food and better conditions being urgently required. We left Bankau with no Red Cross supplies and throughout the march all rations were short issued, the most outstanding being bread of which 2924 loaves were issued to 1500 men for a period of 21 days.

Frank Hitchcock continues.

My most vivid memory of World War Two is not a close brush with death such as a perilous descent in a burning plane into the North Sea. The moment I will never forget is the one when I made myself a solemn vow.

One particular morning we had reached the village shortly after dawn, cold, hungry and exhausted. As we flopped down into the straw of the barn the Germans had ordered us into, we leaned with our backs against the whitewashed walls. We cursed the wall, the Germans and the German private. I was just considering whether to relieve my aching feet by taking off my boots and having the impossible task of donning frozen boots in the morning or whether to just close my eyes and try to sleep when suddenly there came the familiar sound of that hated, strident, "Rouse, rouse!"

"I'm not blood well moving," said somebody. "Not even for that bastard Hitler himself."

When a German NCO [non-commissioned officer] came bursting through the door, we remained sitting, staring at him. He pulled his pistol and waved it at us, but we continued to stare. Then, with a violent gesture, he fired several rounds at the wall above our heads.

A splinter of brick hit me on the back of the neck and for a second I thought I'd been shot. We all got to our feet hurriedly and shuffled outside. Under German orders, we lined up out in the snow on the road that we'd just marched along and there we stood and waited and waited for the Germans to make up their mind about something or other.

The temperature was well below zero and I could feel my heart thumping in my rib cage. I looked at the racked faces of my companions as they shuffled their feet in the snow and it came to me that if they continued to make us march each night in sub-zero temperatures, without adequate food and shelter, some of us would die and I could well be one of the unlucky ones.

And that's when I made my vow.

Eventually the Germans came to their decision and we were marched to the next village about six miles away. I was right. Some of us did die, including some German guards who were then too old to withstand the cold and fatigue.

We were forced along for anything up to 30 miles a day. We were poorly fed and medically unfit. Many collapsed by the wayside and had to be left behind, falling out of the ranks exhausted. The sick were mounting up every day mostly from malnutrition and frostbite. Finally we arrived at a prison camp in Berlin and soon the battle for Berlin was raging in sight and hearing of our camp.

Then one morning, following the departure of the German guards, a Russian Army car drove through the gates. Shortly afterwards thousands of Russian scarecrows travelled excitedly through the gate and disappeared down the road to Berlin. I remember thinking how lucky they were to be set free by their own Army. It was not until 30 years later that I read Solzhenitsyn's *The Gulag Archipelago* that I learned their fate. Russian POWs went straight to Siberia with very few exceptions. They were traitors for having surrendered.

We were released and I eventually got back to New Zealand.

The vow I had made as I gazed across the big German countryside and looked up at the leaden skies shedding snowflakes was that if ever I got back to New Zealand with its green fields and blue skies I would never leave it again.

I never have.

You'll Never Know How Lucky You Are

Hansi Keating (née Silberstein)

Hansi Keating is a New Zealander. She gave birth to three Kiwi children and has three Kiwi grandchildren. But she was born in Germany, a Jew – and survived the Holocaust.

I was born in Berlin in Germany in December 1924. I have a brother, Fred, who is three years younger. My parents had a haberdashery shop. As we were Jewish, my parents were told in 1935 I was no longer to be accepted in a German school. They had to enrol me in a Jewish school.

On 9 November 1938, there was what was called the "Kristallnacht", the "night of broken glass", when the Germans looted all the Jewish shops, burnt all the synagogues and arrested a lot of Jews.

My father was arrested and taken to a concentration camp. We didn't know at the time where he was taken. After six weeks he was released. Why the Germans released some and some didn't come back, we don't know. I was only 14 when he came out of the concentration camp. He never spoke to us about it; all he said was "I have returned from the dead". After that, our shop was taken away from us.

The school I was attending only went to 14 years and I had to leave school then. I did some voluntary work in a kindergarten. The following year I was lucky enough to train as a kindergarten teacher. But the war had started by then and after one year we were forced to leave to work in an ammunition factory outside Berlin. There was a small group of about 50 of us. Because we were Jews, we were in a sort of cage, and we couldn't mix with the others.

In those days, we had something like a passport, an identity card that was stamped "Jude". There were certain things we weren't allowed to buy and we could only go to certain shops. We had a curfew and were supposed to be home by eight o' clock at night. We couldn't go to certain places, and even the parks had special benches marked for Jews.

In September 1941, we started wearing a yellow star, the Star of David, with the word "Jude" written inside. We had to wear that on our left-hand side on our outer clothing. It had to be sewn on, not just pinned on, so we were recognisable to any German. If they wanted, the SS or the SA [the Brownshirts] could assault you or they could even arrest you for no reason at all – even if you just walked on the wrong side of the road.

In December 1942, Germany suffered a setback when Stalingrad was won by the Russians. I was about 17 then and we Jewish youngsters celebrated, but the repercussions for us came early the next year when they decided to arrest all the Jews that were still in Berlin.

On 27 February 1943, we arrived at work and handed in our little work cards as usual. Then somebody whispered to us that something was going to happen and we tried to retrieve our cards but it was too late.

We were asked to assemble in the cloakroom and get our coats. Two or three SS trucks pulled up outside and we were herded into the trucks. Nobody knew where we were going. Nobody knew what was happening.

We were taken into an old synagogue in Berlin that had been bombed earlier. People arrived from all over Berlin who had been arrested in the streets. We were all anxious to find out what had happened to our parents and our relatives.

Nothing was told to us. All the information we were given was that as soon as we handed in our passports we would be given some food. Once we handed in our passports, they were stamped "stateless". We knew then what was going to happen. We had heard of concentration camps. We knew of places that people had been transported to and you never heard of anyone returning.

We were young and we were resistant. During that night there was a very big bombardment. When the sirens and the alarms went off we tried to escape, but we got caught by the Gestapo and told in no uncertain terms that we had no way of getting out of there.

The next day trucks arrived again, and by this time there was a mixture of hundreds, maybe thousands, of people – old, young, women, men, all together. We were loaded onto the trucks and taken to a railway station. At the station, some people from the Jewish community gave us a piece of bread and then we were loaded into a closed-up cattle wagon which was bolted shut. We were crammed in there and the only thing we had in there was a bucket we could use for a toilet.

We set off on our journey. Nobody had said anything, but the direction we were heading was south-east Germany where Auschwitz was. We knew where we were going to.

We came past certain stations where we were greeted by German soldiers singing Nazi songs, songs against Jews.

We were nearly two days in transit. People were getting thirsty and distraught. There were a lot of old people. It was a really distressing journey. There were a lot of young people and we tried to keep our spirits up by talking silly things, but it was very distressing because at the end we didn't know what was going to happen to us. After two days, we arrived at a station in the middle of winter. Snow was on the ground.

The SS soldiers opened the doors and as we were told to jump out I said to one of them ... being stupid ... "We are thirsty, can we have something to drink?"

He pointed down and said, "Drink the snow."

We were shouted at to line up. "Those that can't walk, there are trucks there," they told us.

We were five friends that had worked together in the ammunition factory and we thought if we could stick together, we had a better chance of surviving. One of the girls I was with had her mother with her and we said to her, "You can't walk." We took her to the truck.

We didn't know how far it was so then we said, "Why should we walk if we can have a ride in a truck?" I was next to get up on the truck. The SS soldier put his gun across me and said, "You are too young, you walk," and he pushed all of us young ones back.

We said to my friend's mother, "See you later."

People said, "Goodbye" and waved to each other because we thought we were going somewhere where we would see each other again.

I stood in line waiting to march. I was dressed in a navy coat with a hood on. An SS officer walked past, pointed at me, took me out of the row and said, "What is your name?"

In those days if you were asked your name, you gave it. I said, "Hansi Silberstein".

I went back into the row and everybody said, "What did he want?"

I said, "He just wanted my name."

But just before we marched off, he came back and called me out again. He said, "When you get sorted for work tomorrow, you tell them you work in the dentist station."

I went back and everybody asked me what happened and I said to them, "Look, if we can stick together, we have more chance of surviving."

We marched into the camp which wasn't very far. It was still early morning and dark. We went into a big hall where there were other inmates, mostly from Czechoslovakia, who had been in the camp before us. The first thing we asked was "Where have the trucks gone? Where are the people that were on the trucks?"

The girls pointed straight at a chimney where the flames were shooting out and they said, "That's where they have gone, they have gone into the crematorium."

You can imagine ... we broke down, we cried ... it really sort of hit us. That was the first thing that they tell us ... my friend's mother was in there.

Then the SS women told us to hand over all our belongings. We didn't have much – all we had was our handbags, our watches, our bracelets, necklaces.... Then we were told our hair would be shaven off and we would be given a number.

I don't think at that point anybody worried about anything else that was going to happen. You just automatically did what you were told.

After that, we were told to line up alphabetically. A Czech came in wearing a hat which meant he was a capo. He said, "Was there someone selected last night?"

I thought, "They are after me."

You hear stories about people being selected to go into research, to go into different experiments. I didn't come forward.

He called out again and I didn't let on.

Then he said, "Is there someone here by the name Hansi Silberstein?" He didn't have my name quite right but I thought, "Oh God, I have to go. When they see my name and my number they will know who I am."

So I went along and said, "Yes, it's me. I was told to go to the dental station."

All he said to me was ... and I can still remember his exact words in German.... "You will never know how lucky you are".

He took me straight out. I had my number tattooed. He took me to the sauna, where all the girls had their heads shaved. I saw my friends there, they had their heads shaven ... I didn't even recognise them. I had short hair. My hair was never touched. I was given a scarf and I was told to hide it.

I was taken straight into the dental station which was in the hospital block. The dentist was a French communist. One girl there was an Austrian who had been given a sentence of three or four months because she was engaged to a Jew.

I was told that we were a select group. I remember I was given two odd shoes, but we were lucky to have running water, we could wash ourselves.

There were no toilets, we had buckets. Because I was the youngest, it was my job to clean the bucket every morning. One morning I slipped and it tipped over and one of the women guards made me pick it up by hand. Those are things that you live with.

I was the office girl at the dental station. I had to fill out how many people came through, how many people the dentists saw, what we did, and all that was sent to Germany. I had to take that every week into the camp office and that was filed. The Germans were very precise. Everything had to be written down and recorded.

I learned to speak Polish from the Polish girls I was working with. I was determined not to speak German so we could talk without the Germans understanding.

I got typhoid soon after arriving because there was no hygiene. There was lice, dermatitis, you really had to be careful. Most of the people that came in didn't last very long because they got diarrhoea and there was nothing they could do … they just went down very quickly.

They had selections all the time. Even if people went to the hospital, the doctor would come through and if anyone looked sick, they would send them to Block 25 or 27, and every night these trucks would come through. These people were only skeletons half the time and you saw them, they would be loaded onto the trucks and taken to the gas chambers. There were always trucks going into the crematorium. The flames were burning day and night. You can never forget that smell of burning flesh. I can still smell it today.

We were at the woman's camp at Auschwitz called Birkenau. The infamous Dr Mengele worked there and one time I had to report to him. We didn't have names, only numbers, and I went to report to him after our dentist had been caught visiting somebody in the camp.

The doctor who was there said, "What is going to happen to her?"

Mengele said, "She will be shot." It was punishment for what she had done. I stood there in front of him and I never blinked an eyelid. I looked him straight in the eyes. He was tall and I was tall. I never blinked or pleaded or anything. Then he said, "Can you speak Greek?" I said, "No," and he said, "Well, you'd better learn," and with that he dismissed me.

They brought in a lot of people from Salonika in Greece. Dr Mengele was into experiments. He separated twins. He brought in the twins to the dental station and we had to check their teeth. I had forms to fill out, whether they were identical or whether they were different.

I did that for a short while then they opened a small dentist station at one of the out camps. There were four out camps from Birkenau. We were sent into what was a small camp that had no barbed wire. The SS used to take us there and back every day.

It was there just after Christmas in 1944 that one day word came that the whole camp had to pack up. We knew the Russians weren't very far behind us. We could hear the gunfire.

They made us march out of the camp and after half a day we met up with people coming out from the main camp. There were a lot of elderly people and when they couldn't walk any further and sat down they were just shot … shot in front of us, you couldn't even stop to help them. The Germans were in a hurry to get out of there.

We were on the march for two days until we got to a place where we were packed into open cattle trains … the snow was that deep in them.

We hadn't had any food and we were getting weak. Polish peasants who lived around there came and brought us boiled potatoes. The German guards would take it off us, because they were hungry. They had nothing to eat as well, but we did not feel sorry for them.

We were loaded into these trains and we had our first stop at Dachau. They unloaded the men there and then we were transferred into closed cattle trucks. One night on our journey we were bombed, in Hanover. The guards took off and we were left in the station in these closed cattle trucks with the bombs falling around us. It didn't worry us, we didn't know where we were going but we knew that the war was coming to an end. It was something that gave us a little bit of hope.

From there, we were then taken to Belsen concentration camp where one of the doctors recognised me from Birkenau. She said I could stay there and work in the hospital as a nurse. I wasn't a qualified nurse and we had no medication, but we looked after people as best as we could.

We had to put four people in each of the bunks because there was a shortage of space. These people had typhus and were just skeletons. Once people died, we had to take the dead people out in blankets. I had never touched a dead person before that time. In the end, there weren't enough blankets and we had to physically carry them out and dump them in a heap. That is something you don't forget, you don't treat humans like that.

It was in Belsen that we were liberated by the British Army. About a week before liberation, all of a sudden all the guards were wearing white armbands and we knew then that it was a sign they had given themselves up. But they were still mistreating us, right up till the end.

There were rumours that the Germans were going to blow us up, because they didn't want anyone to find out what was going on there.

The last week, we had very little food. They couldn't bring us any supplies, they were getting short of things themselves. We had a German doctor, Dr Klein, who called us nurses and doctors together and he told us, "It is really hard, we have no medication, but we have to treat our patients with dignity and calm." He was just trying to make himself look good.

We had no water. There was a well just along from us in one of the streets and I asked one of the female German guards to come with us so that we could get some water from the well.

Two of us went with her with a bucket. We didn't have very much strength, and it took two of us to carry the bucket. While we were there it was very quiet because there was a curfew in the camp and I heard what sounded like tanks … a rolling sort of noise.

I said to the girl who had come with me, "Can you hear that noise? It sounds like tanks."

She said, "Oh, it's probably the Germans taking off."

I said, "Listen, it's coming from the other way."

We went back to the camp and I told the doctors. I get emotional when I talk about it.... I said, "I can hear noises, it sounds like tanks coming."

We never thought any more about it. I wasn't very strong. I was so thin, I had to walk on my hands and knees.

The next day was a lovely spring day. It was 15 April. We were keeping ourselves busy, we were attending to our sick ... all of a sudden I could hear someone running along the camp. I went to the window, it was a girl from the office, she was running and all she could say was, "We are free, the British are here."

I knew I had a room full of sick patients and I knew some would die, but I thought they might die in peace, they might know they will be buried like human beings. I had to let them know.

I went across and opened the door and I said to the girls in Polish, "Girls, we are free" and an almighty roar broke out ... laughter, crying....

As I stood there, a guard shot a bullet right through the window. It hit the ceiling. He thought a riot had broken out or something.

I went across to a table and chair there and I sat down and everything went blank. I heard someone say, "Put her head between her knees."

I just passed out with the emotion and everything. I sat there crying and thinking, "I've come through this and I'm all by myself – I'm all alone."

After that the tanks came straight through. I don't know where we got the strength from, but we all went outside and we ripped the gates open, even the gates between our camp and the main camp. We just went mad. And the British arrived in their tanks.

The next morning, a British doctor came and asked if anyone spoke English. I said I had learned some at school.

The British brought big water tanks through and I was so weak I couldn't get up on that tank, they had to lift me up. I was to show the first driver where the rest of the camp was and where the water was needed. I started talking to him and he said, "I beg your pardon, I thought you could speak English."

He was a Yorkshireman. I said to him, "Your English isn't like mine." The trucks behind us were linked by radio and they all laughed.

They gave us chocolate and all their rations, they couldn't do enough for us, but we had to be very careful because we hadn't eaten properly for a long time.

After the war, I tried to find out if any of my family were still alive. I tried to contact a girl I used to go to school with who was in England. My message was passed on to her new address and she wrote to my cousin Henry in New Zealand to say that I was alive.

Meanwhile she also got in touch with another cousin who was in the American Army. One day I was at home and someone said to me, "There's an American soldier asking for you."

It was my cousin. From him I discovered that my brother Fred was still alive. After he was liberated, Fred went back to Berlin looking for us. He had remembered we had a relative in New Zealand so he addressed a letter to Dr Tichauer in Auckland, New Zealand, and it got here.

So we found each other again via New Zealand.

My uncle in New Zealand applied for visas and permits for us to go to New Zealand. It was difficult because we had no papers and no identification. I arrived in 1948. Fred came six months later. Our parents did not survive the war.

I still do not know why the SS officer chose me out of all those people that first night we arrived at Auschwitz. I do realise how lucky I was – I was the only one who came out alive from that whole transport.

At Death's Door
Murray McColl

Murray McColl wrote the experiences of his war years in a notebook. He would write in sporadic bursts as the mood took him, then leave it for a while, before picking up the pen and hurriedly dashing off more of his story. When he had finished one notebook, he started a second one. Then he went back through the blank pages he had left and filled those.

I joined the Army with two great friends, Arthur Brumby and Fred Linstrom, and my brother Allan. Allan and Arthur went into camp with the first echelon. Allan had his final leave for the Christmas holidays of 1939–40 and spent it with us in Tauranga.

It was the unhappiest holiday I have ever had, and at the end of the holidays I headed back to Auckland with mother's message ringing in my ears not to join up. But as soon as I got back I put my age ahead just a month or two and joined up.

I first saw action at a place called Katerini in Greece. A day or so after we arrived, the Germans started their attack and we could see the town of Salonica burning. Our officer went to pieces and during the day an order came around from headquarters to hide all our gear as enemy bombers were starting to fly over our positions. That evening, the officer told us to pack all our guns and other gear onto the trucks and sleep on the ground beside them and be ready to move at a moment's notice.

At about 11 o'clock, there was a shout, "Shift your truck. Jerries are coming this way. Shift your truck." The poor officer had completely gone to pieces and was full of "vino".

Everyone took a flying jump off the ground onto the trucks and took off! We retreated to Olympus Pass and started digging in again in a fairly open position. The second day there, a Maori officer who commanded the Maori Battalion came around and told us to shift, saying if we stayed we would all be killed in five minutes.

That night, about midnight, we packed up our guns and gear and prepared to move to another position. The officer looked around and said that someone would have to stay behind and look after the balance of the gear until they came back. He wanted a volunteer, and he said, "McColl, you will do," but I had never opened my mouth. So they all took off and left me alone.

It was a bright moonlit night with black shadows which made it all the worse. They had told me that the Germans might start creeping up and I should keep an eye open for them.

After about half an hour, I could hear them coming, moving through the undergrowth. The tin hat came off my head about one inch because my hair stood on end. I took my rifle off my shoulder. I had my bayonet fixed. I felt a sudden "Yes, here they are!" movement just over to my left.

Then a little bit of sanity came back to me. I realised it was too small a movement for a man. I took a closer look and saw it was a huge rat eating some porridge that the cook had left soaking for breakfast.

The next day, we dug our guns in again. We had a good range of fire right down the valley and late in the afternoon we could see the German convoys advancing. That night, they started firing flares and our officer was beside himself. I was on picket duty with a chap called Frankie Bruno and the officer could not sleep and was going around trying to hide gear and with every flare that went up he was having kittens.

Next day, we opened fire on them with good result. No. 12

platoon was not far from us on the right and a platoon of the Maori Battalion was right behind us. They were firing off trench mortars. The next day, they attacked us with tanks and artillery. The following day, a mist came down and it was decided that night to vacate our position. We have since found out the Germans nearly cut us off by coming up a road and surrounding us.

We grabbed our guns and took off through the bush. We marched through the bush for most of the night and in the early morning lay down on the ground on our groundsheets. A light powdery snow was falling but we were so exhausted we went straight to sleep.

We carried on at first light and scrambled down a steep bank onto the road to our waiting trucks. What a relief. When we were putting our gear up on the trucks, a message came through saying that there was a platoon of Maoris surrounded in the gorge and that we would have to go back and help them out.

None of us were too happy to go back again. Then around a corner of the road came the platoon of Maoris. Man alive, we were glad to see them. We headed back, not very fast, because of all the convoys of trucks.

The next day or the day after, I cannot quite remember, we passed through a town called Larissa, which is in northern central Greece. It had been very heavily bombed. We turned left here and headed for a coastal town called Volos.

We travelled across coastal plains in a whole line of trucks in convoy. I was sitting on the back of our truck with my back facing the way we were going. We were watching the bombers plastering Larissa. All of a sudden, someone shouted, "Christ's sake, look out."

I turned my head to look in the direction that we were going, and there were three fighter planes screaming down on us. They only seemed to be about as high as a small tree. I could see the flames from the guns spitting out of their wings. They were swooping down on our convoy. I dived off the truck onto the ground and felt a dull, hot pain between my shoulders. After things had died down a bit, they cut my shirt off me and put a bandage over my wound. It hurt a bit, but it really was not much.

Two other chaps were hit at the same time, Bob Steel in the lower back and Les Eden in the arm. Allan was very lucky. He was ahead of us in the convoy and before he could get out of his truck, bullets zipped down both sides – a very close shave. The three of us were loaded into an ambulance and that night ended up at an ADS (Advanced Dressing Station). Allan found me that night and he was quite concerned, although there was nothing to worry about.

We travelled all night and next morning pulled over at a rest area under the olive trees to refuel and have something to eat. It was not long before the fighter planes found us again. They caught us on the road but fortunately did not do any damage. Next day we were loaded onto a train in cattle trucks and headed south again but not at a very fast speed.

That afternoon, we were caught by bombers. The train came to a screeching halt and everyone piled out and took off for cover. We could see them coming in low and open their bomb bays and the bombs would just slowly curl down. That was the end of the train.

There was a road not far away so we all made for that.

A convoy came through containing some large trucks. An English officer who was with us managed to stop them and although they were full of blokes we managed to pile aboard.

I cannot remember if it was the next day or the day after we arrived back in Athens. We went right through the town to a big square called Armonia Square. It was completely lined with Greeks and everybody was clapping not cheering. We were taken to a large building with makeshift beds. I remember we had to walk about a hundred yards or so to another building for our food.

Now that we were back in civilisation again you had the false impression that you were safe. I did not know a soul, but an Aussie bloke and I got together. After a couple of days or so we were over in the mess hall when a bloke came over to tell all of us to report back to our units and (what a silly statement) every man for himself. So this Aussie said to me, "Come on, Kiwi, let's get out of here."

We took off to town to the railway station and here were blokes filing aboard cattle trucks behind an old train. We waited and waited most of the afternoon and still the damn thing would not move. We found out later the engine driver had taken off.

All of a sudden there was a jolt. We stopped again then finally got going. We travelled all night and I have since found out we went down to the south coast of Greece then followed it around in a big curve.

In the late afternoon, we stopped and everyone got off. It was a nice sunny day and the war seemed far away. We had been there only about 10 minutes, we looked back at the train and everyone was climbing back aboard again and it was going back again the way we had come. We all took a flying jump into the boxcars again, and went back a mile or so.

Next morning we had a visit from the planes again and they swooped down on top of us, letting everything fly. I just can't remember how long we were there, a few days, and constantly being strafed by the planes, bullets zipping through the branches of the olive trees. There were rumours, rumours and more rumours.

Then one night we got the order for all troops to form up on the road. We were going to march to an embarkation point. We marched down the road for about a mile or so and some badly wounded chaps were struggling along with other fellows helping them but as we knew we were going to get off we were making every effort.

We finally stopped and the order came – all UK troops on the right of the road and colonial troops on the left. What that was for we didn't know. After about 10 minutes or so, the order came – all troops back on the road – and we marched back to where we started from. What a shambles.

Next day, it was just the repetition of the previous day. Strafed by planes, and more rumours. Then one evening we were told to form up in groups of 55 as we were going off tonight. We still did not know whether to believe it or not. But when it became night, we did start to march down to the beach. At long last, here were the lifeboats on the beach. We formed up in long lines and climbed aboard. They counted us 53, 54, 55, and guess what, of course, just like McColl's luck, I was number 56. I saw another boat a few yards away, so I walked across and jumped in over the side. No one said to get out and I just sat there.

We withdrew to Crete and took up position in Canea. We shifted our positions two or three times before the battle started. We took up positions on a ridge overlooking a coastal road going to the aerodrome.

We had constant air raids but we did get used to them as they were bombing Canea and villages and not us in the open. We were told to expect the invasion on the 17th or 19th. We had a Vickers machine-gun without a tripod and which was sitting on a forked stick, and not all of us had rifles.

But we thought an invasion was impossible. How could they come all that way by air with hundreds of parachutes? The 17th came and went and then the 19th came. I must admit our disbelief about it all started to grow.

But all that ended on the morning of the 20th. We were just starting to eat our breakfast (the last meal I was to have for a long time) when a few planes came over a lot lower than usual. We ignored them but some more came over, so we decided to get into our slit trenches until the raid was over and come back and finish our breakfast.

Then all hell broke loose. They came this way and that way, bombing and strafing. Six to eight planes in line astern came right down low over our trenches, firing with their fore and aft guns. We could just about have reached up and touched them. The screech of the motors and the exploding bullets landing beside us on the banks beside us gave us a helluva fright. I was crouched in a little slit trench with a bloke called Pat Patterson.

Afterwards someone said, "Were you frightened?"

I said, "No, I was just petrified."

After about an hour or so of this continual bombing and strafing, all of a sudden it became quiet and we thought that it was all over. Then there was a low buzzing, droning noise and after a while we could make out all these planes coming. They seemed to be stacked on top of each other. They were full of parachutists, 18 in each plane.

They were very slow moving and as they came over our positions troops came out of the planes. They were just like men from Mars, firing as they came down. They came down with a sound that was like a silent swish. They were jumping out about 300 to 500 feet up and only took a few moments to land.

Had we had proper radio communication, had we had our proper arms and armour, they would not have taken Crete. The first wave of parachutists was about 2000 but they suffered terrible casualties and we should have counter-attacked immediately.

The Maoris were held in reserve for the expected sea invasion, but that is all history now. On the afternoon of the 24th, we went to go and support the 18th Battalion outside Galatas. We took up our positions behind a small ridge about 8 to 10ft high.

As the afternoon wore on, we could hear them coming towards us. It began to get a little chilly so I walked down towards where I had left my jersey about 20 to 30 feet away. As I left, a mortar came over and landed where I had been sitting. There had been a chap next to me and he was killed instantly, so I suppose that was a little of McColl's luck the other way.

Shortly afterwards, we received a lot of mortar fire and small arms fire. Then the Jerries started attacking us, coming towards us with a lot of shouting and firing their Tommy guns and making a helluva racket. The 18th Battalion officer whom we were attached to told us to fix bayonets and we went to charge the Jerries.

I was back about 10 feet or so from the ridge so I could get a better view of them as they came over the top. When we got the order to fix bayonets, I was just about to move to take up my position behind the ridge ready to attack when all of a sudden, *bang*, I was hit in the leg. It must have shattered the bone because my foot was right up under my shoulder blades.

I don't know what happened next but I think the attack was repulsed. The firing, the shouting, the noise was utter confusion. Two men threw me in a stretcher and ran with me for about a hundred yards or so out of the direct line of fire. After a while,

I was shifted again and moved to an ADS. Quite a few of us were collected on stretchers and put on the ground outside the tent. It was starting to get dark by then. After an hour or so, they took us into the tent and bound my wound.

A chap tried to put a cigarette in my mouth, which I promptly refused as I didn't smoke. Later on that night, I was taken into the ADS. We were put into a tent, about 6 or 8 of us. The tent was dug down into the ground about 12 to 18 inches in case a bomb dropped and shrapnel was flying around.

The next morning they operated on me and fitted a Thomas splint with a pin through my shin. Every time someone stepped down on the floor it grated my bones together and I just about went through the roof.

The next day, late afternoon, we could hear firing coming closer. They said we would have to evacuate that night. By this time, my trousers had been cut off me and the tail of my shirt cut off as well to operate on me. My watch was wrapped in my handkerchief on the floor.

About midnight, some blokes came in and started to shift the stretchers out until only one was left and guess who that was? Yes, me again. I waited and waited for fully an hour or more and I thought, "This is it. They have forgotten me."

Then two blokes came in and picked me up. I asked them to give me my handkerchief, which was behind me. I don't know whether they picked it up and put it in their pocket or not but they said it was not there which was wrong.

They took me about 100 yards or so and put me on the ground. There was a bit of activity back and forth and a bloke tripped right over my stretcher. My God ... the pain.

They loaded us into an ambulance. The Army ambulances are a lot bigger than normal ones and from memory you can load four stretchers, two on top of each other on both sides.

Well they jammed us all in, double-banked the stretchers and also put one on the floor between us. The bloke with me had his leg off below the knee and he was waving the stump around.

Then we set off. What a ride! We were bumping into potholes

and shell holes. Blokes were screaming with pain. I'm not sure how far we went – a couple of miles or so – and then they unloaded us and put us under some olive trees. What an experience. I can still hear the blokes screaming and shouting in pain.

As it became light, we could see troops marching through our area. I was not very happy with where I was under this tree and, when a couple of Aussies came through, I asked them to carry us up to another tree not far away which somehow felt safer. They put me down beside a Greek soldier who had had his leg blown off. He was making a bit of a row, moaning in pain. Then he settled down, I looked at him again and realised the reason he became quiet was because he had passed on.

I had not been there more than a quarter of an hour or so when three fighter planes ripped through, letting everything fly. They practically stripped the leaves off the trees where I had been just before.

Late in the afternoon, an ambulance arrived and we were loaded aboard. Just before they put us in, a plane flew over. The ambulance had a big Red Cross painted on the roof and one of the medical personnel said, "He won't touch us."

I was not sure of that. I watched as he flew right around and came back again. I thought, "Wait for it. I'm going to cop it this time."

My stretcher was on the ground behind the ambulance, so I just held my breath and shut my eyes. Fortunately for me he was one Jerry that respected the Red Cross.

We only seemed to go about a quarter of a mile when they stopped and offloaded us at a school grounds in the village of Karlevis. The school was full up so they laid us in rows in the courtyard outside.

We were told that we would be going off that night in destroyers. As I was one of the last stretchers to be put in line I thought that would be good, I'd be one of the first to go. Around midnight, I heard a few blokes take off down the road and I thought we would be next but that was wishful thinking.

In the early hours of the morning, a bloke started to crawl over our stretchers. His head was wrapped in bandages with hardly any clothes on. He had been wounded and had a Tommy gun bullet in the middle of his head right between the two parts of his brain.

Later on, in the prison camp, I became quite friendly with him. His name was Jimmy Blue. The trip he made across our stretchers was very painful and we tried to push him off but with no success. I told him about it a year or so later.

A bloke came around about mid-morning and told us that our friends would be arriving soon and he collected any arms and ammo that we had. As he spoke to us, a Jerry plane flew over, but he said don't worry that is one of ours now. Shortly after we heard a motorbike patrol stop in the village and the clump of feet as the Jerries surrounded the schoolhouse.

An officer and a sergeant went straight inside, had a look around then came out to the courtyard. They were both hyped up and started shouting and screaming at us. They both spoke perfect English.

There was a chap standing in the courtyard who did not seem to be wounded although he did not seem to be quite with it. The German officer asked the Aussie doctor what was wrong with him and he told him that he was shellshocked. The sergeant replied, as sarcastic as hell, "The bombs dropped too close to him, isn't that a pity."

Then he began screaming at us, saying we shot their men as they came down in the parachutes, "You mutilate our wounded." (I think some of the Cretans did that.) He was really winding himself up. He turned his Tommy gun over and bumped the magazine in and flopped it back again.

He came down a bit further until he was right opposite me. He was shaking with rage. His face was livid. I completely froze, not even daring to breathe. I was looking practically straight down the barrel. I was waiting for the crack of the gun and the thud of the bullets ripping into me. Not one of us said anything or called for mercy.

I don't know to this day know why he did not pull the trigger, because he was absolutely beside himself with rage. The officer started screaming at someone close and it seemed to distract him for a second and he went off the boil.

He said he was going to shoot five men for every live round of ammo he found in our pockets. Thank God this threat wasn't carried out. One bloke had enough Tommy ammo to wipe out all the wounded. There were quite a few cases of them shooting the wounded. I met a bloke called Bernie Harris who was in a room lying with a bunch of wounded when a German officer came around with his revolver to finish them off. He shot Bernie and blew his eye out but fortunately did not kill him. They also captured blokes and used them as human screens when they advanced.

We didn't hear from the Jerries again – only when they wanted a swim or when they marched through the village, singing some army song to try and break our morale, but it didn't work.

When the doctor came around to replace dressings he found the bottom half of my leg was at right angles to the top half. I think that would have happened when that bloke tripped over my stretcher or when I was in the ambulance. Fortunately, the Aussies had a good supply of morphine and they gave us a good injection every night which relieved the pain and enabled us to sleep.

Eventually, we were flown back to Athens. I had been on that same stretcher with the same blanket from 24 May to 21 June, and, boy, it was a little "high". After about a week they put me in a splint which was made out of rough timber. They tied it to the bed to prevent it toppling over.

About this time, I mentioned to the doctor that I still had a bullet in my back. Two orderlies pulled me up to a sitting position, then the doctor climbed on the bed behind me and gave me an injection to dull the pain. He made an incision and proceeded to get the bullet out with a pair of tweezers. He kept slipping off the bullet until he eventually grabbed it.

He was about to sew me up, when he noticed something else. I didn't know what it was, but it sure felt like a hay-baling needle. He apologised to me and said, "Grit your teeth soldier."

One of the experts you get in the Army said it was an armour-piercing bullet. The Germans loaded their belts 1 times tracer, 1 times armour and 1 times tracer and so on....

I was very fortunate that another bullet went straight through the rim of my tin hat. Had it been further forward it would have gone right through my brain and it just missed my spine by a whisker. Had it gone through my spine, I would have been paralysed from the waist down.

From then on, my general condition started to deteriorate. When my leg was in the other splint, fortunately I could not see the wound, but in this splint I looked straight at it. They just had it covered by a pad. When chaps came along I used to lift the pad to show them and they would take off like a rocket. The wound was about 4 to 5 inches long with a smaller hole in the back of my leg. It was quite deep but it did not bleed anymore. Treatment for it was somewhat limited as they did not have much to give us. They gave me some sort of tablets which they used to crush up and drop into the wound.

I packed some cotton wool under my thigh to stop the rough wood from cutting into me, but it was not very satisfactory. After about six weeks or so one of the chaps that died had a frame like mine, but a proper metal one, so I was lucky I got his. This was far more comfortable but I still suffered constant pain.

One day in the ward I heard a chap inquiring about me and I received a great surprise. It was Marty Cammick, the first person I had known from before the war to come and see me. He had his arm in plaster and in an aeroplane splint which held his arm at a right angle to his body. He looked very thin and poorly. Someone had told him I was there so he went round ward to ward until he found me. I did appreciate it.

Outside the hospital for the first few months was a stall run by an old Greek, selling fruit. Marty did not have any money but he swapped a pen with an Aussie to get some and bought me a tomato. At that time, a tomato was like a three-course dinner.

They gave me a blood transfusion but unfortunately something went wrong. In no time at all I was shivering and it was a really hot day. I only had a sheet over me but they had to put two or three blankets over me. I tried to stop shaking. I had an Aussie doctor looking after me; he came from Perth and I think he was of Dutch descent. Looking back, my condition must have got beyond him.

I continued my downward slide in health and I must admit things started to become somewhat hazy. I developed a horribly ulcerated mouth, which I suppose was the poison in my system. It was a shocker. My tongue and all over my lips was coated.

A chap called Don Stott came to see me. I knew him from before the war. I played football against him when he played for Grammar Old Boys. He escaped shortly after. He told me he was going to and I wished him well. In the years to come he became quite famous for his exploits and should have won the VC. When he got back to Egypt after escaping from Athens, he saw my friend Jim Barclay and told Jim that he would not see me any more as I was dying!

One morning my stomach was very sore from the constant dry retching and I had developed quite a severe pain at the top of my thigh. When the doctor came around he said he would come in the afternoon and do something about it. What he did was to put me out and make an incision and insert a draining tube. I believe they filled up two kidney bowls of discharge – horrible!

Next morning, an orderly came around to dress it for me. He took the dressing off but was not quite quick enough to put the kidney bowl under the drain tube and it ran on me. What a bloody mess.

From then on they said to dress it twice a day. Unfortunately, my wound started to open up again. As it got deeper, one day a piece of bone was exposed. The doctor was quite interested in this so he got a pair of tweezers and rocked it back and forwards. He thought it was a loose splint. He just about shot me through the roof.

My general condition was getting worse day by day, week by week. I was getting a lot weaker. They put another nick in my thigh a bit higher that the first one. The poison must have been travelling upwards. They used to put a square of cotton wool underneath me for a bedpan and my bedsore was getting worse.

One afternoon, the doctor came along and told me he was going to move me along the ward. My leg had been in that splint for a few months and then they just took it away and carried me along the ward. He should have given me a whiff of something to put me out. I was actually screaming in pain. It was unbearable.

Discharge from my leg went everywhere, all over the floor and bed and I got a bad attack of the shakes. So, I was just on the bed with no splint or anything on my leg and it seemed to me to just be rotting away. This is when my condition got beyond him. I don't think he knew what to do next.

My general health started a real dive. I had my arms folded across me and I could not straighten them out, I could not lift my head off the pillow, I did not have the strength to hold it up. My hair seemed to stop growing and what was left of it started to rapidly fall out. My voice started to fail and I could only barely talk in a whisper. My two hipbones stood out and my stomach went down in a great big hollow.

All that was left of me was a skeleton with skin stretched over it. The old clock must have been just ticking over and no more.

When the orderlies changed over, the first thing they would say was, "Is Mac still there?" I was expected to go at any time.

As some of the POWs who were not so badly wounded had reached the convalescent stage, they were sent on to Germany and also some medical staff, doctors and orderlies. My doctor, Dr Mayhoff, was called up in a batch and sent off. He left in the morning and he had hardly gone when Dr McNamara came down to see me. He had heard about me but could not interfere when I was under the care of the other doctor. He immediately shifted me across the ward (bed and all) out of the draught, because he said I could get pneumonia in my weak condition.

He gave me a blood transfusion but this time my veins had shrunk in size and they had to cut my arm and dig down with some pincers to fish them up. He found me some overproof rum from somewhere which just about blew the top of my head off. A few days after he came to me and said that Chris Rolleston was having his leg cut off, and I might be of the same mind.

At the time I would not have cared if they had taken it off below my ears.

That night, at about 7 o'clock, Dr McNamara came around again with a Dr Brookmore. He had been the head doctor in charge of one of the biggest jails in Sydney. He was a rough customer.

I only had a sheet over me and he just pulled it back and pointed with a pencil where they should cut it and they had a bit of a chat about it. Then he walked off without speaking a word to me. Dr McNamara did give me a bit of a nod and a smile.

Early afternoon the next day, two Greeks came down with a stretcher and said, "Which one is he?" meaning me. They were rough-looking blokes. Then a doctor arrived, one I had not seen before, to give me an injection to put me out before they moved me. He had a hell of a job finding my vein and was digging around for some time.

I took one last look at the toes on my right foot, knowing full well that would be the last time in my life I would see them. The next thing I can remember is early evening and this weightless thing propped up on a pillow which of course was my stump. It was not a very nice feeling.

In 1995, I met a chap called Dalgetty Knight who had been in another ward just through the doorway though I never met him in the camp. At the time, he said, the doctors and orderlies had asked everyone to be quiet as I had had my leg off and I was dying.

That was about the 14th or 15th October 1941. For the next few days, things were somewhat hazy. I did not seem to be quite conscious of my surroundings.

After a few days, they gave me a jab to dress my stump and they repeated that quite a few times. The doctors were absolutely amazed at how quickly my wound was healing considering the poison that was in there before I had had it amputated.

I was a POW for three years and was repatriated in November 1943. On the train back to Auckland, some Red Cross ladies brought in hot tea and refreshments. One said to me, "Oh I do feel sorry for these boys who have lost their legs."

I did not let on I was one of them so as not to embarrass her. When we arrived at the station my family had spread out along the platform to find me as we got off and – blow me down – right outside the door of my carriage was my sister Marg.

She got such a shock at finding me so quickly and I can always remember her saying, "Oh, are you Murray?"

The Cretan Shepherd
Murray McLagan

Murray McLagan started out in working life as a shepherd and ironically that is what circumstances forced him to become once again during the war.

I was born on a farm in Hawkes Bay in 1918. My father was farming there and he gave it up. I went to the Hawkes Bay training farm and then I got a scholarship to go to Massey. When I finished there, I went on to the staff at Massey as stud shepherd and then left for the war. I was one of the first echelon – one of the "originals".

I had artillery training at the Hopuhopu Camp. It was a terrible camp. It was wet all the time and we lived in old tents from the First World War. They were so bad that if it rained we slept with our ground sheets over us to try to keep dry.

Then on 5 January 1940, we took off. About 2000 of us went over on the *Empress of Canada*. There were about seven or eight ships in the convoy. We had Tiny Freyberg on board [General Bernard Freyberg VC, commander of the NZ Division. He was known as Tiny because he was powerfully built and over six feet tall]. We went into Sydney and dropped him off because he flew over. The rest of the convoy had gone on. We caught up with it in the Great Australian Bight.

We had a couple of days in Fremantle and Colombo. We sailed to Port Taufig. We went by cattle truck to Maadi, which was our camp in North Africa. We weren't engaged in any fighting at all to any extent until we went to Greece. We went backwards and forwards for about 18 months before we went into action because we had to wait for the rest of the division.

There were three echelons of the division plus division HQ. The second echelon was diverted to England to try to help over there and then we had to wait for the third echelon because a division was a complete unit consisting of artillery, engineers and infantry.

It was soon after we had a complete division that we went to Greece. We landed at Athens and worked from there up to Mt Olympus which was as far north as the artillery got. The German armour was far superior to ours and we had so little air support they just overwhelmed us and we withdrew back to Crete.

I landed in Crete on Anzac Day, 25 April. It was the same as Greece – the Germans came over and the sky was black with parachutes. New Zealand put up a good fight, but the Germans had the numbers and we didn't have any equipment. We had nothing. I think we had one armoured vehicle and about a half a dozen Spitfires and they didn't last long.

In the artillery, some of us had rifles, some of us didn't. I had a rifle for a while, then a Bren gun for a while. I was on the front line when the sergeant next to me got shot up by a sniper. I had to take over the Bren.

With the first shot the sniper knocked the leg off the Bren and the second shot got me. I was lucky. My tin hat had a hole in it just above my left ear. But the Germans were charging in and I got my revenge by shooting a few of them.

When we realised we couldn't hold the island we had to evacuate to Sfakia on the South Coast and the Navy came in and got as many of us as they could.

There was complete disorganisation. The Navy was sailing back to Egypt half-empty because there were people who weren't allowed to go down onto the beach. We were further up the hill and we never had a chance of getting there. You just weren't allowed to go down to the beach. It was a proper shambles. There were thousands of us taken to POW camps.

After six weeks, another chap, Eric Vickers, and I had had enough of being in a prison camp and decided to escape. We lay alongside the wire for a couple of nights and this particular night a motorcyclist went past and when he got about 100 yards away from us, his bike caught fire. So I said, "This is our chance."

While they were worried about putting the fire out on the motor bike, we took off. We went through a big valley to a place called Theriso up in the hills. The Greeks wanted us to stay there. But we wouldn't stay, and we decided we wanted to get back to the division.

We headed south and stayed in a place called Temania for a few days. We ended up with quite a big group of us there. The Greeks provided some money and we put in money as well to buy a boat but that didn't eventuate either because we had to trust the Greek bloke to buy the boat and bring it back to us. Instead of that, he skipped.

The Germans knew we were in the area and they dropped pamphlets that read:

Soldiers of the Royal British Army, Navy, Air Force,

There are many of you still hiding in the mountains, valleys and villages. You have to present yourselves at once to the German troops. Every opposition will be completely useless, every attempt to flee will be in vain. The comming [sic] *winter will force you to leave the mountains. Only soldiers who present themselves at once will be sure of an honourable and soldierlike captivity of war. On the contrary who is met in civ will be treated as a spy.*

The Commander of Crete

Eric Vickers read one of the pamphlets the Germans dropped and gave himself up. He ended up in Germany. I never saw him again. I tried to contact him after the war but he never joined the RSA. Then about a year ago I read of his death in the *Herald*.

When I read one of the pamphlets I thought, "Oh well, I'll take the chance. They'll have to take me forcibly if they want me."

We were in uniform for a while until we got Greek clothes. Being of fairly sallow complexion, I got away with it. We learned to speak Greek a lot better than the Germans did.

Occasionally I would be confronted by a German. You couldn't avoid it, you didn't know where they were. On one occasion, a little 10-year-old girl and I were watching sheep. They never worked dogs over there. You did it all by throwing rocks at the sheep and turning them wherever you wanted.

We were just sitting down watching the sheep and she turned around to me and she said, "Marcus [my Greek name], there are Germans behind us."

They were only about 50 yards away on the track. So there was only one thing to do – we got up and just quietly drove the sheep. The Germans didn't take any notice. She was a Greek girl and they must have presumed that I was Greek.

We never worried about the German soldiers, we only worried about the Gestapo who could speak truer Greek than the Greeks themselves! If you came into any contact with them, you'd had it.

I became part of the Greek community. I covered quite a big area of the west of Crete, but always went back to the same headquarters. The Cretans were extremely good to me, they fed me and clothed me. You had to be careful that you didn't endanger the lives of the Greeks, otherwise the Germans would shoot up the whole village.

On one occasion, I went down into a village but I wouldn't stay there. I went up into the hills and about an hour later I heard a German patrol coming. They must have been warned that I was there because the face of the hillside where I was hiding was subjected to quite a bit of fire from machine-guns and rifles.

I just crept down into the scrub and stayed there until they went away.

Much later, when I returned to the village, the villagers gave me the works for not coming straight back and letting them know I was still alive.

On another occasion, a Cretan asked me to deliver a message for him to a place about 30 miles away. He said he couldn't go himself because the police were after him.

I said, "Yes, but I want a revolver if I go."

His mother heard this and said, "No, don't you give him a revolver. You'll encourage him to get into more trouble."

So I went and delivered the message and when I came back I had to cross a main road. I had just come down the track and jumped down onto the road and there was a German ute about 10 yards away. Thank goodness I didn't have the revolver otherwise I might have used it. Instead I just followed the Germans across the road. They went to a café and I went straight on.

You didn't worry about bumping into the Germans. It happened all the time.

At the village where I stayed most of the time, there was a telephone line running through. I thought I'd get some of this telephone wire and make chains because these people needed to chain their goats and sheep and there was no way of getting chain or rope or anything. I cut the wire into links and twisted it with some pliers. I went all around the area swapping chains for olive oil, which was a good commodity.

In May 1943, a chap called Tom Moir came in to contact us to tell us we had a boat out.

Unfortunately he got picked up, but the whole thing was already organised and we got the message. A Navy torpedo boat was to come in from Tobruk and pick us up from a particular spot. The idea was that if they got through early enough, we were to take a German post and get a few prisoners. Unfortunately, they ran into heavy sea fog and were late getting to us, so that didn't happen, but we got on the boat and landed back at Tobruk.

It took us three days to get back to Cairo. We were not supposed to be seen by anybody and stupidly they put us in battle dress in the middle of summer, instead of shorts, perhaps to make us more conspicuous in case some of us tried to get away from the party.

But we were well treated. When we got to Tobruk, an

Englishman, Major Simcox, a real nice bloke, gave us a bottle of Canadian Whitehorse beer each. We hadn't had beer for so long.

When we eventually got back to Maadi we were given a big hut and told to stay there. It was the same deal there, we weren't allowed to talk to anybody or move from the area. They wanted to get all the information they could from us before we were allowed loose.

We were interrogated day after day, we weren't even allowed into Cairo until everything was cleaned up. Then we went into Cairo to the New Zealand Club and the girls went mad over us when we eventually got there.

That first night we were in the New Zealand Club there was a very unusual incident. A chap said to me, "I hear you've come from Crete, haven't you?"

I said, "Yes, that's right."

He said, "I wonder if by any chance you know what happened to my brother? We know he was killed on Crete."

When he identified himself, I said "You've just made a mistake boy, there's your brother over there."

He said, "Cut it out, that's not funny."

I said, "Look at him. Do you know who that is?"

It was his brother. He hadn't believed he could be alive.

My aunt was a missionary nurse from World War One. She was up in Lebanon. I thought I'd go and see her. I knew where she was. I went up there and I saw one of the officers and he said, "Oh no, your aunt's up in Damascus now. She's in a missionary school up there. We've got a train going that way tonight. Hop aboard and we'll take you with us."

I got up there and I found out where my aunt was and I went and knocked on this girl's school. She came out and said, "Who are you?"

I said, "I'm your nephew Murray."

She just about collapsed seeing me. She thought I was dead.

I'd got back from Crete in time to join the first furlough draft – the "Ruapehus". Three of us were supposed to be going back into Greece but the New Zealand Division refused to release us to the

British Army. They said, "You've been missing, presumed dead, for two years, you'd better go home while you've got the opportunity. There'll be jobs here for you when you come back."

They looked on us as heroes when we got back to our local towns. My family was very tearful when they saw me, having been missing, presumed dead, for two years.

Instead of having three months' furlough, we had six months. The Government wanted to keep us there because there was an election coming up. They made sure we stayed in New Zealand to vote before leaving again to fight in Italy.

I was one of the few who returned to the war. Anyone whose wife was pregnant and so forth could stay behind. I went to see active service in Italy for 13 months and came back with the fifth reinforcements in 1945 and was finally discharged in August after nearly six years in the Army.

More Interested in Escaping
Stan Martin

Stan Martin was in the medical corps during the war, along with several friends who were accomplished boxers. Trust the Army to give fighters a job not fighting! Technically, Stan was a non-combatant, until he decided to escape.

I was born in Huntly in 1916, the youngest of six. My father was a coalminer. My father was born in Waimate and his eldest brother was the first white child to be born in Skipper's Canyon, which the Shotover River runs through. In about 1920, my father moved the family to Auckland to work. He ended up as a blacksmith on Newmarket Borough Council. He was a good man. He died when he was 80.

I was a relief porter in the railways for four years before the war. On 3 September 1939, I won't forget it, I'd been up north relieving and returned to Helensville. It was a Sunday and there wasn't much work and we were sitting down listening to the news and we heard Germany had marched into Poland and England had declared war on Germany, and so had New Zealand.

We used to say that we must have declared war on them first because we're 12 hours ahead in New Zealand.

Jimmy, the station master, said to me, "What about a ride in on the train and you can join the Air Force."

So I did that, but I didn't hear anything from the Air Force for a while and a few days later they called for a special force. I said to the station master that I wanted to change my shift because I wanted to volunteer for the Army down in Auckland where my mates were.

They put me in the medical corps because I had a St John's certificate. I went back to Helensville and told the station master that I had been accepted as a volunteer and wanted to arrange leave because I had been on the railway about four years. A week after I joined up with the Army, I got notice to report to Burnham Army Camp.

When I told Jimmy he asked what was happening with the Air Force. I told him that I hadn't heard anything, but that I didn't think the war would last long!

He told me my leave hadn't been granted yet. I told him I was going to war and I wasn't going to worry yet about coming back. The day before I left to go to war, my leave was granted.

I arrived in Burnham and saw a lot of men there I knew including one of my best mates, Frankie Bruno, who was the flyweight amateur boxing champion of New Zealand. He was to become a machine-gunner. I sat with him in the train on the way to Burnham. There were about 200 blokes on the train.

The machine-gunners went to a specific area in Burnham and I went to the medical field ambulance. The ambulance drivers belonged to the ASC [Army Service Corps]. I did try and transfer to a combat unit but they wouldn't let me go.

We sailed to Perth and picked up the Aussies. We stopped in Ceylon and then we arrived in Egypt and were sent out to Maadi. They had small tents there and I said, "Christ, they are going to leave us out in all this bloody sand." And they did.

Then we were sent out to the main British hospital in Cairo where they were sand-bagging the windows to stop the shrapnel going through them.

The sergeant-major asked us to line up. There were about 15 of us, in alphabetical order. They were telling each of us what ward we were to be in. Old Alec was six foot one and a good amateur wrestler and he said to the sergeant-major, "I'm not a 'po juggler' [bedpan nurse], I'm a field man." The sergeant-major screamed like hell and they sent for the officers.

They said, "Do any of you others feel that way?"

About five of us did. We all got put in departments that suited us in the end. I chose Sanitation and Hygiene.

I really wanted to go into the field and ended up in the Greek campaign. It was bad in Greece. On Hitler's birthday, 20 April, we were retreating again, being machine-gunned and bombed and this Greek bloke came out and said, "You'd better not go much further back there, that's the pass where the 200 Spartans held back the 10,000 Persians. There is nowhere to stop them if they get past there."

We retreated anyway. At the time, they picked out some of us to go up to 24th Rifle Battalion. Every battalion has a doctor and one medical orderly. When they go into action, they have an ambulance on standby. We went under cover of darkness. We had to use a password. I'll never forget it, it was "Oamaru, Timaru, Waipukurau, hee-haw, blow fly."

I laughed, and said, "Who the hell thought of that?"

They said, "The German paratroopers would be lucky if they knew that Oamaru is south of Timaru, then Waipukurau which is in the North Island … hee-haw, blow fly."

One time we were retreating and were short of trucks, so we had to climb onto the roof of the last truck. They were shelling us from behind and then we saw an aircraft coming, so we threw stones at the driver to alert him. He pulled off the side of the road into what looked like a field of oats and the water cart driven by Lofty Bray pulled up next to us. Someone yelled "duck" as the bombs were dropped.

We all got covered in dirt and old Lofty had some toilet paper in his hands and he was jumping up and down saying, "I've been blown up, I've been blown up."

His pubic hairs were all red and burnt and his eyebrows were singed. Afterwards the doctors reckoned the bomb must have gone right underneath him and blew him out of his trousers!

But Lofty just got back into his water cart and drove on.

We had to retreat back through Athens and drop off our wounded. It was bumper to bumper going through the city but we had a rest there. We were invited to see a mate, Hank, and his brother and stayed there the night. They were going to Egypt instead of Crete and suggested we follow them.

We did, but got lost in the dark in the pass. A lot of mules had been brought over from India and they had been machine-gunned in this pass. Their dead bodies were rotting everywhere. After that we pulled over and stayed put for the night.

In the morning, we heard this weird whirring noise. We crawled up the hill to look down at the Corinth Canal and we saw all these big planes going round and round. Someone said the planes were dropping pamphlets. I said, "They're bloody big pamphlets."

They weren't pamphlets. They were paratroopers.

We raced back down below and told the others. We picked up some walking wounded and pulled out into the road but we were stopped by a German pointing a pistol at us. We were thinking of bumping him off but there was another bloke behind on a motorbike with a machine-gun. They turned us out of the ambulance and put a swastika sticker on the bonnet.

Then they took us down to Corinth Canal, lined us up in a field and they went through our gear. Along with other family photos, I had photos of my nephew, who was only about five, in a motor car.

I also had photos of two girlfriends. I had been engaged to one of them but had a row with her before the war started. I had a photo of another girl that I used to date sometimes too. In the photos, both the girls were wearing evening frocks.

One of the Germans who was holding these photos turned and said something in German to the other 15 to 20 paratroopers around him. He'd said something untoward.

The German NCO got quite angry at that. He said, "That could be your mother or your sister and that's not on."

He had the soldier who had made the comment taken away.

We were then taken to Greek barracks and put in a building

where two guards manned the entrance with bayoneted rifles. They got us shifting papers from the basement. I had found a Sam Browne belt in the basement and put it on.

When I came up from the basement with this nice new shiny belt on and my arms full of papers, one of the guards stepped over and unbuckled the belt. The NCO screamed and yelled at him and made him buckle it back on me. He was taken away for another court martial. I still have the belt today.

I was lucky as a POW compared to others because lice don't eat me. They don't like the taste of me. In the barracks, huge bugs would walk over the roofs and drop down on top of you. If you didn't have a mosquito net on, they would bite you. Morrie McHugh had big welts from them. They stunk like hell if you squashed them.

Eric Baty, Ted Bryant and I decided to escape. Eric was a horse-breaker and New Zealand steer-riding champion.

Baty didn't know German very well and he told the Germans that he was a "Pferdemeister" – horse-breaker – so they gave him a job pulling a horse and cart. The Germans would say "links" (left), "recht" (right), when they wanted to lead their horses. But because he didn't know German, Baty wasn't sure which was left and which was right.

We noticed that the guards would take your boots off you and give you clogs when you went out to work camp, but they didn't check to see if you had an extra set in your kit bag. I told them I was a medical orderly but I worked on farms sometimes.

The next morning, a woman came around and she said she'd have the big strong bloke, Eric. Eric explained he was a "pferdemeister". She looked around to see who else she could have, and she said, "I'll have the little corporal with the blue eyes, just like my husband's." That was me.

She invited us for dinner on the Sunday. I didn't knock her off, but I reckon I could have. I was more interested in escaping at the time.

We had to escape that night because we had just received our Red Cross parcels. They put a bayonet through every tin, so that you couldn't hoard it to escape with. If they did that with soup it would run out. But it didn't matter if they bayoneted a tin of meat loaf because it would last a few days anyway.

Some of the others knew we were going to escape. An English guy said he'd slide the bolt for us and slide it back when we left. We put our boots on and got out. Unfortunately, we left our water bottles behind.

When we got out, it started to rain. Then we heard dogs barking. We followed the railway line in the dark. We crossed some swamp and walked a fair way after this until we came across a field of corn. We rested for a while underneath a haystack and took our boots off to rest our feet. Then we put them on again and took off.

Baty's feet had been giving him grief. He complained they were swollen and he kept lagging behind. Finally we looked down at his feet and said, "You stupid bastard, you've got your boots on the wrong feet."

We were heading towards Hungary. We found a hut, there was no one around so we decided to break in. We lit a fire and had some food. Baty won the bet for the swinging bunk. Ted and I slept on the floor.

The next morning we began hiking it again. We ate blackberries on the way. We crossed a track, and Baty lagged behind to keep eating blackberries. We had to go back to get him.

We kept going and reached a path. As we rounded the corner, we met an SS soldier on a push-bike. He was on holiday, but he had a gun and pulled it out, jumping off the bike at the same time. They put us on the back of a truck and took us to a castle in Hungary where we were thrown into the dungeon and interrogated.

Baty was sent to a place called Graz and he escaped with a couple of Australian sergeants. He got the DCM [Distinguished Conduct Medal] for saving the Aussies from drowning. They were trying to cross a river in the dark to Yugoslavia and the Aussies got stuck in a deep area. So Baty took one of them across at a time. Afterwards one of them told me if it hadn't been for Baty they would have drowned.

Eventually, after the war I ended up in Venice looking for my brother Bunny. Having worked on the railways I thought a railway station was the best place to find someone. I met a mate at the railway station who told me Bunny was down at the hospital. I went down to the hospital and saw him sitting in a deck chair. I hadn't seen him for six years.

The railways paid my superannuation while I was away at war and when I got back I found I had accumulated 13 weeks' holiday pay for the six and a half years I was away in the Army.

War Diary
Bert May

Grateful acknowledgement is given to Kitty May to use the following extracts from the war diaries of her late husband, Bert May.

War Diary of H.K. May – 1940 to 1945

5 January 1940

Left Burnham Camp. As we passed through Christchurch all the loco drivers blew their whistles and created quite a din. At Lyttelton we boarded HM Transport Z6, MS Sobieski. At 1700 hrs, the merchant ships Dunera and Sobieski sailed from Lyttelton to the shriek of loco whistles and sirens. What a row, but a great farewell, thousands of people there to see us off.

27 August

Left for the Western Desert. Here we dug slit trenches, our tents in gun pits, weapon pits, dugouts and communication trenches. It was hard and hot work digging but we were fit and used to go for a swim after work each night in the trucks. We had many good times in the surf and in the lagoon at Bergeta Oasis. We slept in the trenches for protection from the cold and air raids. We found quite a number of snakes here, mostly small ones which would coil up to fight you. Many of the boys were getting dysentery and desert sores, as we don't get many vegetables.

25 November
On the road to Cairo, we made good progress and found the locals chewing stalks of sugar cane in the streets. Just outside Maadi we halted for a couple of hours. We were the centre of attraction as the trucks were covered in dust from the desert (camouflage). We got issued with our first serge battledress. We also had our kit bags, bed, boards, mattresses and worn clothes replaced.

5 January 1941 (Cairo)
We went to El Saff desert with the 6 I.B. on manoeuvres for four days. We travelled across a good part of the desert in the trucks and practised giving covering fire to advancing infantry. Lysanders practised a little dive bombing on us. We got among a couple of stalks of sugar cane. It is terrible sickly stuff, and sticky.

We did a night retreat without lights and what a ride it was. We were going from dark until daylight over banks, getting stuck in loose sand, through local villages and cemeteries. Several trucks overturned and one went nose-first into a ready-dug grave.

23 March (Greece)
We arrived at our new camp, in pine trees, tired and hungry. The boys arrived with the trucks. It took them four days to come over and they were attacked by enemy aircraft several times. They are credited with bringing one plane down.

12 April
Snow had been falling. Nearly into Florina, we reached level land again and found the sun shining and no sign of snow or rain. We took up positions with the Armoured Div, to which

we were attached. We struck good digging and put the gun pit and crawl trench down in record time.

The road was blocked with retreating Greeks and our own artillery, infantry etc in places. We captured a fifth columnist on a push-bike and sent him away in a truck. Shells burst about the road. Could see a Jerry gun flash away up on the hillside. Our artillery soon silenced same though.

A bitterly cold night, we couldn't get warm at all. Keith's gun has a frozen barrel and won't fire. Bullets continually whipped around us. Jack got a good dent in his tin hat. [See Jack Turner's story later.]

1 May (Crete)
We moved up to our positions just above the corner of the road leading to the RAF HQ wireless station. Here we dug our positions on the bank edge, with a good field of fire. The 23rd mortar platoon took up two positions either side of us. Capt. Grant came around and gave us all the dope, the method of attack, how it will come etc. He was only a day or so out in his reckoning of the start of hostilities. Bombing raids last practically all day now.

21 May 1941
We have precious little grub and water. During the morning, great waves of troop-carrying planes came over in threes, dropping parachute troops and gear. There was just one long black line of them down the ridge and over the sea. We got well strafed by snipers, some mighty close calls. Shortly after midday, planes crashed on the drome and beach. Herb's gun stopped a bullet in the feed block but got the gun going again. Keith Newman stopped one through the head and died instantly; Eric Kay got nicked under the nose. A mortar landed in between us and the concussion knocked us all in a heap into the bottom of the pits. The 23rd Mortars did good work, knocked several out of the top of the dome of the Maleme Church.

23 May
At 0500 hrs, we got orders to move, and moved off immediately under British Capt. Grant. Glad to get away from the smell of the dead.

We moved off up a gully and in the darkness two shots rang out and Alf Smith dropped dead two ahead of me and a chap by the name of Turner got one through the arm just ahead of me, a close call.

25 May 1941 [Covers several days]
We went over the hill crest. Air raid, so Mick and I dived down the hill to grapes, in the bottom of the gully. A whole wave of bombers came over, dropping bombs all around. It was then dusk, still under cover of the grapes and sticks of bombs dropping at random. A load was dropped over us and landed alongside where I was, then the first wave came over. I stopped a splinter under the arm. A piece went in the heel of Mick's boot. A HQ Coy lad killed outright. Ralph Morrison legs and arms smashed [he died later in a regimental aide post] and Mick Bailey, HQ Coy, hit badly in the shoulder.

Passed through Suda. My arm now very stiff and sore and festered badly and my knee became stiff. Jack and I moved into a big cave recently occupied by the Greeks for the night. Next morning, the worst day of my life. Knee stiff, I couldn't move it. Jack went away to find a RAP. Came back with word that white flags were another bit of a whisper; then we got the word that the Island had capitulated. The doctors gave me a jab of morphine.

A Greek doctor came to give blood transfusions at the hospital. The place is infected with bugs and some lice and the smell from the wounds is awful. I was shifted to the 5th AGH, near Piraeus. Went by German ambulance through the heart of Athens. Was put in B3, a much better hospital, over 1000 here.

A family portrait taken before Murray McLagan went off to war. He went missing and was presumed dead for two years.

Stan Martin in medical corp uniform.

Bert May snapped in uniform by a street photographer in Auckland in 1945.

Cyril Miles in retirement, December 1999.

Five smiling "Partisans" in Northern Italy. From left to right are Ernie Clark, Ossie Martin, Pat Moncur, Paul Day and Mick Hogan.

Pat Moncur on a commando course at Wilson's Promontory in Victoria in 1940.

Ian Newlands (back row, second from left) at Harewood Elementary Flying School in Christchurch in 1941.

A sketch by Ian Newlands of the inside of Muroran Steelworks in Japan where he was the only POW from New Zealand.

20 August
Everyone in the convalescent camp packed up and was taken per truck to the docks at Piraeus.

21 August
Anchored off at Piraeus, inside the boom once more.

24 August
Arrived in Soliniki this morning. We berthed and were received by hosts of German guards with fixed bayonets. We lined up and were marched through the main part of the town to the prison camp. At the POW camp, we were searched and civil clothes taken off us, also spare gear.

9 September
We got deloused, hair clipped, bathed etc. About 1500, we went down and were registered, Stalag VIII 23194.

21 October
Started work in the factory, bagging sugar etc.

25 November 1942
Bob Freeman went to Cosel for the Xmas parcels today. Some mail, J.P.T. got one from Eric Laird (Egypt) giving us news of the Btn and boys. Bill Hakaria, Cliff Buckridge been killed. Deb Coulter wounded again. J.C. Leslie (Lt) back in NZ married Deb's sister. Piece snipped out of the letter, looks like he's gone too.

29 April 1945
"Possibly the day": All night long, heavy explosions and heavy artillery shook the ground, at 0400 hrs, at 0600 hrs, heavy MG Fire, then silent for several hours. American Lt. Colonel takes check parade this morning. Yank fighters come over the camp very low rolling etc. The boys cheer etc, then things start to move. Artillery, demolition tanks,

MG fire and small arms fire, also mortar.

The battle for Moosburg lasted about 3 hrs. Went around the camp, saw a piper plane. A spent piece of shrapnel came through the tent. Jerries getting out by the sound of the fire. Our officers up the sentry tower. Reports have tank and motorised infantry coming along the road.

YES, SIR, IT IS THE DAY. YANKS ENTER THE MAIN CAMP AT 1245 HRS. After all these years. Still odd booming about, possibly artillery. Planes, USA, overhead. It calls for a celebration.

Monday 1 October 1945
Folks awaiting at every station for their boys. Got a good view of Ruapehu smoking as we came past. Got into Auckland at 1340 hrs, all the folks down there to meet me. And so, home sweet home at last. It sure has been a long time.

Inhumane Treatment Prevailed
Cyril Miles

Cyril Miles has been a New Zealander for the past half a century, but fought his war in the Royal Navy.

I was born in Buckinghamshire, England. Dad was a professional thatcher. I used to help Dad with all that thinking I would learn how to do it, but I wouldn't have a clue today.

When I was old enough, I borrowed £10 off my aunt and ran away from home to join the Merchant Navy. I had 10 weeks of training at the Gravesend Sea School. You had to have a trade certificate, including life-boat drill, to get on board ships at that time. At the end of that 10 weeks you had to pass out and they found you a job on your first ship. After that you were on your own.

It was inevitable there was going to be a war. In 1935, when Hitler walked into Austria, I was on an old tramp steamer [a freighter that takes a cargo when and where it can] coming back from Argentina. It took us five weeks to get there and five weeks to come back. The old thing was condemned.

We took coals to Argentina. We used to go right up a tributary of the River Plate. All the farmers and residents from all around would come down with baskets to unload the coal. This was my first introduction to shifting stuff with baskets. I didn't know that later I would be doing that for three-and-half blasted years, shifting thousands of tons of earth from A to B and back again [in a Japanese POW camp].

I was in the Navy two years before the war broke out. I had a brother in the Royal Marines. He seemed happy there, so I joined up too in 1937. I thought I wouldn't like to be on a ship with the war looming and nothing to hit back with. Sooner be in something that you'd at least morally feel a bit happier in.

When my training was complete, I was assigned to several ships but I didn't get on them. One was an aircraft carrier. Something happened. I think it was sunk. Then I was assigned to a small cruiser called *Phoebe* which carried 5.7-inch armaments. But I had a boil under my arm and I couldn't make it. That was lucky because *Phoebe* got torpedoed on its first trip.

I went to the *Exeter*, which had been in the River Plate battle. It used to have three eight-inch turrets on it, twin turrets, A and B, but in the action the German warship the *Graf Spee* hit the marines turret and blew it clean out, like a tooth coming out. They had to flood the magazines because there was a fire on the ship that they couldn't control. Everybody that was there copped it, so they were short of marines and I was assigned to the *Exeter*. But she had been smashed to bits by that battle. It took 12 months for her to be refitted and re-altered.

In the meantime while I was waiting, I went onto the 15-inch battleship *Resolution*. I did all the things that marines do on there, polishing bloody brass and other chores....

We were off to the Mediterranean, going to Gibraltar. While we were there the Vichy French broke out. Our ships followed them but they got away. They were going pretty fast and got ahead and went to Dacca. I missed that action.

On Gibraltar we never sent radio signals because the enemy was so close. All messages were hand delivered and I was one of six that had to take the hand-delivered messages to the ports around Gibraltar. The ships left without us and the six of us ended up staying there for about four months, waiting to catch a ship. That was a good break. I went back to barracks and was finally commissioned onto the *Exeter*.

We went in a big convoy to Africa. It was one of the biggest convoys that went out with troops for the Libyan campaign.

The *Exeter* was fitted with the latest radar. We only had a 300-mile radius to work with which spotted aircraft, not submarines. We had depth charges for submarines, but you don't know the depth and they used to preset the depth charges at a depth that they guessed the submarine was at.

We had an encounter with a sub in the Sunda Straits. The Sunda Straits are not very wide. It's a deep and narrow channel and the sub must have got under us. Then he decided to come up. We don't know why, but we suspect he'd hit something, maybe a rock which forced him up … I don't know if somebody went mad or something. It does happen in those subs.

He was safe when he was underneath us in the deep channel, but as soon as he came up and had a go at us with his 4-inch gun, it was hopeless. He copped it something terrible.

We were trying to get through the straits to come out of the Java Sea. The *Exeter* had too much draft to get through the Sunda Straits. The only way we could get out was through the Sunda Straits. We didn't get there in the end. We ended up in battle and sunk a ship. We had several battles with the Japanese and in one of them the *Exeter* went down.

There was some humour when the ship was going down because one of the bombs went into the stores and struck the flour, so that we were covered in flour. We were asking each other if we were still alive or ghosts.

We jumped into the water. Normally the Japs would just leave the men in the water to die. When they sunk American ships, in lots of cases they would set fire to the fuel oil that had spilled into the water and burn them or machine-gun those that hadn't died.

Fortunately, they didn't do it with us. It was because it was the *Exeter* and they thought we were very brave men. They thought we were the same people that were in the *Graf Spee* battle. I didn't tell them any different. We were bloody lucky that's all.

The ship went down on 1 March 1942. We had been on our

way to New Zealand. The Japs took us to a captured Dutch hospital ship which they'd blown the bows off and they'd slaughtered everybody. There was blood everywhere.

They found some old empty beer bottles on board and they gave us one bottle of water which had to be shared between 10.

We got a fright. They told us if we wanted to go to the toilet, they'd put planks over the bow for us. After all we had been through they wanted us to walk the plank!

We had not had much to eat or drink so we weren't keen to go out there anyway. We found it amusing afterwards.

Anybody that was injured they couldn't be bothered with. They just cut off their heads with the bayonets on their rifles. They'd just saw them off and dump them over the side.

I had a little monkey on board the *Exeter*. Jenny I used to call it. She was still alongside when I got up on the Jap ship. First thing she did was to bite a bloody Jap right on top of his thumb and he chucked her over the side.

They took us to an Army barracks that the Dutch had vacated. They paraded us through the streets and made all the Indonesians throw their slops and everything at us. If the Indonesians wouldn't, the Japs would beat them.

I was trying to help an old cook. We were both getting behind, so we got bayoneted, kicked around and beaten. We finally got to this blasted barracks. It was a well-built thing with concrete flagstone flooring and one-man rooms. Ten of us were put in each of these one-man rooms.

We were naked. What clothes we did have on when we jumped off the *Exeter* – shorts, singlet and shirt – we had to dump because they were soaked in fuel oil from being in the water. We could hardly breathe; it was poisoning us slowly.

The Japs threw some Army clothing in a heap outside each of the barrack blocks. When I reached for a jacket and trousers a Jap beat the hell out of me.

The next day they said, "You can have those clothes."

After that, beating became the order of the day. There were no reasons. We deduced that they were baiting us all the time, to try to get a reaction so they had an excuse to mow us down.

We had been talking to Indonesians on one working party and the Japs beat the hell out of us. They used pick axe handles. They had six sort of corners on them in a hexagon. They had "Indonesian" written on one strip, "English" written on another, "Hollander" on another one ... they would hit you with whatever nationality you were.

The American prisoners had a compound of their own. The Dutch had a compound. The Dutch were "honourable surrenderers". The Japs had promised the Dutch that if they surrendered they would look after their women, and that they would be fed and clothed, so the Dutch surrendered and they were allowed to keep their uniforms on, they were allowed to have sidearms on and they had stacks of money. We used to call them "bloody Jerries with their guts kicked out". They were never addressed as anything higher than "f...ing Dutchmen".

They used to say, "Is there any difference between us and other Dutchmen?" And we used to say, "Dutchmen from Holland we call Dutch and you we call the f...ing Dutch."

The Japanese didn't speak English. Their pigeon Malay you could understand. We all learned it. Their rules were very simple: no work, no food. And if anyone tried to escape, 10 got killed. It's amazing what you can learn when you are under fear.

There was a big sumo fellow in a warehouse there and we called him a Jap and he said, "Not Jap, Nippon, Nippon, number one."

I made the mistake of saying "Churchill, number one." Oh shit, I should have kept my trap shut. They beat the heck out of me.

One of the jobs we had to do was to clean out houses. We'd have to chuck all the furniture, lovely furniture, smash it and burn it and all they put inside was a little bed about a foot off the ground. They did that because they had only had the island three weeks and they were afraid the houses were booby trapped. If they had been of course, we would have got it.

When we cleaned out the houses there were half-eaten meals left on the tables by the previous occupants who had left in a hurry and in that hot climate they were pretty rotten by then. But they weren't feeding us, so we'd eat them.

And down at the wharf we found old tins of milk that had blown in the heat. They would probably kill you today, but we would eat anything like that. We were starving.

They expected us to lift bags of cement. It took five of us to lift a bag of bloody cement. We got one cup of rice a day ... well, we used to call it rice. The base was rice, but it was boiled that much to make it go that far, it was really like dish water or the paste you use to put wallpaper on with. Everyone was getting as skinny as could be.

They made us dig a grave one night because they said we'd been speaking to Indonesians. Well, we scratched a hole, then we had to kneel down over it and they had swords they had made out of car springs. They wanted to try them out. One of them was standing next to me saying, "Momma, papa...."

We thought we were going to be killed, but then they made us stand up and gave us a bloody hiding. There was nothing left to beat, but they beat like hell. You were damn lucky to get through the day, any day, in that three and a half years without getting a wallop ... you just counted yourself lucky.

Blokes were dying all the time. There were continual burials.

It went on until June 1944. We knew the date because somebody used to mark off days and dates.

We were alongside a secret aerodrome that had dummy planes made out of bamboo all round the place and one old Dakota that used to come in there.

One day as we were running down to the job, the bloke alongside me who was one of our pilots said to me, "Don't look now but we are being followed."

I could hear this plane. We were just alongside the tower where they had one Messerschmitt and the old Dakota and then we heard ... pop, pop, pop ... and the Messerschmitt went up in bits and the Dakota was on fire and the bloody tower was all blown to bits.

And the pilot said, "That's got four engines. They haven't got any four-engined planes."

We had built a ditch alongside of the road which we had turfed the day before and pegged down with slivers of bamboo and the Japs jumped into the ditch. As they jumped in, some of these guys gashed their legs on some of the pegs.

The Allies dropped leaflets showing the Japs being kicked out of Indonesia. We got hold of these, but we had to be very careful not to be seen with one of them. If they searched you and you had one, they'd do you on the spot.

They dropped a few bombs after that near the camp and the shrapnel took a Dutch bloke's face right off. Three Dutchmen escaped. Within 24 hours they got them. They took 30 guys from that hut and stuck them in the guard room. Every change of the guard, they'd beat them. It took 22 days for them to die.

The guard room wasn't any bigger than a kitchen. It was standing room only. I don't know how they could stand the stink. And they thought that was bloody good fun.

They gave us a hell of a beating one morning. And then all of the guards had to fall in and they were crying their eyes out. They used to have soft toys, dolls and things for presents. They were cuddling them.

The next morning there were no guards at all. They'd gone.

They didn't tell us anything but a plane was very high up over and he was signalling. "Who are you?"

One of our old signalmen picked up a piece of glass and signalled back, "Survivors HMS *Exeter*."

The next day, the Red Cross planes came over and they dropped a message to say to clear an area for a dropping zone.

We told the Indonesians to keep away from the football field. Some Dakotas came over and dropped supplies. About 15 Indonesians got wiped out in the first drop. They were hit by the stuff because they were trying to get there first.

An American Air Force plane came over and dropped a radio set into the camp and then they parachuted in a civvie Yank and an Australian major. We were freed, but the war has never really ended for us.

Originally, there were 860 men on the *Exeter*, about 300 in the camp and 129 of them finally got home. Afterwards some of them did themselves in. One of them, a sergeant, was married with five kids. When he got home, he shot himself.

When the war ended, I was still in the Marines, because I had signed up for 12 years. Because I was a POW of the Japs, you could apply for release at no cost. If you bought yourself out, at one time it would have cost about £30,000.

A bloke in the barracks said, "You'd be a bloody mug if you don't get out with the jumped-up little bastards that are in charge now. They haven't even seen a shot fired and they are telling you what to do."

[After his discharge Cyril applied to emigrate to New Zealand but was told it would take about three to four years. A few days later, he got on a boat and jumped ship when he got to New Zealand.

He had signed a contract to serve on the ship for three years and was sentenced to a month in prison. When the magistrate asked Cyril why he was willing to spend a month in prison to save the three to four years spent waiting to come to New Zealand, Cyril replied that he couldn't wait because he had already wasted that length of time in a Japanese POW camp.

When he had served his term, he took New Zealand citizenship and his son later carried on the family tradition and served 20 years in the New Zealand Navy. But he never fired a shot in anger.]

You Do It Because You've Got To
Pat Moncur

I met Pat Moncur in his den at the bottom of his garden, a caravan full of pictures of family and friends on the walls, as well as the odd funeral notice of an old comrade who had passed away.

I was born on 14 March 1920 and joined up in Rotorua in 1940. I was selected to go on a commando course in Australia. It was all very hush, hush.

I saw three battles. At Belhamed, we did a bayonet charge there ... a bad one ... and I fought at Minqar Qaim and Ruweisat Ridge.

In a bayonet charge, the MPs [Military Policemen] go out and put lamps up, green and red, facing towards us, not facing towards the enemy, and we all line up. The first thing you do is get rid of everything that impedes what you want to do – gas pack, groundsheet ... all that sort of thing.

The bayonet is fixed on the end of the rifle. When you're charging and you see the enemy, you shoot first, then when you get into close quarters you use the bayonet.

The Germans were great on fixed-line firing, you could see the tracers going over. They had one machine-gun going one way and the other machine-gun going the other way. They would traverse every now and then. They would go three feet to the left and three feet to the right. When you were advancing towards this, you'd have to go under it and when they traverse, you have to go with it and lay down, because when it comes back over your head, you're through. Then you make towards the area where the firing is coming from.

When you were doing the bayonet charge, a lot of the Germans you ran across feigned injury. You wouldn't shoot a wounded German, but some of them fired at your back after you'd passed them.

We were running along on one occasion after we broke out and the bloke beside me went down, he'd been shot from behind. From then on, everybody who was lying down, you just made sure they were dead. It was self-preservation. There was nothing enjoyable about it.

The first time you do a bayonet charge it's exciting. The second time you are doing it you are frightened and the third time you are scared stiff. It's a shocking business. The first one's exciting because you don't know what's happening. The second time you know what's happening, so you're frightened. The third time you're scared stiff, but you do it, because you've got to do it.

They sent us on a bayonet charge at Minqar Qaim on 27 June 1942 and we were a hell of a mess. We were cut to ribbons and Rommel went round behind us. We put in a bayonet charge that night to break out. There were trucks all over the desert, all heading for Cairo. We pulled up at Alamein and they reformed a division there and that's where I was captured on 15 July 1942.

The 18th Battalion had been formed in 1939. They were infantry up until 15 July 1942 and after that bayonet charge there weren't enough members left to keep the battalion going so they sent the remnants back to Maadi and formed the 18th Armoured Regiment. All of us who were captured at this stage were not allowed to wear the 8th Army medal because the 8th Army wasn't formed until 1 August 1942. We missed out on that.

I was now a POW. We had no water and were given one meal a day. The only shade was palm trees. We were transported to Greece first, then Italy. On the way, a British submarine sunk the ship in front of me, full of prisoners of war. Ninety per cent of the people on that ship went down. Our ship went to the Corinth Canal, and hid in there. There was an Italian ship in front of us and an Italian warship behind us which were also hiding from the subs.

In Italy, I was selected as one of the fitter ones to go out on a working party. One night, Ozzie Martin and I decided that we didn't like working there, so we decided to escape. We cut through the bars of our hut and went down a steepish valley. There was one guard, outside a farmhouse. We got on top of the fence, jumped over and ran away.

The commando training that I had in Australia came in very handy when I escaped. I had learned how to live on the land and how to conduct myself in a tight spot.

Up in the mountains, we stole anything we could. We broke into houses and demanded food. We got very good at breaking into houses. Most of the men were away. They gave us what they could. We were pretty brave when there were only women in the house.

I wouldn't do it again. I think I'd stay nice and comfortable in a prisoner of war camp and wait for somebody to let me go.

We ate a lot of grapes. We stole pigs and eggs. I was stealing eggs from under a haystack and this voice behind me said, "What are you doing?"

I said, "I'm stealing the eggs."

It was a woman and she said, "Poor man."

She went away and came back with some food. She asked me where I was living and I said in the haystack. She gave us regular food for a while. We were very lucky in that first fortnight after our escape. I got to know that family very well and we kept in touch after the war.

Another Italian woman gave me clothes. An old lady came up to me last year when I was back in Italy and told me that she was the woman who had given me the clothes because she had heard that her husband was killed in the war. But he was actually still alive. She said, "When my husband came home he was very angry because I gave his clothes to you." She was a lovely old lady.

We went up into the mountains and contacted a Welshman who

was in charge of a group of partisans. We did two raids. On one about 15 of us attacked a cheese factory. We took all the cheese and distributed it among the partisans. The other attack was on a convoy that was coming through the pass down to Venice and it wasn't very successful at all. It wasn't well planned.

We opened fire and the convoy stopped. The next thing we could hear the mortars coming in. I thought, "This is no place for Patrick." We left there and scattered.

I got back to where Ozzie was and he said, "What are you going to do?"

I said, "I'm going to Switzerland." I wanted to see the war out and I thought I could do it better in Switzerland. He said he'd come with me. Six of us went off, Paul Day, Ozzie Martin, Pat Moncur, Mick Hogan, Jock McKay and Ernie Clarke. We travelled only by night, and slept during the day.

We got through several frights along the way. One time we were on bikes and we went past a local Italian policeman. He waved to us and we waved back. I don't know who he thought we were, but as you're pedalling along, you don't look back and your shoulders feel about as wide as the road until you go round a corner.

On another occasion, we dumped the bikes. We were going through the fields and we decided to go through a village. It was night time. Not a soul was out because there was a curfew. Just as we were walking through the village, the village clock struck one. Jesse Owens wouldn't have caught us. We took off like rabbits, our nerves were that brittle.

Finally Ozzie said, "Who the bloody hell are we running from?"

I said, "I don't know."

We stopped running and had a laugh about it.

For a while I had a pistol which I had pinched when we escaped. Later I lost it. I must have taken it out of my pocket to use to defend ourselves. I don't know where I dropped it.

On the way to Switzerland, just before the Brenner Pass, we were going along a mountain pass, and we went through a bush and out of the other side and there's a guy hanging. You have no idea how frightened I was. Oh dear, dear, dear … that body just swinging there and turning. His neck was broken, his head was right on one side, his mouth was open and his eyes were open.

He couldn't have been hanging for more than 24 hours before we got there. I took off into the bush and Ozzie came straight after me. We stayed in the bush for two days. We didn't go near the body, but ... oh gee whiz ... I didn't want to be hanged.

I had a second pistol that I had got from the partisans. I think that's where I lost that one. I must have dropped it to push the bushes apart.

The Brenner Pass was absolutely crucial to the German war effort in Italy. The Germans there were as thick as fleas on the back of a mongrel dog. Ozzie Martin and I got through, but Mick Hogan and Jock McKay got captured. They had a hell of a time. Paul Day and Ernie Clarke got through and we climbed over the mountains into Switzerland.

In Switzerland, I spent 90 per cent of my time at a place called Arosa, which was a health resort. I was a very sick boy. Paul Day joined the British Consul's staff in Geneva and went on to Oxford University where he became a professor. Ozzie Martin became a telephone operator at the British Consul. Like me, Ernie Clarke was in hospital.

When the Americans got to the French/Swiss border, we jumped border and went down to Marseilles. There was a bit of fighting still going on down there. We joined up with some Americans. This big, black American sergeant said to us, "Would you like to help?"

I said I would, so he gave me a gun and we went into action to flush out some Germans who were holed up in the wharf.

Then the sergeant asked me if I would like to go to Monte Cristo Island. I did. I'd read the book *The Count of Monte Cristo*. But when we went along there the American in charge wouldn't allow us to land. We returned to Marseilles where an officer instructed us to go back to our own unit. So we got a ride on a tank transporter. While the tanks are on, it sails perfectly; when there's no tanks in, she rolls like a son of a bitch.

Finally the doctor checked me out and he said, "You've got to go home."

I said, "That would suit me fine."

I had no idea what I was letting myself in for when I joined up. I thought I would get a cook's tour and see some of the world. Everything was fine until the first bayonet charge. Then the whole thing went topsy-turvy.

You'd come back after a bayonet charge and there were a lot of fellas missing. All of a sudden you are thinking, "I wonder what it's like in Rotorua now?"

But you couldn't just say to the General, "Look, I've done my bit, I'm going home." You kept at it and did what you could.

Mad as Maggots
Ian Newlands

I came early to meet Ian Newlands and found him working in his workshop. Today he's just the same as he always was, forever beavering away making something. It's a good habit. It got him through hell.

I was 19 when the war was declared. I was doing stage one mathematics in engineering, as well as physics and chemistry. At the end of the year, I went home and volunteered for the Air Force but there were so many who had applied that I had to wait until the following December, 1940, before I got into camp.

In the meantime, we learned Morse code over the radio, navigation and more mathematics, which I already knew about, vector diagrams and that sort of thing. Then we did elementary square-bashing at Levin, marching and getting fit and attending lectures going over the same thing again, projectiles, machine-guns and rifle drills. The main thing was to get fit enough to last the distance.

They told us, "There are four main training aerodromes. You mostly will go near your home town."

We drew lots to see who was the unlucky one. It was me. I ended up going to Christchurch. I learned to fly in Tiger Moths.

Then we were the second course of pilots to go on the Empire training scheme to Canada.

Going over there, we went as first-class passengers on the *Aorangi*, a big passenger liner. We had menus about a mile long, there were lifts and swimming pools on it. We had one steward to two tables, the very best of everything.

In Canada, we flew on planes that were made for the French. All the instruments ... metres, kilometres, litres ... were all in French. Then we got into the Harvards, which were much faster.

It was near the end of winter. The snow was coming up off the ground. The aerodrome was between Lakes Erie and Ontario and almost every day we'd be flying over Niagara Falls. You could see for hundreds of miles once you got up. It was blue skies for miles and miles.

We did a lot of night training flying (as well as day flying) where they pulled a screen right over the top of you and you had to fly by the instruments the whole time. Plus we did link transport work.

Our wings were presented at the end of the course and then we got on an AMC (Armed Merchant Cruiser), which was a passenger ship armed with eight six-inch guns. There were 108 ships to the convoy altogether. When we went up through the Newfoundland Straits about three ships struck icebergs. They had to put back to Halifax in Canada.

There were very strict rations in Iceland. You hardly got anything to eat, you only got about six biscuits and a bit of porridge and a cup of tea for a day's rations and it was freezing cold. The only way to keep warm was to keep running the whole day long. Once, in England, we played the Poms at soccer with about 20 or 30 of us New Zealanders against only about 12 of them. We were used to playing rugby and we weren't a match for them but we kept warm.

In England, they put us on operational training at a place called Usworth, near Newcastle, which was just a grass drome. The first time they sat me in a Hurricane fighter, they said, "This is this, this is that ..." and of course you'd forget half of what they'd said. Coming down, I did a couple of circuits, trying to remember how to get the wheels down and how to put the brakes on.

While we were there, the Yanks arrived. This was before their war started. They were neutral at the time. They came over in a big convoy. The first ships must have had the cooks, because by about midday they had their own bread made. They were all walking around in their number one uniforms, with great bloody medals, bars down their arms and they hadn't even been in the war yet.

One time I was up near Edinburgh and had some leave so I went to see one of my mates down there who I hadn't seen since I'd left New Zealand. He was flying bombers. When I got down there he was doing solo circuits and bumps (practising take-offs and landings). He had to do so many of these so I went up with him and we had a good yarn while he was doing them.

When I got back to the drome I found that my squadron had moved. I just caught the last transport out. This bloke said, "Hop on and I'll give you a ride down."

We started off on operations doing reconnaissance and patrol work with 43 Fighter Squadron. At night, you slept out on the edge of the drome in huts, called dispersal huts. In the morning, you hopped straight into your aeroplane, which wasn't parked that far away.

But we didn't really a fire a shot in anger in England. We did patrols in England but there wasn't much daylight stuff coming over. There were still the night bombers coming over. You'd wake up in the morning and there'd be craters outside your window. We saw plenty of air raids but we didn't actually shoot anything down.

They decided after about three months that we were to go to Africa. We went from 43 Squadron to 232 Squadron. After about a week, we got all our injections. On my birthday, 6 November, I was in bed with headaches and God knows what from the injections. Not long after that, we were sent in a convoy to Africa.

We had Christmas at sea and we didn't even get a plum pudding or damn all. So on New Year's Eve, we decided to make a night of it and really got worked up on whatever was available. We all went down to the beach and tried to launch these native canoes into the surf at Takoradi on the Gold Coast.

The next morning we were half out to it and they said, "Right, everybody to be down at the drome at daybreak and off on a DC3."

It was a Pan American Airways civilian plane with American pilots, all first-class accommodation. At lunch time, they would land in the desert in a little town, a tourist stop. All you could see was mud huts and it was hot as hell. Then you'd go inside and there were all these beautiful dining rooms, natives with white turbans and silver trays with food on. Incredible!

We'd take off and land in another one again at night time. We slept out in the open in four-poster beds under mosquito nets because it didn't rain at all. There were no trees, no grass, thousands of miles of nothingness, completely barren.

The second night we reached Khartoum, staying about a week and flying Mark II Hurricane fighters in the desert. These had 12 machine-guns carried in the wings.

We were then flown in Blenheims to Port Sudan where we boarded the aircraft carrier HMS *Indomitable*, which took us to within 800 miles of Java. 258 Hurricane Squadron were also on board making 48 pilots and planes in addition to the carrier's crew and aircraft. None of us had flown from a carrier before!

To save space, the wings had been removed from the planes and were reattached for flight. We took off in three groups of 16 Hurricanes escorted by two Blenheims to land at Batavia airport. Unfortunately, the brake pressure hose had not been connected on my plane, or the gauge was faulty. When I came in to land, the petrol was showing just about empty and I didn't want to do another circuit if I could help it. I had no brakes, so I thought I'd cut the motor on approach and then I'd definitely be able to get to the start of the runway and hope for the best. But with the heat coming up off the runway I had a lot more flotation than I expected and the plane took a while to settle down and I ended up about a third of the way down the runway before it touched.

At the far end of the runway I could see a Hurricane sitting on its nose and I thought, "Hello, he's got no brakes either, I don't want to bang into him or I'll damage my plane." So I tried to get the speed down to about 20 miles an hour.

I got it off the runway by hard rudder wiggling it a bit and tried to get in between two parked planes but unknown to me it had been raining and the grass was very slippery and so instead of getting in between the two I crashed into one of them.

The damage wasn't too bad but it kept both our planes out of action for a few days. That was the start of the bloody shambles. We lost more planes on the ground than we did in the air.

On the way to Singapore, they told us on the carrier that the Japanese only had obsolete biplanes. Later on we found out that the obsolete biplanes belonged to New Zealand. We were hopelessly outnumbered all the way through.

On 5 February, we were flown up to Singapore and they wanted half a dozen pilots to go up to bring back some planes that had been repaired in the jungle. We were told to leave all our kit bags behind, except for our toothbrush, razor and wallet. I never saw my kit again and I lost my log book, which had all my details in it.

We climbed into two Lockheed Hudsons belonging to the Australian Air Force and had several Hurricanes as escorts and flew up to Singapore. But we didn't know that the northern dromes were under shell fire.

The first one we landed on was Sembawang. We were getting hungry. It was lunch time so we went into the cookhouse and there wasn't a soul anywhere. The place was deserted, but we could smell the dinner cooking in the oven. We opened the door and there was roast beef and roast potato ... so we grabbed a plate each and piled it up. We were half way through this meal, when ... *boom, boom, boom* ... we were under shell fire. We all rushed out and got in the plane again and took off to Tengah. The wheels had only just left the ground and shells were exploding everywhere.

We had to operate from Kallang, which is near Singapore City, on the south side of the island. All we could see when we first landed there were great big oil tanks on islands outside of town. All of them were on fire. The smoke was going straight up in spirals and spreading out in a black cloud about 2000 feet up. And the *Empress of Asia* was lying on the bottom and smoking away but still upright. It hadn't sunk because it wasn't sitting in enough water to sink.

Kallang was just a grass aerodrome, no concrete runways. It had already been badly bombed. The whole aerodrome was just a mass of craters about 20 feet in diameter and about eight feet deep. You couldn't land in a straight line anywhere, you had to zig-zag. It was more or less a banana-shaped runway.

The control tower and administration building had been flattened by bombs and we operated from a little old bungalow on the side of the drome. It had a telephone and the barest necessities. We thought this was a bit of fun.

At the most, we had about 10 or 12 operational Hurricanes and there were a couple of little Buffalo fighters there. There were plenty of pilots because a lot of them had gone direct on a different ship, getting there before us. There were a few New Zealand pilots and a few odds-and-sods Australian ones.

The Japanese bombers would come over about every hour, starting in the morning from about 8am until about lunch time. They seemed to pack up in the afternoon. By the time we got warning, we couldn't catch them up. They would overfly the drome and come back and drop their bombs as they were heading back to base up north in Malaysia.

We had trouble with their Zero fighters, which were one of the best fighters produced in the war. Our Hurricanes had inline motors and had glycol for the cooling system whereas the Japanese had radial motors and relied on air cooling. They didn't have the same problems as we did with overheating on the ground. The Zeros were very light. They had only about two cannons and two machine-guns as armament. The Japanese were very accurate and very capable pilots – again, the opposite to what we'd been told when we first came out to Singapore.

It was very hot on the ground. We just had shorts and short-sleeved shirts, and miniature pith helmets, narrow-brimmed to keep the sun off our heads, and goggles and New Zealand flying boots. Once you got up to 25,000 feet, it would be freezing cold. Then you'd come down. You'd spend the day being hot, cold, hot, cold, which was very exhausting. You'd do two shifts a day – one in the morning, the other in the afternoon.

We only had a few planes and after a few days there weren't that many left. Our Commanding Officer crashed on take-off one day, as he flew off from the drome. He had to fly over a little basin in Kallang harbour and he hit the mast of a barge. That was the end of him and the plane.

A lot of the pilots were shot down but managed to get away with it. The planes had masses of cannon holes in them. Then we started running out of different stuff. Oxygen (for the oxygen masks that pilots wore) was pretty scarce and we were short of hydraulic fluid. When we ran out of glycol some of them filled the radiators with water in the finish. Anything would make do.

As a sergeant pilot, I usually got called up as a number two and would guard the tail for the number one, the officer. On 6 February 1942, I was up at 25,000 feet with a New Zealand pilot. We spotted this lone dive bomber flying along and we opened up our special throttle (called "pulling the tit") that for about 10 minutes allowed the engine to go over the designated spot before it would overheat.

We went hell for leather for this Japanese. We got up pretty close to him. My engine was overheating a bit, but I had to have a crack at him. I pushed the machine-gun button and at the same time I could hear, *Rat-a-tat-tat*, and I thought, "Is that me?"

I was getting hit myself from somewhere. He got me through the motor and the engine seized up. I couldn't see who hit me, and I had no motor, so I couldn't get away. I had to make out I was dead. I rolled the plane over and put it into a spin and dived for the deck from about 25,000 feet.

The cockpit got full of fumes and I was going that fast that the speed dial indicator went hard over right and jammed. I think I was almost approaching the speed of sound. I started to pull out of the spin at about 6000 feet, because I thought, "He's not behind me now."

But the plane wouldn't pull out of it. I was going straight down.

The day before, my friend W.A. Moodie had gone straight in, crashed and died.

All I could do was to use the control trim. You should never do that because it puts your tail into a high-speed spin. But I had no other option. About 500 feet off the ground, I managed to pull it out of the spin.

But I still had to land and I had no engine, no air speed and no hydraulics – nothing was working – you have to have your motor working to give your hydraulics pressure. I don't know whether I had brakes or not. Luckily I was above the aerodrome. I circled the aerodrome until my speed got down and I managed to get down on the ground and headed for the boundary fence.

I can still see the fence today. It had six wires and upright posts like a normal New Zealand fence.

The wheels weren't down, which they call a belly landing. I knew I wouldn't be able to pull up because it wasn't a very big aerodrome. I selected the wheels down and kept pumping the hydraulics as I was coming over the fence. I just cleared the fence by inches and waited for the crunch.

Nothing happened. I just kept going along and I thought, "Oh, the wheels are down."

Now I had to keep steering in between all these bomb craters and the next boundary fence was coming up and I had hardly any brake pressure again. I pulled up about 20 yards from the far fence, in one piece and not on fire. The fire engine came out and all they could find was two bullet holes in the side of my motor on the right-hand side.

They send you straight up again to get your nerves right. I went up by myself and I was really mad that I had been shot down. I was looking around for anything to fire at. If I couldn't find an aeroplane, I'd always fire guns off into the jungle somewhere on the far side of the strait where it was lousy with Japanese troops. You couldn't see them for the trees.

[A book, *The Bloody Shambles*, was later written about the Japanese invasion of the Dutch East Indies, Malaysia and the Philippines and the pilot is mentioned in it who shot Ian down. He claimed a kill for the incident.]

A few days later, on the 11th, I went up with a New Zealand officer to bring back two planes from a northern aerodrome that was under shell fire. In order to get the planes off the ground to avoid shell fire, we had to get them off first thing.

We had an early cup of tea and were told we would be back in time for breakfast. We went up by taxi. It was pitch black and we were driving this taxi down a jungle road and every now and again there were Gurkhas on guard. They'd stop us and we asked if it was still okay to go on and they'd say, "Yep, away you go."

Finally we got to the drome and they showed us the two planes to take.

Sometimes they are buggers to start, but mine started quickly and I couldn't be bothered waiting for the officer, so I took off.

The Japs had an observation balloon on a wire and they could see all over the island. I thought I'd see if I could find that bloody thing and shoot it down for a start. My guns were fully loaded, but I couldn't find the balloon. I strafed all around the perimeter until the guns were empty. I landed back at the drome again. My mate got back eventually and I didn't tell him I'd been strafing. I used to keep it all to myself.

I went back to the hotel for breakfast and to spruce up. Then back down to the drome again ... well, there wasn't a bloody plane left ... they'd all gone off. All the officers had gone and left us sergeants there.

We knew we had to get out of Singapore. One of my mates had been shot down and bailed out in his parachute and landed in the Johore Strait, between Singapore and Malaysia, and the bloody Japs had machine-gunned him when he was in his rubber dinghy. He was fairly badly knocked about. We knew he was up in the local hospital, so we thought we'd see how he was getting on and if he could come with us.

So we went up there and, "Oh what a mess." The whole hospital had people lying in bandages, all down the corridors, doctors stepping over them. There were not enough beds for everybody.

Our friend didn't look too good. We thought we should leave him there. He was saying, "Take me, take me." But we thought he'd be well enough and left him there. It turned out later that the Japs visited that hospital and bayoneted half the people there, nurses and all. But he got out. We saw him later on.

As we had no planes to get out with, we had to get out by ship. We looked for a ship or a barge to pinch – anything that would float to get out of the country. We got a hacksaw and a hammer and other tools in case we needed to cut an anchor chain or something.

We were having trouble finding a boat, when someone said, "There's an RAF boat going out tonight, the *Empire Star*." It was a big cargo boat. We got on that, it was full of nurses, RAF, and a few Aussies.... I think unofficially they were deserting – they'd had a gutsful. The conditions were awful.

We didn't sail until almost daybreak. Ridiculous! We were waiting for the last people I suppose. We got out and had a bit of a convoy with a lot of smaller ships.

For four long hours we were hit continuously by 54 Jap bombers and fighter escorts. The Japanese bombers always came over in formations of 27 in a V formation and they let all their bombs go at once.

They scored three direct hits on our boat and the cruiser got three hits. There were about 18 men killed on the *Empire Star*. There would have been a few more because some of them would have got blown straight over the edge.

I only had my shirt and shorts on in Singapore and one of the officers left his jacket behind with a couple of stripes on it and I put it on, not thinking. When I was on the ship everybody thought I was an officer. I was screaming around the deck, saying, "Clear the decks, man the guns, and fire!" and all this. That's the way I used to carry on anyhow.

I was behind a wire which held the mast up and had a revolver firing at this dive bomber coming down. All the deck was like a hail storm, bullets hitting the steel and bouncing up. One bomb had gone through the deck into a cabin and hit eight Air Force officers playing cards. Another bomb, just a little bit away, landed right in the middle of the spare propeller and didn't do any damage.

Everything was covered in this yellow dye. Another bomb hit on the side of the boat on the front of it and knocked out a big hole and I was shouting, "Man the fire hoses."

I looked down and all the fire hoses had been knocked out and all the pipes were hanging over the side. Luckily, the fire was put out.

There was an officer next to me and a blast knocked his vision out. I don't know if he recovered. I took him down below to the cookhouse for someone else to look after him and went back up the top for more action.

There was a naval officer marching along in his white uniform, looking immaculate and swinging his one arm like he was on the parade ground. He wasn't swinging the other arm because he'd been shot through the elbow. There was only a bit of skin attaching it. He was going down to the sick bay. I thought it was pretty cool the way he was doing it.

The deck I was standing on had bodies on it everywhere. I was dragging them over to one side, clearing the decks. The cabins were behind the bridge and I didn't want the women and children to see all that.

First of all, the three dive bombers had come over and made three direct hits, then they came over in formations of 27. They were dropping their bombs from about 12,000 feet. Twenty-seven bombers would come from one direction and the other 27 would go from the other direction at a higher altitude. One lot would let their bombs go then the other lot would let their bombs go. That was 54 lots of bombs coming down, four or five bombs from each plane.

It would take about a minute for the bombs to reach us after being dropped. The captain of the ship would do a hard left to avoid them, so there were quite a few that missed. Then he just cut the motors and stopped the boat. He just sat there and of course they were expecting us to zig-zag. Not one bomb hit and the whole ship lifted up in the water and down again from all the explosions as the bombs hit the water.

The next day was Friday the 13th. We thought it was going to be a black day, but nothing happened on that day. By then, about 90 per cent of that convoy had been sunk. Afterwards, we heard all sorts of stories about that convoy, like some of them got on an island and the Japs found them and shot them. Some of them got over to Sumatra. There were very few survivors.

We got to Batavia and funnily enough the bloke who owned the blooming jacket was there waiting and he got his jacket back. I ended up with just a shirt and a pair of shorts again. On the 20th, I was flying again.

There were a few dog fights, then we heard that they had captured an aerodrome about a hundred miles east of us so we went over and strafed that. They were strafing us and we were strafing them back.

We moved to Bandoeng, which is halfway across the mountains. We'd no sooner landed there than they were bombing us again. We scrambled and I had only just got airborne and the whole cockpit was full of white fumes. I couldn't see a thing.

I almost did a circuit around the aerodrome boundary fence to land again. I swung around and landed in the bomb bays, which were big piles of dirt to park up to four planes in.

I slammed the brakes on, jumped out and dived into the nearest slit trench, which was about six foot deep. I could see the four bombers coming straight at me. They'd seen me park the plane. And on the other side of the bomb bay was a Dutch bomber.

The Japs started dropping their bombs ... one two, three ... I could hear them coming and the next one went over my head and landed on the bomb bay a few feet from me. Then the Dutch bomber caught fire and activated the machine-guns. Every time I poked my head out of the trench, the machine-guns were firing right over my head. I was trapped there for about half an hour.

When I finally got out, I was able to find out what had happened. The fitter had left the cap off my glycol tank. If I'd caught him I would have shot him on the spot with the revolver that I always carried around with me. I was that mad. Mad as maggots.

We evacuated from there the next day but the Japs were right down the island by then. There was only one plane left to fly and they asked everybody who wanted to fly it because there was a Dutch pilot in a Buffalo who wanted to go and strafe some of these Japs in a gorge where they were fighting the Dutch troops. They wanted someone to go and cover for him. I thought, "Oh, the bloody plane would hardly fly...."

A few minutes later, they capitulated and waved the white flag. They told us to hand over our guns, no escaping and all that jazz which was confirmed by the CO. If anybody escaped, 10 or 20 other prisoners would be shot and also tortured.

I was now a POW. I was working in Batavia for seven months, fixing up all the damage we'd done. We'd put about five great bloody bombs right down the middle of the runway, and they had made great big craters. Our first job as POWs was to get truckloads of boulders and fill up the holes near to the top and put about a foot of concrete on the top of that, all mixed by hand.

We dug up all the petrol tanks from all the petrol stations out of the ground. All the scrap iron had to be taken back to Japan. By that time, I'd got dysentery and had to go to hospital.

About one in four came out of hospital alive. I'd seen them cart them out and then the orderlies used to go through their kit bags and help themselves to what was in them. Then I got a fever and felt intoxicated. I was out to it for about three to four days and then we got tropical skin rashes. All the skin around our private parts came off. It was just weeping raw flesh.

There were about a thousand men with this and you'd get out in the sun to try and dry it up, all naked sunbathing. Some of them got great ulcers, great big holes in their legs. A lot also got malaria, all sorts of tropical diseases.

Then one day the Japs came to us and said they wanted volunteers to work in a big steel factory in Japan. I was a sergeant and I said to the others, "Let's get the hell out of this."

It was too hot for one thing. I thought Japan would be the same climate as New Zealand.

We got on a ship as far as Saigon and one of the boilers burst and the sea was as rough as guts. We went up the Saigon River and got it fixed up. Then we had to trim the coal [bringing the coal forward to the furnace] and feed the boilers. You'd be covered in dust from the coal, then everyone got sick with typhoid – you name it, they had it on that hell ship.

We started off in a convoy of about half a dozen ships and a few Japanese destroyers. A lot of them got torpedoed. We got out of the convoy then, we were on our own. But then we struck a really bad typhoon.

The toilets were on the side of the ship. All the droppings would go into the water. When we struck the typhoon, people were in the toilets and were washed overboard never to be seen again.

Everything was done by wooden buckets in those days. They would lower the rice and soup down from the top by rope in a wooden bucket. When it got to your deck, you'd pull it in and feed all the people around you. When the toilets went over the side and people couldn't climb up the ladder from being too weak, they used the empty buckets for toilets.

The ship was going up and down and the people that were sick would fall over and end up down the bottom of the holds. By the time we got to Japan, it was shocking, you couldn't believe the stink. We were out to it. When we got some fresh air, we sort of came to.

Then the white-coated Japanese came along, and they moved us onto another ship temporarily. They told those who couldn't walk to get on a truck. So I got on the truck. This was in Moji, South Japan. They took us to an old building with concrete floors, with rooms that would take eight people lying down.

We all had dysentery. You couldn't stand up because you were too weak. You would crawl down to this toilet place and you would squat over a hole in the floor Japanese-style. You spent half your time squatting over the toilet and you were just passing blood and slime and stuff.

If you had some of these round little yellow beans, within 20 minutes they would pass back through. We had nothing in our stomachs.

With beriberi, you lose all sense of touch, taste and smell. Some go half-blind or lose their hearing. This fella with beriberi shat himself. After about a day or two, we said to him, "You must have shit yourself."

He said, "I'll put my hand down and look."

He pulled his arm back from underneath the bedclothes and it was just covered. He couldn't feel it and he couldn't smell it. We got the orderlies and they came and carted him away, so there was one empty bed.

A few days later, we had a knock on the door and a bloke says, "You got an empty bed in there?"

We said, "Yep. Come in."

He said, "All the others in my bedroom are dead."

That was one that had survived out of eight.

The ones who died got cremated. They put them into wooden buckets, just pushed them in similarly to how you are in the womb before you are born and then they cremated them. Then the ashes went into a box with the person's name on it.

After three months, some American orderlies came along and they said, "We're going to give you a blood transfusion."

Our veins were hard to find, there wasn't much of us left, we were wasting away. We were just skin and bone. They put these great thick needles in and gave us all a dose of saline and blood plasma. It took about half an hour and you won't believe this, we just got up and walked around, immediately. Two days later we got another dose and they said. "Okay, you're going up to North Japan to work now." But I got a lump under my arm, which was some sort of reaction from the blood transfusion.

Eventually I got to the steel mill I had volunteered for. We went up by trains and when we changed trains at Tokyo all the kids were hissing and booing us. We arrived at the steel mill in the middle of the night. The steel company had their own ships in port and they owned the railways and the village. One day, everybody got a new umbrella, the whole village. They were all walking around with a new umbrella.

If there was any misdemeanour in the camp and nobody owned up, the Japs would have the whole camp standing at attention out in the cold, snow or rain. The treatment could be very brutal and most of the men did break. I survived by making things and doing sketches, by designing yachts, by keeping my diary and being orderly sergeant in charge of the working parties, a sort of a go-between.

The only way to get away from the Japs was to climb up a guard tower because the Japanese never used it. I did a sketch of the steel works from the top.

Shovelling was too hard on me, so I got a job in the workshop repairing wagons. I used to make knives and spanners on the quiet. Any time that I could have got out, I could have used the spanner to undo the nuts on the railway lines and let them all go. I had a map and everything, all prepared to escape. But I never did because if you did try to escape the whole hut would suffer.

We had no news. We didn't have a radio, we couldn't read Japanese, so we had no idea what was going on.

The Americans started bombing all the ports near the end of the war. By then we had been moved inland to a coal-mining camp. Up until then they'd had Koreans and Chinese labourers going down these mines. We'd pass them sometimes and half of them would be bloody dead because the mine had collapsed on them or blown up.

One night we were supposed to go in and it was cancelled the next day – the mine had collapsed. It was as close as that. At the end of the war, the guards all walked out and left the gates open.

On the way home we flew over the part where they had dropped the atomic bombs on Hiroshima and Nagasaki. There was just nothing but a few shells of buildings and a few power poles. It wasn't that long, but it seemed to me like we were flying over those ruins for several hours. It looked totally desolate.

The Glamour Boys
Maurice O'Connor

Approaching his 80th birthday, Maurice O'Connor, otherwise known as Morrie or "Lofty", still retains some of the twinkle he had in his eye when he was younger. He has an energetic way of talking, his voice tending to gust with enthusiasm when he makes a point. He lied about his age to join a war that he was finally happy to leave behind.

I was born in 1922. My father and his brother had a trucking business between Island Bay and Otaki until his brother lost his life going over the old Paekakariki Hill and, from then onwards, the business went down.

After that we moved from Wellington to Napier then back to Wellington because my mother's parents lived there and my father got a job in the Government.

I was only 17 years of age when the war broke out. I was working for a tailor in Lambton Quay, learning to be a cutter. I lied about my age to get into the Army. I was big, weighed about 13 stone and was playing 1st XV rugby, so I got away with it.

When I went into Hopuhopu camp, a couple of the officers must have known that I was under age because every time I went on leave to Wellington they used to ask me to bring back my identification.

You weren't allowed to go overseas until you were 21 and every time I came back from leave, they'd say, "Well, where's your dole book to say you're 21?"

And I'd say, "Oh, I forgot to get it" and one thing led to another and they just eventually forgot.

I was at camp about three months and then we went to England. I was in the second echelon, 7th Anti-tank Regiment. I was three weeks in Egypt before we went to Greece and ended up in Crete.

I was an artillery man but we were trained to be infantrymen. Some of the others were taken off before the battle but unfortunately I was left there and so I went through the Battle of Crete.

Over 50 years later, you don't mention what happened. You don't go around like some guys that come back from the war ... they're still wiping blood off their bayonets. But I would say that those types of guys, they've never seen any action, because you don't talk about it ... because dreadful things happened.

Every time I visit my doctor, even when I go in with my wife, he wants to know all about the war. And one day he asked me if I killed any Germans. I said, "Well, you're in the front lines, it's very rare if you don't."

In Crete, it was a different scene because most of them when they came down out of the gliders and the parachutists were dead before they landed. It was like shooting ducks.

I went back for the 50th anniversary of the Battle of Crete and I was with a couple of mates. We ended up with two Germans in a bar. We had a couple of drinks with them. One of them spoke very good English and the other one only knew a few words. The one who spoke good English said to us, "When we were here 50 years ago, you New Zealanders fought unfairly."

Their argument was we should have let them land on the ground before we started fighting. But all three of us laughed at that. If it had been reversed and we were coming in, look at how brutal they could be. They're more brutal than we are.

I was lucky to get off Crete the last night at Sfakia.

Then we trained for the desert campaign, what they call the

Crusader Campaign, in October, November and December 1941. That's where I was wounded and captured.

Before I was wounded we'd been in a bayonet charge with the 24th Battalion. Then we got a message to say that we were expecting an advance by friendly troops from another sector. We could see them all coming and all of a sudden they were bombing us and shelling us and mortar fire and everything. And next thing they were in our lines and they were telling us to get our hands up.

The Germans had actually advanced with our own equipment which they had captured previously. When our officers looked through their binoculars they looked like our troops. They had our square 15cwt ambulances and our armoured cars and everything. They were in shorts the same as we were and they had little peaked caps on like some of us used to wear. Some of them had their steel helmets on but they weren't German, they were British. When they got into our lines and the guys behind us realised what was happening, they opened up.

So I don't know if I got three bullets in the leg because I got caught in friendly fire. The guy who was the bombardier on the gun I was on, Ray Pilling from Petone, got shot in the leg and lost it.

My leg just bled and it wasn't until three or four days later that I realised I had been shot in the leg. I didn't even know that it had happened.

But I knew it was happening when I broke the bone across from my ear to my eye. That was from shrapnel. My eye was infected too.

I was in hospital for a couple of days. Then they took us to Benghazi. There were 18 of us and they put us on an Italian boat and they took us to Crete again. There was actually an English surgeon who was still there from the battle who was now a POW and he operated on me.

I was there for about six or seven days and then they took us back to Benghazi. We arrived on the late afternoon of 8 December 1941. Late that night we sailed on a boat called the *Jason* and about 2.45pm the next afternoon we were torpedoed by the British Navy.

They fired three torpedoes but the first two missed. And the third one hit No. 1 hull and all the hatches and beams fell on the guys in the hold, plus the explosion of the torpedo going off blew the bulkhead into No. 2 hull. All of them were dead too and the bulk hull from there to the engine room had a big bow in it but it didn't burst.

There was panic stations going on with everyone, especially with the Italian captain and the crew and they took to the lifeboats. It was a German engineer who came up from down below in the engine room with a big Luger in his hand. He ordered us all at the aft end of the ship because the propellers were still going around and by the weight of everyone going at the aft end he was able to jam the ship onto the rocks off the coast of Greece.

There were 2000 on that boat and there were about 500 dead. Out of the lot, I think 45 were New Zealanders.

We eventually got ashore and were in Greece for a few months. Then when we actually left Greece to go to Brindisi in Italy, the Italians were a little bit decent to us because they knew that we had been torpedoed. They didn't keep us down in the hold all the time. During the daylight they used to let us go up on deck, but lock us up down in the hull at night.

I stayed in several camps and then they asked for volunteers to go to work and they preferably wanted New Zealanders and South Africans. We were digging a canal for a small hydro scheme.

It was quite an enjoyable camp because we'd got quite friendly with the guards and they used to take us down to the river for swims. When we took the food out to the job site, on the way back there was a guard who'd always stop at a farmhouse and we'd get on the vino.

One day in the camp they all went on strike because the food wasn't any good. We'd had a bit too much vino and this Italian captain was in a bit of a panic and he was running around with a revolver in his hand because we were all on strike. He couldn't imagine it, us being prisoners, and he was the one holding all the revolvers and rifles to keep us in line. I was a bit wild when I was in the Army. I went and called him a brave *capitano*, in Italian, and he locked me up in the jail.

The other prisoners used to say, "If you want anything, you just go and see Lofty. He'll get it for you." I used to barter for anything with the guards.

When the winter came again they took us back to a big permanent camp with about 15,000 prisoners in it. I spent the winter there then when the summer came again I had to go back out to a labour camp. I thought I'd be going back to the same one, but I ended up going down south to a camp called Aquafreda in the Apennine Mountains where we worked in quarries digging out slate.

When Italy capitulated in September '43, we all marched out of camp with Red Cross parcels and what food we could get and split up into little two or three-men bands and we went up into the Apennine Mountains.

I lived with Italians for about a month in the town of Carnico. Then with the other three guys I was with, we made our way over the Apennine Mountains. The highest part we were up was over 7000 feet. We stopped for the night in a big alpine hut in an old skiing resort. It had wire-sprung beds in it and mattresses.

We finally got down through the German lines to our own lines in a place called Termoli which was occupied by a battalion of the famous English Buff regiment.

We were taken before the officers, who wanted to know why we were in civilian clothes. We could have been anybody because a lot of Germans could speak good English and we could have been spies, but in the finish they believed what we were saying. They took us to a town called Foggia and we were put through a delousing plant and we got a change of clothing.

We were lousy most of the time we were prisoners. If you were a smoker, you turned your trousers inside out where the underlining is and there'd be eggs all along there. You just pricked them with the ends of the cigarette or you could squash them between the fingernails of your thumbs.

In Italy I went into the city of Taranto every day. I used to hate wearing a hat and a Red Cap MP doing traffic control in middle of the road said to me, "Where's your hat, soldier?"

I told him I had lost it in the desert two years ago.

A couple of weeks went by and all the guys I was with wanted to go to the brothel. And by this time, unbeknownst to us, they had put the brothels out of bounds because they weren't controlled like they were in Egypt. And when we got there, these Red Caps were there and the same guy said, "You – where's your hat?"

I said, "I told you, I lost it two years ago in the desert."

"Why haven't you been reissued with a new one?"

"I've been a bloody prisoner of war for two years."

He said, "Well, how did you get here?"

I said, "We got through the German lines."

And the guy was so sympathetic, he told us we could go into the brothel, but we didn't, because there was no control there of disease and all that sort of thing and we knew we'd probably get back to New Zealand and we didn't want to be getting into that sort of thing.

The brothels in Cairo and Alexandra were controlled by the military. The women were examined by doctors. They called it the Berko in Cairo. Even in that street they had a place where you'd go after having intercourse and get washed in special ointment.

When Montgomery took over, he put it out of bounds. He also cut out the beer because he was a teetotaller himself.

Eventually I got back to Egypt and they wanted me to go and have a couple of weeks' leave, then have a refresher course and return to my unit.

I said, "Not me. I'm going home to New Zealand. I've had the war."

They asked me, "Why should you go home? There are guys who have been waiting here two years to go home."

I said, "Well, yeah, they got three meals a day. I was starving in Italy."

I arrived back in New Zealand in January 1944 and I was still only 22. I had my 21st birthday in the POW camp.

When I went home, if they had wanted me in another year's time and I was fit I probably would have gone back but I had to wait for an operation on my eye.

At the time we went to war, the Government said we were fighting for the mother country but most of the men came out of the Depression. It was an outlet. They wanted to get away.

The first echelon they called the "wife deserters". When I went to England they called us the "glamour boys" and they called the third echelon "one jumpers away from conscription".

But under different circumstances I don't think they'd get people to volunteer in the masses we did. I don't think they'd get them today. I wouldn't advise my son to go to war....

He's Alive, He's Alive
Bob Russell

Bob Russell is another who wrote up his war-time experiences in a notebook. Then other family members wanted a copy so he ended writing out several more notebooks. His second wife, Betty, whom he married when they already had a clutch of grandchildren between them, kindly lent me her copy in order to tell Bob's tale.

I joined the Army in December 1939, aged 21. I received my call-up in April 1940. It was early May that I reported to the drill hall in Rutland St. It was the first time I had met Howard Marx, who was to become a good friend. Also there was Lloyd Theyers, a bloke whom I knew slightly, mainly because I had played rugby against him. We formed a very strong friendship.

There were 500 rookies in this draft. We had to march down Queen St to the railway station. It was just on midnight and it was amazing to see the number of people there to see us off. As my dad was on the railway staff, I knew where he would be along with my family so I broke away from the group and went and said my farewell.

Along to see me off were my mum, dad, two sisters, brother, current girlfriend and some close friends. There were plenty of tears. I finally made the train and sat beside Howard Marx.

After a long trip, we arrived at Burnham Camp. We were the first draft to make up the third echelon. The fitting-out of uniforms was hilarious, some too big or too small. We had three months' training and naturally we all got pretty fit. It was winter and it was awfully cold.

After about a month, I was called into the orderly room and asked if I would like to go to the Trentham Camp for an NCOs' course. As I had made such good friends I said no. It was a decision I have always been happy with.

The No. 1 character in our outfit was Bluey Smith. Nothing much was happening on the parade ground at our first day in Burnham Camp. Bluey asked Captain Barnard, who was on the permanent staff and a good guy, where the nearest pub was. He was told Templeton, nine miles down the road.

Bluey's reply was, "When you want me, that's where I'll be."

Bluey was true to his word and was picked up there at 9pm. He spent the first night in camp jail.

Each parade ground has a small neat lawn with a flagpole in the centre. Our adjutant was a Duntroon-trained officer, a real fine-turned-out man who liked to wear spurs with his uniform.

He went on parade one morning and found someone had tied a horse to the flagpole. What a laugh! Three days later, the horse had gone but in its place next to the flagpole was a large pile of horse dung. Both incidents were taken in good spirits. However there is a sad ending to the story. This young adjutant, who was only 21 years old, was killed in action but not before he had won the Military Cross for outstanding bravery.

The infantry training was very extensive. Then without any warning, 500 of us were sent to Fiji. We never really found out why, but I think it was something to do with the Japanese. Even at this stage, the Japs were showing signs of entering the war. We were not there very long. Then we went back to New Zealand for 10 days' leave before being sent to the Middle East. Our ship was the *Aquitania*, which was the third-largest passenger ship in the world. We travelled in style, having nice cabins to sleep in.

Our first port of call was Fremantle and as our ship was too big to berth, there was no leave. However we had made friends with some of the crew. Howard and I borrowed some civilian clothes and we slipped over the side of the ship into a lighter boat and off we went for a bit of AWOL. We spent two days in Perth, had a good look around the city, then went back to the ship and were never caught.

We finally arrived at Port Said, then travelled by train to Maadi camp. There we had a revision course on rifles and Bren guns. The instructor suddenly picked on a hard-case West Coaster for a definition of a "fine sight". As quick as a knife the answer came back, "My girlfriend sitting on the Lyttelton Wharf with her pants down."

You can imagine the laughter.

One evening, Bluey Smith came back from a day's leave in Cairo and he really had a skinful. He could not make parade next morning. Our officer then called out, "Marx and Russell follow me."

We followed him into Bluey's tent, where we found Bluey all covered up and in a deep sleep.

Finally, the officer managed to wake Bluey up and yelled at him to get up. No chance! Bluey just looked at the officer through two bloodshot eyes and said, "Sir, if I ever get over this hangover I'll promise you I'll never drink again."

Luckily, this officer saw the funny side of it.

One time, our company was doing a short guard duty on a large ammunition dump in Syria. The company was paraded and were addressed by the Pommy officer. The boys were told that at all times they were to be most vigilant. Apparently there were many attempted break-ins by the locals. The boys had to challenge twice only.

One night Len Lane, who was our best shot, was on duty about 9pm. He heard sounds and he challenged. No answer. He challenged again. There was no reply so he took aim and fired.

He shot dead a Syrian who was trying to crawl through the high wire fence. There was no fuss.

Len was on duty again three days later. It was about the same time as before. Len again heard noises somewhere near the wire fence. He challenged. There was no reply. He challenged again. No answer. So he shot.

Oh boy, what a fuss followed. Len had shot the Pommy captain's dog. We Kiwis were not very popular for a while.

In our spare time, we kicked a football around and chose a battalion rugby side. We had the trials played in the sand and I made the team at second five-eighths. We played three games of rugby in the Freyberg Cup. We won the first two games but lost the third 6-3.

On our way to the front line we tasted what real war was all about. Our convoy got dive-bombed and we had a good taste of being strafed. It was all very scary. I never got used to being strafed.

We were now frontline soldiers in the Eighth Army, which consisted of British, Indians, South Africans, two divisions of Australians, the 51st Highland Division and, of course, us. Our New Zealand Division consisted of three brigades – the 4th, 5th and 6th (we were in the 6th).

The Germans were at full strength and they were now giving the Allies a very hard time. At this stage, they were a far better-equipped Army than ours. Their Tiger tanks were really awesome.

Our task was to attack the Germans and by doing this relieve the Australians who had held Tobruk for 10 long months. The attack was successful enough and the Aussies were able to get a well-earned rest. The South Africans took over Tobruk. However we all felt the full strength of the German Army and it did not take them long to take Tobruk back again and send the rest of us backwards at 100 miles an hour. We got back to Bagush Box and dug in. Our 4th and 5th Brigades got completely surrounded by the Germans and they were confident they had two-thirds of the New Zealanders beaten.

However, they were mistaken. The 18th and Maori Battalions joined forces and they put up a remarkable bayonet charge which split the Germans wide apart and this enabled the rest of the troops to escape.

It was a great victory that really shattered the Germans and also stopped their advance. There were many casualties on both sides and there was a lull in the fighting while both sides licked their wounds. It was Christmas and in 1941 there was no ham and Christmas pudding but "yummy" beef and rice, and, for sweets, tinned fruit.

After three weeks' duty on the Turkish border, we were rushed back to a place called Kahonga Box. Then we were pulled out and retired back to El Alamein where we dug in. Each evening as the sun sank, we got bombed heavily. Then on 15 July, our 5th Brigade attacked the Germans. We, the 6th Brigade, were held in reserve. The 5th Brigade did a fine job but suffered many casualties.

On 22 July, it was our turn to attack. We spent all day getting our arms ready then as the sun went down we started our attack and all hell broke loose. By dawn, we had reached our objective and dug in.

For a short while all was quiet, then we heard the sound of the tanks coming. We had no answer to them. They simply rolled over us. The British tank brigade was supposed to have come up and helped us but we never saw one.

General Freyberg had been wounded and Brigadier "Whisky" Bill Inglis had taken over our division. He was a very angry man with the support the British had not given us. He then made a statement that the NZ Division would never go into action again without the support of our tanks.

Maybe if we had had tank support on the 15th and 22nd, things might have been very different but we were now POWs. We had, of course, thoughts of being wounded or killed but none of us ever had thoughts of being taken prisoner.

We were kept in the front line all day without food or water with shells raining down around us from our own side. It's not very nice being shelled by your own people.

When the evening came, we were put on trucks and started our trek to Italy. After five days of terrible conditions, we arrived in Benghazi and were put in a POW camp. It was a shocking place. Many men were ill with dysentery. We nicknamed this place "Dysentery Cave".

We stayed in this camp until 16 August, then we were put on a ship called the *Nino Bixio*. There were three holds, two up front and one at the rear. We were packed into the forward hold. Five hundred of us – mostly New Zealanders, a few Aussies and Englishmen.

The 17th of August was my mother's birthday and at 3pm it came ... a torpedo against our hold and also one in the engine room. I have no recollection of what happened in the next five days.

There were 17 of us, all from the same company, 24th Battalion, and only four of us survived – Howard Marx, Bluey Smith, neither of them injured, Doug Truscott who had all fingers on one hand nearly severed, and me with head injuries.

Jim McAlpine, whom I had worked with before the war, was lying very close to me when the torpedo hit and his body was never found. When I finally got home I had to go and see his mum. What an upsetting experience. Jimmy's dad had died when he was a young boy. Even now as I recall this I am filled with grief.

The ship did not sink and we were towed into a port in Greece and I was taken off the boat along with many other wounded men to a German naval hospital. Luckily my injuries were not too severe – just concussed and a bad cut over my left eye.

When I finally was able to take notice of what was going on, I was terribly upset to see so many men with bad injuries. There was a terrible loss of men, all killed from our hold, 122 of them. I was now separated from my two close mates.

From the hospital, along with other walking wounded, I was housed in an empty warehouse. There was no clean water and no food. Dysentery struck again and I lost a lot of weight. After seven days in this hell-hole, we were put on an Italian hospital ship and sailed to Bari, Italy. Into another camp and who was there to greet me? My two close mates Howard and Bluey.

Next came a time in my life I have always wanted to forget. The health of all the men was at a very low ebb and most of us had body lice and crabs at the same time. It was a very degrading time. With constant washing and shaving the hair from our bodies we finally got ourselves rid of these nasty bugs.

Then we were on the move again, however this time without my close mate Howard who had got very sick and been put in hospital. This was the last time I saw him until after the war. We travelled up to northern Italy to camp number 57. This was a very large camp with six separate compounds.

Coming over from Greece to Italy, the guy in charge of us had to take down all our particulars as our papers had all been lost. My turn came and when he asked me my occupation I said, "A warehouseman."

He said, "A what?"

I told him again.

And again he said, "A what?"

I then retorted, "A bloody farmer."

By saying I was a farmer, I was sent from camp 57 to 107, a working camp. In this camp there were 500 South Africans and 500 New Zealanders – you can imagine the rivalry that went on.

One job we had to do there was digging drains. They were four feet deep, three feet across the top and about 8 inches at the bottom. The Italians got very frustrated at our slowness as we were out all day long and not very much got done. Naturally, in the camp there were some guys who knew all about drain digging. These guys met the Italian bosses and got them to agree to a contract.

What a change and what a laugh. Now all the groups went out to work at 7.30am and by 9am the job was done. The Itis were really not at all happy with what had happened. They wanted the contract broken but with no luck. Finally it was agreed that we would make the job spin out until 10.30am. It was a great victory!

We had now settled down to life in a POW camp. However, I, along with many other boys, never did come to grips with being locked up and determined to escape.

The first escape attempt in the camp was a bit silly. A South African calmly walked away from where he was working. Two days later, the guy got recaptured and brought back to camp.

The next escape was really well organised. Two South Africans and myself were called into the Camp Leader's hut and asked if we could run an athletics meeting. The only thing we were told was that it was for something really important. While it was going on, two blokes were being carried out of the camp in two large rubbish boxes. Right outside the camp there were two large holes dug for camp rubbish. Sex is of great interest to male Italians and while the guards were being shown rude photos of sex scenes, these two guys were being dumped in the large holes. Two more guys got out in the same manner and the escape was a complete success.

However, the four escapees were later caught right on the Yugoslav border.

The weather where we were was very similar to the South Island's. At times it was very cold with some heavy falls of snow. Spring was on the way and two South Africans, Bill and Brian Leech (cousins), Dick Hunt and myself decided we did not want to spend another winter there. We began to make plans to escape.

We had managed to get hold of some wire cutters and cut through the fence. We got out without too much trouble but we did have to watch out for the fascist guards who were now in charge.

We quickly made our way to a small village and found a man who had worked as an overseer on the fields where we worked. We swapped some of our gear, mainly our woollen underwear, for civilian clothes, and set off south. At about 11.30pm, we decided to get a little sleep. In the morning, we all felt good at being free at last but were all still very nervous.

We thought we were well hidden in the middle of a cornfield but then we were found by two Italian teenagers, a girl, Assunta, and her brother Severino, who came wandering through and found us.

Big Bill Leech spoke a little bit of Italian, and he and the two young ones took off and soon came back with some bread and fresh water. Assunta tried to tell us not to travel at night as there was a curfew in place in all the villages, but we did not understand what she was saying.

Before we moved on, Assunta gave me a small snapshot of herself and brother with her address on the back, which I still have. We took off and by midnight we were back in a civilian jail. We had been caught breaking the curfew. Our freedom had not lasted long.

We were desperate and it was now 2am. We just had to get out and get out we did. The big South African was the tough one of the four. I do not want to go into the details. It was not very nice, but I don't think there was any loss of life. It's those things that you feel guilt in yourself about. It just had to be done.

When we were free again, the first thing we did was jump on a train. This turned out to be a very lucky move as it got us over the Tagliamento and Po Rivers, the last one becoming a big stumbling block to the British Army later in the war.

By now there were a lot of people on the train so we decided to get off. It was a wrong move because we walked slap bang into a large contingent of German troops. We guessed the troops were on the move south. We quickly got back on the train and very quickly decided our only option was to stay put. Eventually the train moved on but very slowly. It was a real stop-start affair. Our patience was really tested.

We got off the train at the next stop and decided that from there on we would have to walk.

Our big trouble was hunger. However, being free just kept us going. We headed for the comparative safety of the hills where we found that some grapes were now getting ripe. Stealing them became our daily diet. At odd times we found a fig tree, not too bad. We started to feel a little bit healthier. After a few days, we decided to come out of the hills and head for the coast. We were not completely sure where we were but did manage to discover we had passed Venice.

We kept going. Our next bit of excitement was that we had come to a big town, Rimini. We could see the railway station and guards. We were tempted to go for another train ride but just as we were about to make the decision to get on the train there were suddenly bursts of gunfire all at the train.

Our luck was still holding. We hurried back inland.

We kept going day by day and sleeping at night. We came to what we later discovered was the Sangro River and as it was a lovely sunny day decided to strip off and have a wash. We also washed our clothes. It was lucky I had kept a cake of English soap from a Red Cross parcel. The clothes dried in no time.

We had now been free for 24 days. On we went, averaging about 24 miles a day. Our big trouble now was Dick Hunt. Some time before he had swapped his boots for an Italian pair. They were now falling apart and Dick was having terrible trouble with his feet. He showed a lot of courage and struggled on. We began to hear the sounds of the front line and awoke one morning to find ourselves very close to a German infantry company.

We began to travel in single file. Brian was leading and suddenly we came on him being searched by a German. I don't know what made me do it but I threw the cake of soap and my wallet in which was the snapshot that Assunta had given me.

As all this was happening there was the sound of engines and overhead came 20 or more British dive-bombers giving the Germans a real hurry-up. All the Germans rushed for cover and my mates also took off in a big hurry. But I stopped to find my two possessions.

I was on my own for about 15 minutes before I heard a call from some undergrowth. It was my three mates. Together again we settled down and had a talk about our situation. We decided that we now must be in "No Man's Land", the area between the opposing British and German forces. There was gunfire going on all around us.

A German plane was shot down by flak and crashed to the ground only about 800 yards from where we were hiding. The pilot baled out to safety. We found out later that he was taken prisoner by the British. We also saw the Germans drive a train into a tunnel then blow it up. We had earlier walked through this tunnel.

Had we been found at this stage by the Germans we could have been shot as spies as we were travelling in civilian clothes. We had now been hiding for about four hours and it became evident to us that if we did not move on we would be caught in British artillery fire.

We went forward very slowly and carefully. We saw infantry troops coming down a hill towards us. They trained their guns on us. It was really scary! What an eternity it seemed for us to convince them that we were escaped POWs. We had walked into the Canadians. We were free at last. What a great feeling.

We were taken to HQ. Firstly, we were all interviewed, one by one, by the Canadian intelligence officer and he was satisfied with our story and that we were two South Africans and two New Zealanders. We were now fed and clothed and we were all given a medical check. Dick had his feet dressed and bandaged and he was also given a pair of boots.

The whole escape had been a terrific experience that I shall never forget. For us the war was over, but getting back to our base in Cairo became a real hassle. We were now in British hands and they showed no interest in us. Eventually, we were taken by truck down to the foot of Italy across the Messina Straits and into Sicily.

We were kept there for over two weeks until we were put on a ship and ended up in Malta (we were going the wrong way). This gallant island had endured 1100 air raids during the past two years and suffered a lot of damage. At the end of the war it was awarded the "George Medal".

We were then put onto another ship that was going the wrong way and arrived in Algiers. By now we had had enough of the treatment we were getting and really kicked up a fuss. We were met by an English major and we told him our story. He finally got us off the ship and sent us to a transit camp.

We explored Algiers, but did not like what we saw. Eventually, we were put on a ship and headed back to Malta and another four days there. However we were now heading in the right direction!

Finally we got back to Wellington – what a tremendous feeling.

We spent only four hours there and were then on a train to Auckland. My entire family was there to meet me, plus many close friends.

There was also another reason why they were so pleased to see me. In August 1942, the casualty list in the *New Zealand Herald* had me and a few others as "missing believed drowned". My family and friends were completely devastated by this news. They had thought I was dead.

You can imagine the great joy eight months later when the news came through that I was safe and well in a POW camp. My sister ran down the street shouting, "He's alive, he's alive."

What a welcome I received when I got back to Auckland. My mum would not let go of me. The welcome for me more than made up for all the strife I had had in the past three and a half years. Our home in Epsom was an open home to all. It was amazing the number of people that called in to see me, some I really didn't know.

The Army days were well and truly over for me but in their way the effects of war lingered for decades afterwards.

I had not been home long when I had a breakdown in health and was quickly put in the military hospital. I spent just on three weeks having lots of examinations. I was diagnosed as a malaria case. I was well looked after but I continued having mild bouts for some time.

Dick Hunt, who escaped with me, did not fare so well. He got married and they had one child but soon afterwards he fell ill and was diagnosed with TB. He died soon afterwards.

Thirty-two years after the war ended, I decided I would make a trek to South Africa, partly to try and locate the two South Africans whom I escaped with.

I travelled up to Rhodesia to visit friends in Salisbury. They told me to go and see their parents in Transvaal. The luck I had with my escape was still holding. They knew a friend who knew a friend and within two hours I was talking to one of my old mates. In a matter of weeks the three of us were able to get together for a wonderful weekend.

I also went back to Egypt and spent a whole day at El Alamein. It was very sad for me to visit the cemetery and see all the headstones with the silver fern on them.

I returned to Italy to see if I could find the area where I was kept a POW and also to see if I could find the two Italians who managed to give us some food and fresh water. With the snap of Assunta and her brother that she had given me, I went from village to village to see if I could find someone who could recognise the two youngsters.

I went into a local coffee shop. Many of the people there were naturally interested in us and there was a lot of talking going on. An old lady appeared and with a lot of hand-waving managed to tell me I was in the right village.

Luckily a man came in who spoke reasonable English. He took us to a house and who was living there but Severino. What a reception we received and were given an enormous lunch with lots of pasta, bread, salads and red wine. Many of Severino's family came around to join in in that warm and vibrant way that only the Italians can do.

I now discovered the whereabouts of Assunta. She had married an English soldier and was now living in England. She had presented him with two daughters and then he had left her and she was too proud to go back to Italy. Eventually, she married an Italian who was a POW in England and did not want to go back to Italy. Just prior to me going there, he had had a heart attack and died.

I found her and she knew me as soon as she saw me. She came out to New Zealand and spent time with me out here and I went back over there and stayed over there.

But I never married her. I wasn't sure and Italians are very family-oriented and she wanted to see her children and grandchildren. She came out to New Zealand twice. The second time she went home I went back with her and took her to Canada to see her brother whom she had not seen for 32 years. We stayed in Winnipeg for about three months, which has an Italian quarter and we had a ball.

Then we went to England and after three weeks I was homesick for my family. We discussed it and we discussed it and after 10 months I came home. She recently died. Another chunk out of my life.

Unforgettable Arch
Arch Scott

Arch wrote a book about his wartime experiences called Dark of the Moon. *He lent it to a priest who "laughed like blazes" because he knew what Arch really meant when he said he was "ship" scared. Today Arch still retains a sharp and slightly rebellious wit.*

I was born in Hamilton on 14 January 1916. I can't remember it very clearly [Arch is being humorous here]. I was the youngest of 10, five boys and five girls. My brother Maurice Scott, 20 years older than me, was wounded in the First World War.

My father was a farmer and a dealer in land and stock. We were in Kawhia for a number of years on the North Island's west coast. At the turn of the century, there were three Scott brothers who had the local store in Kawhia. They all bought and/or leased land around the harbour and Dad had all sorts of land too. We had a number of sheep and every year while I was going to primary school we used to shift the fat lambs on a big, flat-bottomed pontoon with rails around it from our no-road-access, Maori-leased land at Taharoa to the steamship that took them to Auckland freezing works.

Dad died when I was only six. My mother used to sign cheques: "Estate of TB Scott, BA Scott, executrix" on every cheque and I remember she ran the outfit all the way through. We all helped of course.

There were about as many Maori as there were Pakeha at Kawhia school. I have a great fondness for the Maori. They were one of us and we were one of them. Marvellous people. You find out that as you go through life that's what the whole world is like and as the Italians say, "Tutto il mondo e paese" – "The whole world is one country."

I volunteered in 1939. We were all volunteers. We just had to go. There was nothing else for it. We weren't told to go, on the contrary, you had to be stopped and that was why it was so dreadful being taken prisoner of war because you were there fighting for the freedom of the world, but you lost your own freedom which was almost too much for a mind to take.

But we never really knew what we were letting ourselves in for. We didn't really think too much about the fact that men would die or lose limbs. The other force was so strong. It was a general feeling among everybody.

I had met Joy, later my wife, in 1937, in my first year teaching in Hamilton. We were very close before the war. She knew of our secret overseas departure from Papakura and was waiting for me in Frankton, in a phone box. It was raining like hell. I had been handcuffed to a bloke that had escaped the last two drafts. They wanted to make sure he went this time.

I said to him, "I want to meet my girlfriend here tonight. Will you wait for me?"

He said, "Yeah, I'll wait for you."

I met Joy. She had a lot of little boxes of sandwiches and other "goodies" to take back. I went back and the chap was still waiting for me on the train.

Originally, I wanted to join the Air Force, but my eyesight was not good enough. So I went to the recruiting station and joined the Army and waited. I was finally called up in January 1941 with the 5th Reinforcements. I don't know why it took so long. I was in it a long time and I still can't work out how the Army works at times but I do maintain steadfastly that it felt good to belong to a unit of 2NZEF.

Maurice "Lofty" O'Connor (centre) relaxing with friends after the war.

No, this is not "Checkpoint Charlie" in Berlin but Maurice O'Connor (wearing glasses) at a reunion in Wanganui.

Bob Russell (back row, centre) eating an enormous sandwich at Port Said. Lloyd Theyers is back row, right and Howard Marx is front row, centre.

Guard duty at Papakura camp in 1941 – Arch Scott is second from the right.

Arch Scott (left) with Gino Panont, partisan brigade leader – this photograph was taken in the Piazza di S. Marco soon after liberation.

Arch Scott stands on the left. On the right is Paul Day who escaped with Pat Moncur to Switzerland.

Allan Smith (top right corner, with pipe) with his squadron while stationed at Lille.

The painting of 146 Typhoon Wing that Allan Smith found hanging in The Royal Academy after he returned from a POW camp.
Back row: John Deall (266 Squadron), Guy Plamondon (193 Squadron), Bob Rutter (263 Squadron). Second row: Johnny Baldwin (Wing Leader), Allan Smith (197 Squadron). Foreground: Johnny Johnson (257 Squadron).

Irene and Allan Smith at an investiture in 1946. Allan is wearing the Distinguished Flying Cross and Bar.

Frank Snelgar (left) with his brother Jim who served in the Occupation forces.

Like the time we were taken prisoner, that was just a proper RABU [Real Army Balls Up]. Many things that happen went like that in the Army. The orders from the top filter down through a purification system where they come right down to the coal face to the privates and lance corporals and corporals and then work back up and by that time they're not a RABU anymore, they've become a SABU [a Self-Adjusting Balls Up].

By the time they know some things won't work they've also lost so much from doing something bloody stupid. Later when our company asked the English why the tanks hadn't turned up they said it was because we hadn't asked for them through the correct channels!

We had basic training before we left camp and I also went to the NCO school because I had a lot of cobbers going there. Prior to that we were in a hurry to get overseas, but there was a lot of camaraderie between us and we talked it over together and we thought it might be better if we went to NCO school first.

Then I went to Egypt and was captured in the first action.

I was in a mortar platoon, driving in a Bren carrier on which we carried the mortars. I was very lucky. I just rode through that night attack on the Bren carrier and I wasn't fighting at all whereas the infantry, foot soldiers, had to fight their way right through and it must have been just hellish.

In the actual advance that night, we didn't really have anything to do with the fighting. I did damn all. We started just before dark and just got down there and it went through all night until daylight in the morning when Pop Mendelburn and I dug a slitty [slit trench]. We got down about nine inches and we struck rock! We couldn't get any further and we thought, "Oh, she's tight, digger."

But when the bloody tanks shoved their turrets over the cliff in front of us and started firing down on top of us I thought, "Holy smoke."

We were just pressing down in the slit trench. Every now and again you'd look up and see these things that looked like red hot oranges jumping around you. They struck an ammo truck and it just went up and the whole place was an inferno. Then the tanks just rolled forward and came down among us and we were in the bag.

It was one of worst moments of my life. I hadn't done one bloody thing ... was just handed over on a plate. I never found anything as bad as that. I've never felt so useless, absolutely bloody useless.

We were taken prisoner and put in big trucks and taken away by the enemy. From there, it took four to five days to be trucked to Benghazi.

There we were given blue cards, A-M, and red cards, N-Z. We didn't know what those were for. All people with the red cards went on the boat called the *Nino Bixio*, which was a cargo ship with three or four holds on two levels.

Most of the men went down to the bottom hold, but my friend Don McDonald and I went down the ladder only as far the mezzanine floor. We sat on a ledge with our backs to the bulkhead. I was behind a pillar which forced me to sit with my knees hunched up. From time to time, Don suggested we should change places, but I said I was okay.

A lot of us had dysentery but for several hours no one was allowed up the ladder to use the toilet. The odd individual would climb up the ladder with his "doings" in his tin hat only to be sent down again by the guard.

Later when the guards realised we were not dangerous, we were allowed on deck and I recall meeting one of our mortar platoon, Jim White, who came from a family of seafarers. He said how happy he was to be on the sea, but I told him I was ship-scared.

The second day at sea, in the middle of the afternoon, the odd shafts of sunlight were coming into the hold. Don used this as an excuse to again try to get me to change places with him. He said I could stretch my legs out, but I said, "No, no, she's tight, digger, I'm all right."

So Don stretched out and fell asleep.

I was awake when the torpedo struck.

I was thrown forward with a bit of a bump on the head but Don had a hatch cover hit him right over the head. He died instantly. If I had changed places it would have been me. My uncomfortable position behind the pillar had protected me.

There was another twist on this I found out later. When the cards had been issued, Don and Paul Day had considered swapping cards so that Paul and I could remain together. In the end, they decided against it.

On each side of me were half a dozen men lying dead. One of them had his rosary beads around his neck and the shaft of sunlight had now settled on him.

I walked past Don and saw a hole in the hold big enough to drive a truck through. In front of me was a bloke with his legs blown off. A man looks so small without his legs. He wanted a smoke so I gave him one. He said, "Thanks mate," and puffed on it as his life ebbed away.

Then I met a bloke I knew who was from North Auckland. He had lost a foot and his leg to about halfway up the shin. He had a rifle that one of the guards had left and he wanted someone to kill him with it. He was a bushman and said he was no use any more. He had been magnificent in the hand-to-hand fighting on the night of the attack. "You'll do it for me, won't you Scotty?" he said to me.

I tried to talk him out of it, then I just left him alone. He survived the war.

I went up on deck. Everything was a shambles. There were human entrails on the rigging and rails, pieces of bodies splattered and squashed against winches … blokes were jumping in the water. Some were throwing hatch covers over to make rafts for themselves. Some of the hatch covers were hitting men below. It was bloody chaos.

There was one bloke who was blown straight out of the ship into the sea. There was a rope hanging over so he climbed back on board. The thing I remember about him was he had a black-and-white football jersey. I don't know where he got it from.

I met a cobber from home up on deck. He was a Niue Islander from just over the harbour in Kawhia. I had a big long yarn with him. He seemed quite all right, but then he just died the next day. I talked to his family after the war and told them about it. His history says he died of wounds. No one's really sure. I think he died from shock.

The ship listed a bit but it didn't go down. Then the captain came up with his pistol and he saw we weren't antagonistic or anything and we helped him get the rope out to an Italian destroyer which put us on tow.

We were towed away to Navarino in the south of Greece where we remained on board until they decided what to do with us.

I had a soldier's prayer book and just by myself, without getting a group around me or anything, I sort of prayed for the dead and gave them a burial service.

Over the next few days, more bodies floated to the surface of the water in the hold. Finally the dead were taken off the boat and buried.

You don't really get used to people dying in war. It's just something that happens and you have got nothing to stop it, so you just have to live with it.

We were taken to Bari in the south of Italy and we were next to officers' camp No. 75. We were in a canal with no water in it and which had concrete sides.

They fed us for a while then moved us to the big camp, No. 57, Gruppignano, near Udine. There were thousands up there and we went out in working parties to work on farms. It was there my cobber Paul Day and I decided to learn Italian. Loudspeakers used to blare out the news all hours of the day and we had books. We learned from newspapers and some available books around. I had done French for three years at secondary school and Paul was a Master of Arts with first-class honours in English and French.

As I was the only one in my group in work camp that spoke Italian, I became the interpreter. We got to know a lot of Italians when we were in the working camp, though one of the sergeants was a bit offside with us.

We played some football there and then he came and stopped the second game because he thought we were trying to kill each other.

When we played the first game the sergeant wasn't there and so that went off all right. The second game was a bit more competitive because the place we were in we had a group upstairs and a group downstairs. The top storey was playing the bottom storey and that second game was a bit more fair dinkum. There were a couple of blood noses.

I don't think it was quite true in my book where I said, "I found the sergeant running behind me yelling at me and I went to pass him the ball, but stopped when I saw his face" but it was something like that. He ran out onto the field and said we'd get hurt and he'd be in trouble. So he took us back to camp.

The Italians changed sides on 8 September 1943 and that sergeant was quick to leave, but the other guards stayed and the place was open all hours. We got rid of the barbed wire and we stayed there because we had nowhere to go.

I knew the Italians were bloody good people but then POWs started coming to me and saying, "This bloke here, I think he's asking me to go and stay with him" and things like that.

People were wanting them to go to their homes to live as POWs – usually in sheds, lofts, haystacks, or cane huts. That became my job, just to go and talk to these people and okay them. I kept a note of people and where they were. Sometimes I'd get word back that it would be too dangerous in one of these places and I'd have to shift them to another place. It became a full-time job.

The Germans weren't too far away then. They were around and I don't know why the hell they didn't pick us up because for a while I just stayed there where the camp was and they didn't come there. But they pounced on some camps straight away. But after a while I moved out of the camp to stay with Italians.

I met a priest called Don Antonio Andreazza. He was a mighty chap, a magnificent man, who would do absolutely anything for us.

Once he came to me very excited that there was a Spitfire pilot hiding out in the area. We got on our bicycles and went to see him, but as soon as I looked at him I knew he was not an Englishman.

I was concerned when he suddenly dived under the bed to retrieve a gun. But then he gave it to me and said he could get some more. There were some doubts about exactly who the "Spitfire pilot" was and one of the local Italians wanted to settle the matter by digging a hole under the grapevines and putting him in it.

Finally we discovered that he was a man who had killed another after some romantic entanglement and was hiding out.

I used to go to meetings of the local Liberation Committee. I could take part to some extent. I knew enough Italian to get by. I went to a meeting one day and was asked questions which I answered. Then one of the other delegates from somewhere else burst out, "I know who the Englishman is."

There was an Italian there who had ginger hair and he pointed straight at him. He thought I was Italian.

By October 1943, I had collected about 80 escapers and arranged with partisans at Ronchi to take them to Yugoslavia. The Italians provided two people to go with me. An old engineer was one. Suddenly he came through the railway car and said, "The militia are coming through from the next carriage asking for documents."

I got the people we were escorting to walk on out and they all followed and got off the train and we walked back along and we got on it again. We finished our journey, then we all got off and apparently the Militia all walked past us inside the train.

One day I was hastily called up into the hills behind Monfalcone to meet a Yugoslav partisan leader who spoke Italian. He only had one eye and looked ferocious. In fact he seemed the personification of a poem I had once heard called "Jack the One-eyed Terror".

"Are you really called The Terror?" asked the leader of our Push.
"You make no fuckin' error," said the Bastard from the Bush.

Even as I was wondering how he had lost his eye, some shots rang out and "Jack" disappeared into the "bush" [the Italian scrub]. I was left alone in the middle of nowhere as darkness began to fall around me.

After half an hour, I was just about to push off when "Jack" came back. His explanation of his disappearance was that they had been sorting someone out, which I took as a veiled threat.

The reason I was there was to try and get him to escort some of our men out of occupied territory. But instead "Jack" wanted them to fight for him. But this was out of the question when we ran across five men who had already been fighting with his partisans. Three others had already been killed and these five were living skeletons. "Jack" was not quite the "Bastard of the Bush" and released them to me.

As I took on more responsibility as a liaison man and helping people to escape, so I became a target for the Fascists. One morning I was at a house where they made clothes for escapers when I was warned that the Fascists were coming. I quickly went to the door and took my bike from the wall and met them as they ran towards the gate. I pushed the gate open for them and they rushed madly past into the house in search of me. I paused a moment, as any ordinary Italian would have done, and then cycled away.

In those days of always being in enemy-occupied territory we developed survival habits against being caught. One was that on entering a room we would invariably "con the joint" and take up a position of scrutiny and of easy escape. This habit remained with me for many years after the war.

One incident caused me great sorrow and worry. There seemed to be a strong connection between some of our chaps being picked up and an Italian who was ostensibly very friendly and always seemed to be prepared to do everything I asked of him. One day, when talking to the partisan brigade leader, I just happened to mention my gathering doubts about this chap.

The next day I again met this brigade leader who told me that I needn't worry any more as they had shot the chap the previous evening. He seemed amused at how much the chap had protested our mutual friendship and at his saying how annoyed I'd be if anything happened to him.

I just felt sick and thought, "You can't win. You can't even discuss things with anyone. Poor bastard. He could have been okay."

I met Dave Russell in October 1944. He was very active helping others to escape. My last meeting with him was when we were given information which turned out to be false that one of our chaps had been shot by the Germans. On hearing this, Dave said,

"By hell, Scotty, those bastards are getting bloody personal." It was the last thing I heard him say.

Shortly afterwards, he was picked up by Republican soldiers. On 28 February at about 2 o'clock, he was taken to the German HQ where he was interrogated, but his answer was, "I will not tell you my job here nor where my companions are."

When told that he was to be shot, Dave stood to attention. They led him outside and told him to stand against the concrete wall. He asked for a cigarette and smoked part of it. They asked him if he had anything to say.

He shook his head, threw away his half-smoked cigarette and stood up rigidly to attention. They left him where he fell and at about 6 o'clock in the evening a bullock wagon came along. They bundled the body into an Italian groundsheet, took it to the cemetery and buried it. Later the villagers erected a headstone to commemorate his courage and fierce loyalty. After the war, Dave Russell was posthumously awarded the George Cross.

Much later I went back and saw the bullet marks in the wall.

I eventually escaped from Italy. It was on Friday 13 April 1945. I got out on a boat escape route that I had set up which got a total of 47 men out of northern Italy.

I received a permission to go back behind the lines. I wanted to fight again. We made three attempts but I couldn't get back there.

I finally returned by following the Allied advance through Italy. It was good to meet up with my old Italian friends again. Each tried to outdo the other by boasting about how much he or she had known of our clandestine operations in the few months before my departure.

I was temporary military governor of the area until a trained military governor could get there to take over. When he arrived, he asked me to remain as his interpreter.

There was one incident that occurred at this time that was possibly the most dangerous thing I did and also probably the most stupid. The Allied military government had posted notices that all arms were to be handed in. One partisan leader refused to hand over the revolvers he was wearing and said that if anyone wanted them he was waiting in the piazza.

I went straight to the piazza. I was wearing an American uniform and had a big Colt on my right hip. When I got there, the piazza was almost deserted except for a figure standing with the sun at his back and arms loosely folded and two white-handled pistols standing out of their holsters.

I looked at him and walked slowly towards him.

He didn't move.

I came close to him, pointed a forefinger at each side of his body, slid them in beside the triggers and lifted the pistols out of their holsters.

I arrested him, but he escaped from jail during the night. The jailer explained this by saying, "I have a wife and two children, and I have to go on living in this country."

Much later, I found out about another partisan leader who had refused to give up his weapons and had killed two carabinieri who tried to collect them. He was still doing his 30 years.

In the war, I fought on behalf of New Zealand, the Italian resistance, the British and the Americans. At one point I possessed British and American uniforms at the same time. I wanted to stay in Italy but was told that I was to be repatriated.

I found this most unfair after an ex-POW friend succeeded in staying by getting his Italian girlfriend pregnant. Since my many written applications to stay had been refused it led me to consider that "the penis is mightier than the pen is".

When the war ended, I was on leave in Inverness in Scotland. I went to the "Best Pub in the Highlands". That night, the barman pointed at a notice on the wall that said no singing was allowed in the bar. I stood up and did my bun. I said, "Come on, let's sing." I danced on the floor. I had a mate with my hat on and I had his on and we danced all over the place. The whole place was really stirred. It seemed so stupid that they wouldn't allow people to sing in a bar when they had just won a war.

After the war, I found I couldn't go back to teaching initially. I seemed a bit bomb happy, and hearing loud noises bothered me. I worked in a country store for the first year. Then I returned to teaching and married Joy in 1947.

In 1966, Joy, our four children and I returned to Italy. My family was amazed by the reception from people who had not seen me for 21 years but would recognise me immediately and weep openly.

When I was made an honorary Italian, my illuminated scroll from a primary school read, "Certain men do not succeed in making themselves forgotten."

A Man of Integrity
Allan Smith

Allan Smith is an exceptional man. He went to school with Robert Muldoon. Muldoon became Minister of Finance, but Allan was better at maths. Later Allan used his focussed and straightforward common sense to manage Wilson Meats for 30 years.

During the war, he came up with some crucial innovations for low-level dive-bombing tactics. As he modestly described them to me, I listened with growing respect while quietly calculating just how many lives they would have saved.

I was born in Auckland on 12 January 1921. I went to Mt Albert Grammar School. After leaving school I worked for Wilson Meats (now known as Wilson Foods). I joined the Royal New Zealand Air Force in March 1941.

I loved flying right from the start. I had the feeling of anticipation and excitement when I walked out to fly an aeroplane and that feeling has never left me. Every flight is a challenge – the smell of the aircraft, the feeling you are becoming part of it as you strap yourself into the cockpit … the taxiing to the end of the runway, the cockpit drill, checking wind directions and then you get a feeling of power as you open the throttle and take off and feel the exhilaration of the rapid climb upwards. Every time I got out of the plane and walked across the tarmac and I knew I'd had a successful flight, then I would walk a little taller.

I obtained my wings on Harvards at No. 6 SFTS in Canada. I came top of the course and I was very proud when the wings were pinned to my chest.

When we got to Britain we were asked what type of aircraft we wanted to fly. I made my three choices. As is usual in the Forces, I was given my third choice – fighters. I was sent out training on Hurricanes at Sutton Bridge.

I went solo on a Hurricane on 17 January 1942. It's always strange going solo for the first time because most of your instruction is done dual. I specifically recall being pressed hard against the seat as I opened the throttle. When I looked down at the ground, it was covered in snow and I didn't know where I was, so I flew east until I hit the sea. I found my way back to the aerodrome which had been closed soon after I took off because they had decided the weather was too bad for flying. The instructors had to come out firing Verey pistols to help me locate the airfield in the snowstorm.

I had my first flying accident on 12 March. As I took off, I felt a tyre burst, but the undercart locked up all right, so I carried on. When I came back in to land, it was confirmed by the tower over the radio that the port tyre had burst. I was told to land with the wheels down. As the Hurricane started to lose speed, the weight started to settle onto the damaged wheel. The fairing on the undercarriage cut into the ground like a plough, tipping the machine on its nose.

For what seemed like an interminable period, the Hurricane stayed balanced on its nose before it began to fall backwards again, with me falling upside down by the straps. I had to wait to be rescued, hoping that the plane wouldn't catch fire.

The instructors decided I had to get back into the air as soon as possible. I went up on another exercise, but by the time I came into land, I had delayed shock from the previous accident and was shaking like a leaf. That day the Air Force came very close to losing a second Hurricane.

On 16 March, we were posted to No. 486 (New Zealand) Squadron, based at Kirton Lindsey in Yorkshire.

On 21 May I was flying not far from the aerodrome when I saw the tallest, blackest cloud I had ever seen. I sailed straight into the middle of it. When I was in it, the cloud started to take control of the aircraft. It rose and carried out some very violent manoeuvres until finally the cloud spat the plane out again. I found I'd lost both gun panels and damaged the tail plane and the elevators. The fuselage was also partly missing on the starboard side. I immediately carried out the fastest landing I had ever done in a Hurricane.

On 25 May, I was doing formation flying, following a Havoc plane which had a radar and searchlight for illuminating enemy aircraft. That night it guided me through the blackness until I again saw the grass airstrip and the familiar lake near it of my home aerodrome, Wittering. I followed the landing instructions from the tower which came over the radio, but I thought it was odd that as I landed the grass seemed smoother than usual.

I had actually landed at Cottesmore, which was 20 miles away, while taking instructions from the control tower at Wittering.

I had made the error of not checking the aerodrome identification beacon. I was then taken to flying control at Cottesmore, and I was confronted by a very angry wing commander, who informed me I had landed in the middle of 12 bombers, any one of which I could have collided with. When I got back to Wittering, I received another dressing-down from the CO there.

In November, I was stationed at Tangmere. By this time we were flying Typhoons. We used to fly two patrols a day, about 50 feet above the water, about 20 miles out to sea, where we could be picked up by radar. We flew low to avoid the German radar. We would tend to fly with the same people, to get used to each other. I used to fly with Frank Murphy as my number two. We built up such a good relationship that we could almost read each other's thoughts.

On 19 January 1943, there was thick fog. We took off in

formation and about halfway down the runway we ran into the fog and had to convert from visual to instruments. This should not have been a problem as I had plenty of night flying experience, but some instinct told me I should look up on this occasion.

You wouldn't normally look away from your instruments, but I did and I suddenly saw trees in front of me. I pulled the stick back hard and we just got above the trees. I was so glad that my number two stayed in formation with me because it meant he missed the trees too.

That day we chased some bandits, but they turned and ran. By now, the fog had thickened and all the dromes on the South Coast including Tangmere had been closed. Now we had to get down again. I was told to keep flying and to try and conserve fuel, hoping that the fog would lift. If we ran out of fuel, we would have to bale out into the sea. I made a couple of attempts to fly into Tangmere at roof-top level with a distinct memory of the gasometer at Bognor towering 50 feet above me.

We had to turn back for fear of flying into the South Downs, which were located behind the aerodrome. We went back out to sea and waited. I think someone up above must have been looking after us because the fog started to roll back from the coast near Ford aerodrome. We saw a gap in the fog and we flew in. Even as the aircraft landed on the runway, the fog closed in on us again and stayed that way for the rest of the day. The flight had lasted an hour and 25 minutes and we were very close to the end of our endurance.

On 29 April 1943, we were on patrol and were told by those watching radar that bandits had been spotted coming in from the south. We headed towards them and then I saw two aircraft low in the water and radioed "Tally Ho to Black Gang" (which is the controller).

As we approached them, the bandits turned back towards France. We gave chase, tucking in behind them at no higher than about 50 feet above the water. As we flew into firing range, I instructed Frank to take the second aircraft because his gunsight wasn't working properly. I zeroed in on the leader of the two planes. As it came into my sights, I gave it a couple of bursts with my cannons and struck the fuselage and the tail. I then closed in on the leader and opened up with my guns. The plane burst into flames. I moved to port to avoid the debris.

As the Messerschmitt lost air speed, I finished in close formation 20 feet to the port of it. The pilot turned and looked at me. It was the first time I had seen a German ["the enemy"] face to face. I will never forget that face.

At the time I was thinking that if I were in his position, I would have pulled the aircraft to port to try to ram me, but he didn't do that. Perhaps his controls were damaged, perhaps there was another reason ... I pulled away and watched as he hit the sea. I did not feel any feeling of elation. Instead I felt that God would strike me from the sky for taking the life of another human being.

It was my privilege to fly with several outstanding pilots and wing leaders – Des Scott, Johnny Baldwin and Denys Gillam. Des Scott and Johnny Baldwin were two of the best pilots that I ever flew with. Under Scottie, we learned to take the battle to the Germans.

Johnny had a quality of leadership that made you fly well above your normal standards. He expected the best from those around him and he earned everybody's respect by his own high-calibre performance. The further we flew into enemy territory, the more relaxed I felt. Flying with Johnny, I felt invincible. It wouldn't have worried me if the entire German Air Force had taken off to attack us. He had an infectious enthusiasm for operational flying. Under his leadership, morale was very high and we developed a pride of performance.

Denys Gillam was a legend. When we were shown training clips on film, time and time again the name Gillam was mentioned and it always seemed to be in a hail of flak, taking the plane in so close that it seemed he must hit the ship or the mast.

He flew over 2000 operational missions throughout the war and it seemed impossible that he continued to survive. He was very aggressive and very determined and he always seemed invincible.

He remained distant from the other fellows and was a loner. In the air, we found him difficult to fly with and that was why the

Germans had such a problem shooting him down. He had the same restless quality in the air as on the ground and I don't think he or anybody else knew what was going to happen next when he was flying.

When he flew at Tangmere, he always asked for a number two to fly with. The number twos couldn't keep up with him, so we often put number ones on with him. Even they found it difficult to keep up with him.

On 29 April 1944, I was married to Irene Duddleston. She was a very beautiful girl. We met when she was a WAAF transport driver on 486 Squadron; she used to drive a tractor that would pull a tanker that the "Erks" [the ground staff] used to refuel the aircraft.

I had trouble getting to my own wedding because movement was prohibited because of the invasion preparations.

I attempted to obtain a pass for myself and my best man, Vaughan Fittall, from the Chief Constable of Portsmouth. However, he said to me, "Sonny, you will just have to come down and take your chance."

Luckily we had no problem getting in and out of Portsmouth and Irene and I were duly married.

I was never frightened during the war because I had long accepted the fact that it was most unlikely that I would survive it and as a result flew without fear but was determined to last as long as possible and make the most of each day.

About every seventh mission, my plane would get hit. I'd feel the shudder. And think, "Oh, where have I been hit?"

Though there was one occasion, after I was married, that I did get a reaction to combat flying.

I was in France and I didn't want to be away from the squadron for any period of time but I had a deal with the wing commander [Johnny Baldwin] that if things were quiet I would take some leave.

I flew back to Culmhead in England where my wife was stationed and we had two wonderful days together.

When I returned to the squadron, it was preparing to go on an operational mission, attacking a German strong point.

I told the bomb crew to refuel and bomb up my aircraft. I then led the attack. We went in at dusk and it was one of the most spectacular attacks I ever participated in.

In the half-light, the explosions, the bomb blasts, the flak being fired by the enemy and the tracer shells flying through the air created a magnificent fireworks display that seemed larger than life. The target was destroyed, but as we flew back to base I found I was shaking like a leaf. It was the only time this had ever happened, and I think it resulted from being with my wife in the comparative peace and quiet of England in the morning and being pitched into the middle of battle the same day without sufficient time to adjust.

I found that what I used to do was just focus completely on the task at hand without any distractions. I used to just block everything out of my mind except the task at hand, and then at the end of the day when the missions were completed, I would go back and relax.

The pilot who used to worry us the most was the pilot that could not relax at the end of the day, but stayed under tension worrying about the next day's missions. The way to beat stress was to live every day at a time, worry about things when they happened and then to unwind at the end of the day.

Among the pilots was a number of "maverick" and "wild ones" and while some of them caused problems on the ground, in the air they all got on with the job and some of the "problem children" were the best people to have alongside you when the going got tough.

I had a total sense of commitment, both to the pilots of 197 Squadron and to destroying every target we were given. We only ever had to go back to two targets a second time, both bridges, and destroyed each one of them on a second attempt.

I had taken up command of 197 Squadron after receiving a telephone call from Denys Gillam inviting me to do so. I was full of enthusiasm and went to my Group Captain at Gloster Aircraft Co, where I was flying as a test pilot, to inform him of this. He stopped me in my tracks by telling me that I was too valuable and that he would not let me go. We discussed it at great length but there was an impasse and I left his office, packed my bags and took off. I don't know what the Group Captain thought but I suspect he would have done the same thing in the circumstances.

I had little experience of leadership before joining the Air Force apart from being captain of rugby and cricket teams. I discovered that the Air Force training did little to encourage the pilot to use his own initiative.

In the early days, as I flew more missions and became more experienced, I started to become fearful that I might be asked to lead a flight. My fears were realised when I was asked to attend a flight leader course and in return was appointed Flight Commander on 486 Squadron.

I was determined to give the job my best shot and it is surprising how the acceptance of responsibility makes you perform above your normal level. Provided you earned and retained the respect of the pilots, I discovered a very special bond developed which continued long after the war.

I gradually became involved in the personal lives of the pilots of 197 Squadron and I used to work closely with the adjutant and the doctor to keep a close watch on individual morale. The only job I could not reconcile to was writing to the next-of-kin of the pilots we lost in action.

I had considerable help from the adjutant but felt sick in the stomach every time one of these letters had to be written. A few years ago, I came across some letters that had been sent to my wife after I had finally been shot down myself and taken POW and I realised how important these letters were and how much they were appreciated and treasured by the recipients.

During 1944, 197 Typhoon Squadron flew from Normandy, Beachhead, Lille and Antwerp as support attack for the Canadian Army which was on the ground. In Normandy, we operated from an airstrip in the Beachhead only a few miles from the front. I had to sleep in a slit trench at the back of my tent with my tin hat over my head in case of shrapnel.

At night, the Germans were pounding the Mulberry Harbour with a long-range gun from a hidden position. Intelligence discovered that the gun was hidden in a railway tunnel near Pont L'Eveque.

It was planned that I would lead a group of four to attack one end of the tunnel while Wing Commander Johnny Baldwin would do the same with the other end. We would fly down the railway line and release the bombs at the last moment.

The flak map showed the flak would come from the western end of the tunnel and before we took off we tossed to see who would get it. I lost. So then I suggested to Johnny that in that case I should go first. I was surprised when he agreed. So we flew in and I was so intent on what I was doing that I hardly noticed the flak and we effectively sealed the end of the tunnel.

Then Johnny led his four Typhoons in. Maybe the flak maps had got it wrong but they came under heavy flak and though they were successful in closing that end of the tunnel, Johnny's plane was badly damaged. He just managed to get back and crash-land on the airstrip. Happily, he walked away without injury but perhaps rueing winning the toss of the coin.

During that period, I started to exercise my mind to take some constructive action to try to reduce our losses from flak. Most of these losses seemed to be coming about during attacks when the pilot was using the speed he'd built up in the dive to get up above 6000 feet and to get out of the light flak.

In his anxiety to get out of there as soon as possible, he was giving the German gunners, who seemed to be training their guns on the exit path, a relatively simple shot from dead astern. After giving the matter some thought and applying some of the principles that the squadron learned on anti-shipping attacks, I made the following recommendations to the 197 pilots:

1. After low-level attacks, the pilots would stay on the deck until well away from the target area or any known flak concentration in the vicinity. The theory was that an aircraft travelling at high speed close to the ground is very difficult to hit because the trees and buildings would stop the gunner's line of sight. From all the dive-bombing attacks, as soon as

the pilot has released his bombs, and started his climb away from the target area, he should apply as much rudder as he can in alternate directions, gaining his height in a zig-zag fashion. This is most uncomfortable for the pilot but the resulting skid cannot be detected from the ground.

2. What looks like a simple shot will miss because the aircraft is skidding away from the line of flight of all the shells. The only real danger is from the gunner who can't shoot straight.

These two recommendations were not easy to sell to the pilots because they involved staying down in the light flak area for a longer period. Eventually I was able to persuade them to try it and they were finally convinced when they saw the tracer going past them on the side they were skidding away from.

The result of these changed tactics on the casualty rate was quite dramatic. Our losses fell to six a month while the next lowest of the other squadrons was 29. The Wing Commander soon came to find out what we were doing and this technique was spread through the whole wing with similar results.

We had also observed we had lost several pilots during dive-bombing when their planes blew up right at the point of bomb release. Walking around the planes one day, I noticed marks on the trailing edge of the wing on several planes right behind the bomb racks.

We developed the theory that some of the pilots were starting to pull out at the same time as they pressed the bomb release and their plane was squashing into the live bombs. We instructed them to continue their dive until the bombs were well clear of the aircraft before starting to pull out of the dive.

Whether the theory was correct or not we never knew but it almost certainly was because we didn't lose any more pilots in this fashion.

After the breakout from the Beachhead, I took my squadron to Manston Aerodrome in south-east England, from where we could still reach the front line.

The 3rd of September 1944 is a day that will live long in my memory. I went to an intelligence briefing and when I saw the target I immediately noticed the bomb line marked on their maps. It was a couple of days old and I discovered that the target we'd been allocated was an area that we'd been working the previous day and the target itself was inside the Allied lines. I informed them of this but they were insistent that their information was up to date and there was no way I could budge them.

I finally brought matters to a head by refusing to attack the allocated target. There was no way I was going to go in and knowingly bomb our own troops. I was then taken before the wing commander who wanted to know what was going on. I told him I was not prepared to attack a target that I knew was inside Allied lines. He again reiterated the point that the intelligence advice was that this area was now German occupied and in fact it had been several days before.

I still refused to carry out the attack. He then put on his hat and formerly ordered me to attack the target. I refused again. They brought in another of the pilots, Guy Plamondon, and ordered him to attack the target. "Plum" had been one of my flight commanders on 197 Squadron and I told him I was senior to him and ordered him not to attack the target.

Next I was summoned before the station commander. Again there was an impasse and I started to realise things were turning serious. I sent a signal through to Denys Gillam to let him know I might need some help.

It definitely was getting serious because now they flew in an air commodore. He kept his hat on throughout the interview and he wasn't very friendly. He accused me of being "yellow livered".

By now I was starting to get a little mad about this whole thing. I told him to select any target he wanted, no matter how dangerous, and we would attack it, even if we lost the whole squadron – but we wouldn't attack this one.

I don't know whether that got my point across, whether Denys supported me or whether updated intelligence reports revealed that the area was not, in fact, in enemy hands, but that was the last

I heard about the matter. I must have come perilously close to receiving a court martial.

The Germans started the Ardennes offensive while we were stationed at Antwerp Airport. They were attempting to capture the port of Antwerp and shut off the Allies' source of supplies. Part of their plan was a concentrated attack of V1s and V2s on the city. I've never seen so many V1s in my life. They were mostly fired at night and often there were three or four of them shooting across the airfield at the same time.

One of the V1s hit a cinema in Antwerp, killing a large number of civilians and a number of personnel from the airfield. There was also a danger of flying glass. I slept next to one of the remaining windows and kept my head in a sleeping bag to protect against flying glass. I was relieved when the window was finally blown out even if it did make the nights colder.

On 23 October, intelligence informed us that there was going to be a high-level meeting of the German 15th Army at Dordrecht in Holland. The following day, I led an attack which consisted of 48 Typhoons from five squadrons. The attack was very successful and killed two generals and over 70 officers.

Ground attack work by a Typhoon squadron was a dangerous occupation; we were regularly hit by flak. I knew that sooner or later I would be shot down but I never actually thought that I would become a prisoner of war.

At one point, we were given a talk by a British officer whose job was to interrogate captured German pilots. He had told us, "You mustn't say anything, because as soon as you say anything you are finished. You have to be polite and answer every question with name, rank and number."

On 31 December 1944, we were flying over the River Maas, on the way to making a low-level attack on a bridge at Culemborg, south-east of Utrecht. I was hit by heavy 88mm flak. There was a puff of white smoke and I was sure the glycol in the radiator had been hit. The glycol cooled the engine and I knew it was only a matter of time before the engine overheated and cut out.

I probably could have made it home at this stage, but I still wanted to carry out the attack which had been designated "destroy at all costs". Also the navigation was difficult because of dense cloud and snow on the ground. It seemed to me that I had to continue because I was the only one who knew where we were.

Soon after, I was able to locate the target and led the attack and made a direct hit with my bombs. I had managed to pull the plane back up to 600 feet when the engine cut out.

Once you know you are going down, the first decision you have to make is whether you're going to bail out or crash land.

I did not have that choice. I did not have enough height to bail out. I crash-landed on a small lake that was frozen over. The weight of the plane broke the ice and the plane started to sink. At least I did not have the problem of worrying about destroying my aircraft so that the enemy couldn't use it.

I quickly got out onto the wing and ran towards a small wood, slipping and sliding on the ice. I was only about two-thirds of the way there when personnel from the flak unit who were guarding the bridge captured me. At least I was still alive. I still remember that feeling of relief. I knew for the first time since the war started that I had a reasonable chance of surviving it.

I was also intrigued to meet "the enemy".

I was taken to the officers' mess of the flak battery. Inside was a Christmas tree. They were very friendly to me, they gave me drinks and cigarettes. Then the officials arrived and I was put in a cell and given sauerkraut. I was taken to a civil prison in Utrecht and escorted by two World War One soldiers and taken by train to Germany.

The railway line we took was well known to Typhoon pilots. We had attacked it frequently, but this time I was lucky, there was no attack on the train.

The war wasn't quite over for me, however, because when we arrived at the small town of Bad Homburg I had a battle with a German major about who was going to take the last available seat in the station restaurant.

We'd only just managed to get that sorted out, when there was a bombing raid on the town. Then I was told by one of the guards who was guarding me that the nasty-looking characters in khaki uniforms with swastika stickers on their armbands were the Hitler Youth. They had decided to organise a lynch party. Guess who they had decided to lynch? My guards hid me in the ladies' toilet until the danger had passed.

I was taken to the interrogation centre. I was booked in, photographed, and my identity established. The cells were bare and small. There was a wooden bunk but no toilet. If you wanted to go to the toilet you had to activate a lever system, which nobody answered sometimes for up to four hours. The trick was to learn to signal in advance.

The food was some sort of bread and a thin, watery soup. There was no medical attention and I was told I would have medical attention when I provided the interrogators with the information that they wanted, which of course I wasn't going to do.

The interrogation started in a friendly manner, with coffee, drinks and cigarettes. They then tried to trick me by giving me information that they already possessed to try and make me think there was no point in holding on to the information I had. When that didn't work, it changed to threats. I was accused of being a spy, even though I was wearing a uniform. I was threatened with being shot.

When that didn't work, I was told I would be handed over to the Gestapo. One piece of good luck for me was that I was not flying my usual plane that had a distinctive OV-1 marking and German intelligence would probably have some record of the attacks I had taken part in. But my normal plane had been damaged by flak the day before and the plane I was flying when I was shot down had no squadron markings on it.

I did as I had been told and answered all questions politely with only my rank, name and serial number. This continued for several days, with increasing degrees of aggression and excitableness from the guards. There was no suggestion of physical torture. It was a psychological game.

However, the guards would turn up the heat in my cell to unbearably hot temperatures, and then turn it right down again with the windows and shutters left open to let in the freezing cold air, in what was a very bad winter. When I was almost blue with cold, the temperature was again turned up to an unbearable heat.

Finally, when they had got no more out of me than my name, rank and number, I was sent to the POW camp at Nuremberg. I was surprised that my valuables were given back to me, including my gold wedding ring.

On the train, I was given some Red Cross parcels, one of which contained milk powder. I decided to make some ice cream out of it by mixing it with snow, but the result was a severe and ultimately life-threatening attack of dysentery.

When we arrived at Nuremberg, we were marched through the town and stoned by the local people. In a way I understood their feelings because their city was being bombed day and night.

In every American prison camp, there was a man of confidence, who was basically the intermediary between the guards and the prisoners. At Nuremberg prison camp, which was mostly full of Americans, I met this person in pitch darkness. I couldn't see him, but he had a deep voice, and he seemed to be over six feet tall. I had this image that he probably looked like John Wayne.

In the cold light of day, I discovered he was a very thin character with horn-rimmed glasses and a receding chin. But what he lacked in appearance, he more than made up for in intellect and guts.

Because of my rank, I was placed in charge of a group of Americans. When an American major arrived, I turned my troops over to him. I was quite surprised when they refused to accept him. They had become quite attached to me, but I walked off and left them to it.

The diet at the camp consisted once again of watery soup and one-seventh of a loaf of bread. It was quite difficult to cut a loaf of bread into seven equal pieces. The rule was that the person doing the cutting had last choice which meant they would get the smallest piece. For this reason, some people took up to an hour to complete cutting the bread. Their efforts would have done credit to a diamond cutter.

It was mid-winter and the camp was very cold. At night, we could hear the bombing raids on Nuremberg. One night, the RAF dropped target markers on the camp and we sat there listening to the drone of the approaching bombers, certain that they were going to drop the bombs right on us.

At the last moment, cancel flares were dropped and most of the planes averted the strike. But one of the bombers still dropped its bombs and one of the walls was blown out of our hut.

My health continued to suffer, the dysentery was endless and I became a walking skeleton. I might have died but for a new POW who had some medical knowledge. He burned wood and dipped it in water to produce a charcoal paste. He made me eat it until it was coming out of my ears. But it solved the dysentery and I started to recover.

As the front line approached our camp, we were marched away from it. At night, the German officers used to take over a farm or a group of farmhouses and the prisoners slept in the barns. One night, I was sleeping in a hayloft and needed to go to the toilet, I lost my bearings in the dark and fell through the loft floor 15 feet to the ground.

The next morning, I was taken to the medical centre where it was discovered I had no broken bones. I tried to trade some cigarettes with a German nurse for some bread. When she disappeared, I thought I was going to be reported, but she returned with a loaf of bread which she gave to me. She refused my cigarettes and burst into tears.

I was returned to the column, my back gradually improved and I was starting to walk properly again. We arrived at a place called Moosburg, where I fell asleep from exhaustion. I awoke again in darkness and saw some figures standing around. Gradually my eyes became used to the light and, to my amazement, I realised that one of the men standing before me was Trevor Harvey, who lived about six houses away from me in Marsden Ave, Auckland.

As the Western and Eastern fronts moved towards us, we stopped marching and were squeezed into our small camp. The battle moved so close that a ceasefire was declared while there was a meeting between the German Army and the United States Army and our camp was declared neutral territory.

On 29 April 1945 (which was my first wedding anniversary), General Patton broke through the perimeter of the camp with pearl-handled revolvers on each hip. He had a surprisingly high-pitched voice. He told us that he'd have us out of the camp in 48 hours. It took a little longer than that.

On 8 May, which is VE day, we were taken to Landshut Aerodrome north of Munich and flown back to the UK. It was a beautiful day. Many German pilots had decided that they preferred to surrender to the Americans than to the Russians. They started flying their light aircraft in. The German planes began to block off the runway preventing the Allied planes from landing. The Americans fired warning flares, but the German planes kept coming in and the Americans had no choice but to start shooting them out of the sky. Aircraft were falling to the ground all over the place.

We flew back to the UK where we were deloused by a white powder which was pumped all over us. It was different to the welcome we had expected but it was definitely needed. I had been wearing the same clothes for four and half months and my hair hadn't been cut for six months.

I found it hard to readjust after being a POW even though it had only been for a short time. I don't think anybody can really appreciate freedom until they lose it.

After the war, I returned to New Zealand and rejoined Wilson Meats Limited. Luckily I was almost immediately taken around the country by the firm's head livestock buyer and the travelling and the outdoor work detached my attention from the war again.

At that point, I can say, the war ended for me.

Tears and Laughter
Frank Snelgar

Frank Snelgar has a gruff voice through which he does not so much tell a story as breathe it and then when he lets loose his laugh ... oh what a laugh! He tilts his head back and it rumbles around the room. And then suddenly it is replaced by waves of emotion and the tears of a compassionate man who has lived a real life.

I was born in Auckland. My mother was up at a farm in Whangarei and she met my father and came down to Auckland. When I was born in 1917, I was three months' premature and weighed only 3lb 4oz.

Soon afterwards, my mother took off and Dad couldn't find her for four years. She was with the Salvation Army because she had no money. They were bastards. Mum used to have to get down on her knees and scrub and scrub at the Salvation Army.

My first job was working in a chocolate factory in Newmarket. The first day working inside the factory I ate so many chocolates, I was bloody near sick.

Later I got a job at the produce markets. I was there right up until the war and I fell in love with a beautiful girl in Herne Bay ... oh, she was beautiful. Her name was Lynn Boyd. When I was about to go away to the war she said to me, "Frank, will you marry me?"

I said, "No, I mightn't come back."

Much later, when I was a POW, one of the guards came up to me and said, "Frank, we've got news from abroad. Your girl's dead."

I was shocked. She had something wrong with her chest and she died. It was very sad, very sad. Even today I miss her and I think of her all the time.

[Frank's voice choked with emotion and he looked at me through tears. The sudden surge of emotion filled the room. Later, when the typist transcribed this section of the tape, she wept.]

I joined up with the Air Force in 1940. I came back and said to Mum, "Hooray, I'm in the Air Force."

She said, "Frank, you might get shot down. Don't go in the Air Force."

I didn't know what to do. The first echelon came, then the second echelon came and then the third echelon came up … I ended up joining the Army. [Laughs.] By cripes, I don't know what was the best, up above or down below. Bullets and shells went everywhere.

We finished our training and set sail on the *Orcades*. It docked in Bombay. We were there for three months. We went to Egypt. I was one of the drivers. Bombs would come down everywhere. Bloody awful, I tell you.

We then went over to Greece and we went to fight the Germans up the pass but they pushed us back, and we came back and we got on board the boat to Crete. We were lucky.

At about 6.30 in the morning, we were having something to eat and over came the planes. It was the invasion. I went up the hill with my mate to watch and they came down by the thousands. The big bombers came down almost as high as the ceiling. They came down so low, because they found out there was no opposition … bang, bang, bang, all the way.

In the end, we made our way up to the embarkation point in fives, fours and threes. Then at midnight they packed in the island. Brigadier Inglis, who was in charge of the island, said, "Well, boys, I'm sorry, we're going to leave you. Good luck, boys, I'll see you after the war." Away he goes over to Egypt. [Laughs.]

There were 5000 men left on the island. Then the Germans came. The next minute I was ducking dive-bombers. *Boom, boom, boom* … every bugger took off. They were going everywhere, diving and ducking everywhere. So my mate Bob and I and about six others took everything off, swam over the bay and went down the island. We marched for an hour or two with nothing on.

Then we met a Cretan officer who offered to get us off the island by boat. This was great, we were happy as hell. And about 4.30 over came the dive-bombers … *boom, boom*. There goes the boat.

A Cretan gave us some clothes. We marched for a while then we later fell asleep. When we woke, we heard these Germans shouting. We were captured. They got us onto a boat and we went back to Canea, which they had built a big fence around on the beach and we were in there. I got a bad case of malaria. I was shivering hot and cold and they had nothing for it at all, so I said to a mate of mine, "Bugger this, let's go out."

One night, when it began to rain, we shot out. He went this way and I went that way and we agreed to meet at a spot and I fell down over every bloody barbed wire on the island. And I fell down every ditch.

In the end I met him and he said, "I'm going back in."

I said, "Well, I'm not."

He said, "You're a sick man, you must go."

I said, "When I'm out, I'm out."

So we had an argument and he pissed off back. I covered myself over with olive leaves and about 8.30 it was dark and I heard this, "Shh, shh, shh."

There was a fellow standing there looking at his watch and he said something to me, but I don't know what he said. About an hour later, four men came and picked me up and put me on a donkey. Well crikey almighty, worst thing they ever done … up and down, up and down.

We stayed in the same place for a while. There was Bob and me and Eric Owen and another joker. After six months, I said to Bob, "We'll amble on for the Cretans' sakes" because the Germans were very active around this spot.

So we moved on and went up the island, over the mountains and down the other side.

We met up with a Cretan fellow who took us to his home. He had a big old house and his wife was marvellous. We were there for about four or five days. We decided to go for a walk. He advised us not to, but we had our minds made up and we got recaptured.

So we were taken to a prison camp, all barbed wire. I was there for six days. The Itis were bastards. I didn't see my mate Bob for a week.

The Italians put us on a boat and took us to Rhodes. We arrived there about 6.30. And Christ almighty … when we looked, our beds were made, the table was set with knives and forks, pepper and salt. By Jesus, it was good. They came in with a menu and said, "What'll you have, boys?" He wrote down our order and we had a great feed.

About 9.30, another joker came in. He said we had to meet the admiral. We went along and the admiral gave us a great time. He said to us, "Boys, I am very sorry for you, but while you are under me you can have a marvellous time." And we did.

We were there about six weeks then we got on another boat and went to Italy and from there we went on to a place just over the Austrian border.

My first job was in a sugar factory and after that I went to an iron [smelting] factory, working with big hammers. It was hard work. Then I went to a paper factory.

They had a big alternator there and I said to my mate, "If I had some sugar, and threw it on the alternator it would go bang and put the whole factory out of order." Midday came and nobody was around.

I said, "Right, Tom, the sugar."

We threw in the sugar and nothing happened. The alternator was still going, all the machinery was still going. We couldn't work out why nothing had happened. Then up it went … *bang*. It put the whole factory out of action. It took months to repair.

They brought the SS in to question us.

"Me know nothing. I know nothing," I told them. Luckily they believed me.

As the Russian forces approached we went on a march. God, that was tough. How I managed to survive I don't know. We went backwards and forwards ... everywhere. In the end we were coming down the hill and we were going backwards and forwards over the hill. Nearly six months had gone by this time and we were buggered. Then we were going to go over it once more when an officer said, "Halt, halt."

He said, "Nobody's coming over this bridge."

But the officer in charge of the POWs still wanted to march us over it.

"You're not," said the first officer. "Nobody's coming. This bridge is going up in four minutes."

So they argued about it until ... *Boom*! Up she went.

The Americans were only five miles away and coming down fast. They were going 30, 40 miles an hour. They all went past but one vehicle.

They asked us if anybody was sick.

We were all sick.

The American officer said, "Have any of you got smokes?"

Of course we hadn't.

The Yanks must have thrown us every cigarette they had. Gosh, talk about smoke, it was thick in the air.

About an hour and a half later, a truck arrived and we all boarded. It took us to a town called Landshut and we were put in a big posh hotel.

I decided to have a shower. It was beautiful.

After that we were going to fly to Amsterdam but there was heavy fog, so we came down about five miles out of Paris and ... oh, what a time we had.

We were in Paris about a fortnight then we were stationed at Broadstairs in Kent. From there we used to go back and forwards to London on the train. I spent six months there and then caught another boat home.

Grantie
Irene Stembridge
(née Grant)

"Grantie," as she is known to her cobbers, originally wanted to become a surgeon. In the theatre of war she came as close as she could get at that time as a nurse, seeing active service in the Pacific and Europe.

I was born in Christchurch. My ambition was to become a surgeon but I was living with my grandmother and we just couldn't afford for me to go to Otago University for six years. A lot of people were able to work in between while studying but you needed money as a standby and we just didn't have it.

I thought I'd be a nurse instead, so I went to technical college. The principal, who was a doctor, said to me, "Academically, we'd like you to be a French teacher." I had a French grandmother and I loved French, but then I found that I'd be living at the hospital and the pay was very, very small which meant I wouldn't be able to help my grandmother at all.

So I left the academic part of the college and went to night school to learn short-hand typing and book-keeping. In those days, they used to ring the colleges and say, "Send four or five girls and we'll choose one." The first time I went to an office to be interviewed by the manager he gave me the position, which amazed me. I worked for him for some time and then I applied for a Government position because I had qualifications. I worked there for quite a while and then I got a position with Hays in Christchurch, a very popular Christian firm.

Hays was a great place to work. Sir James Hays was a very good managing director, his twin sons, Hamish and David, were very interesting, and David was an accountant who eventually became Mayor of Christchurch for three terms. Hamish was a very competent heart surgeon. I got on very well there. I was in charge of mail order for a time.

But I also loved nursing and had been doing voluntary nursing at Burwood Hospital for a long time. The Red Cross persuaded me to go overseas. You were asked to go to the main hospital in Christchurch for three weeks at a time, so they could receive a report of how you got on. We had to pass examinations and I got honours in them.

The matron, Miss Widdowson, begged me to stay. She could see I loved nursing but I told her I couldn't stay because the wage was far too small. By that time I was working with book-keeping machines and I was getting double a nurse's pay. But then the Red Cross found out that my eldest brother who was in 75 Squadron had been killed in 1942 and before that, in 1941, my other brother had been wounded and caught in Crete. He was eventually sent to Stalag 8B in Germany for over four years.

So I went and asked the managing director of the firm where I was working whether he would mind if I went away overseas, through the Red Cross. He was a First World War man and married a nurse from the war and he was quite excited that I was going away. He told me my position would be there when I came back.

I was a Red Cross nurse, which means I was a VA, a Voluntary Aide. In Wellington we were called WAACs, but when we joined up the Red Cross said we were Voluntary Aides. We didn't like the word WAAC, we were VAs. But we were very friendly with the WAACs. They did a wonderful job.

I went away and served at No. 4 General Hospital for a year in New Caledonia. When I came back on leave I was told that the hospital was going to be dismantled and I was sent to Trentham Military Hospital for a few months. Then I went away with the 14th Reinforcements to Egypt but I was transferred to No. 3 General Hospital in Bari. I worked there for about six months and then I was transferred to a clearing station in Florence.

We started right from the bottom even though I had been nursing. They don't appear to do the menial tasks that we did after technical college these days, which I think is a shame. We helped the orderlies. I helped with the outside "fireworks" as we called them, to sterilise the instruments outside in a "copper".

I did a lot of night duty. I got on very well with the patients. When I worked on night duty in a ward in No. 4 General Hospital, these boys had been out in the open fighting the Japs. We all thought the Japs were suicidal. The Japs were snipers and some of these boys were very young and they couldn't take it for very long.

They arrived in the tin huts and after they left the tin huts they convalesced in the ward that I was nursing in on night duty. We always had a sister in charge and I got on very well with all of them.

The soldiers came from all walks of life. Some of them were qualified, were well educated and some were officers. Some weren't and had been doing ordinary work before the war. They were all good soldiers.

The second hospital I worked in at New Caledonia was only about five miles from Noumea. We would get permission to go in by Jeep and shop for the patients so they could send little presents home. When I came home eventually I went out to two or three suburbs and took the presents around myself.

Some patients accepted their injuries and some didn't. We always did find that the patients who were really ill or badly injured didn't moan as much as another who had been "sniped" as we called them, but hadn't gone through the trauma like the badly injured soldiers. And some were very badly injured.

I recall being quite excited when we were told that we were to give penicillin injections every four hours. That was a step up for us, not being qualified nurses. Penicillin was very new at the time and it got excellent results.

Some of the soldiers who had limbs amputated would be terribly worried about going home. I found that more so in Italy – that was a different kind of war. They were terribly worried how their wives and children were going to take it. They were also worried about how they would get a job. A lot of these men were really interested in sport and they were concerned that they wouldn't be able to play sport again. But they were good patients in the main.

I had known one or two of them in Christchurch before I went overseas. I remember one who was particularly thrilled to see me. He was a cricketer. I was playing cricket at the time, or trying to, and I would always go over to him and say, "Are you going to teach us how to play cricket?"

We always used to say, and it was very true, that a lot of these patients were guinea pigs. Some of the younger surgeons over there were learning such a lot and made very good surgeons when they came back home because they had been right through it and learned a great deal about many different kinds of operations and drugs.

You knew that some of the patients were past recovery and were going to die. We were young and we could take it. This is the point – it's no use being in that kind of position or job if you can't take it. We were sad, of course, but we were well aware that it could happen. We were young and we could take it, otherwise we wouldn't be nursing – it's a simple as that.

I think the only difficulties that some of us girls had were with some of the qualified sisters ... not very many of them ... but we felt from the atmosphere that we were resented. They thought that perhaps we were taking their jobs away from them but then they found we weren't, we were doing the menial jobs. Then as we bettered ourselves we were asked to do more, to help to take out stitches and give penicillin injections.

I've got some great friends who were in charge of the wards overseas and they come to our reunions here and joined the Returned Servicewomen's Branch of the Auckland RSA. The friendship never stops.

Irene Stembridge (née Grant)

Towards the end of the war, the clearing station in Florence where I was nursing was turned into No. 6 General Hospital to get the Army ready to go to Japan. I applied to go to Japan and was turned down. I was told I'd had sufficient service, so I said I would like to be discharged to England. They asked me why and I told them eventually I wanted to get to Germany to see my eldest brother's grave.

They talked me out of that, they said it would be ages before I would be able to get to Germany. They said I would be down for leave in England and I could go round to where my brother had been serving and where my other brother had been camped at Aldershot.

So I had 15 days' leave, two girlfriends came with me, we had a wonderful 15 days. We went to Scotland and England and over to Ireland and back again to Bari, in Italy.

I met my husband, Ned, in Bari and we became engaged there. He was sent over to Japan with the forces but on the way the ship had an epidemic of measles. I think about 200 soldiers were put off at Singapore and he was one of the officers sent off to look after these soldiers. He managed to get home through his MP because his father had a transport firm and required him to work in Pukekohe. They were doing essential work with market gardeners, etc.

So he didn't get to Japan. He came home from Singapore and we were married at Labour Weekend in 1946. We've been married 53 years.

I'm very RSA-minded. I found that I was the only girl in Pukekohe that had joined there. There was nothing there for me so I joined the Auckland RSA, the Returned Servicewomen's branch, and used to travel through at night time to their reunion dinners which were excellent. The girls always had a wonderful committee. When we shifted from Pukekohe to Auckland in 1970, I was still a member. I did mainly welfare work after that, particularly with girls to begin with.

Unfortunately, our treasurer was drowned in an accident and I took over the books in 1974. I've been doing the treasury work for the girls ever since. We had a wonderful crowd of girls who belonged to the Auckland branch. They had to belong to an RSA to join the Auckland women. We've had women join our branch from Invercargill and Whangarei while still belonging to their own RSAs.

We had a couple of reunions a year and we still have it. I do welfare work for the girls and the Auckland committee. I've been on the committee for about 10 years. I've really enjoyed it, particularly the welfare.

I visit anyone who's sick or in hospital or transferred to different homes. I'm very fortunate, I have one or two RSA girlfriends who will do that visiting for me if it's too far out from my home. In 1999 I was given a merit award and certificate for my services to the RSA.

Quite a number of our girls that returned to New Zealand took up nursing and were qualified within a year. They begged me in Christchurch to continue nursing, I said no because I was getting married that year, but they would have taken us without hesitation.

I've never regretted my service overseas. Unfortunately, I came home with a bit of a disability in my health but I'm still driving, I'm still walking, and still do welfare. God has blessed me.

Navy Jack
Jack Tomlinson

Jack Tomlinson has the most remarkable energy for a man who is part way through his ninth decade. Everything is done and said with immediacy and gusto. When I interviewed him, he looked like the old sailor he is, with his alert eyes, clipped beard and tattoo just visible under his rolled-up shirt sleeve halfway up his forearm. He fought in the Royal Navy but emigrated to New Zealand in 1950.

I left school at the age of 13 and a half. My parents were only too glad for me to contribute something to the family budget. I did a few odd jobs delivering bread and newspapers. At about age 14, I went to the South Coast of Bexhill and got a job as a page boy in a hotel. I was up and on the job by 6 o'clock every morning, washing the front steps and polishing brass handrails, etc, and it didn't matter if it was snowing, it still had to be done.

My parents could not afford to put me to a trade, so I went and joined the Navy. My parents knew nothing about it until I arrived home one day in uniform. At the recruiting office, I was asked what branch I wanted to go into. I didn't have a clue, so the boss man said, "I'll put you down for seaman." I did a nine-month training course including plenty of parade ground stuff, seamanship, rifle drill and many weeks in the gunnery school.

Those who couldn't swim had to learn. The swimmers were told to hop in and swim two lengths, the non-swimmers were told to line up at the 15ft end and in turn were told to "Hop in, lad."

On coming to the surface the first time, the instructor said, "Here, lad, grab hold of this," and offered me the end of an 8ft pole. I made a frantic grab but he pulled it away and I went down again to have another go at emptying the pool. The second time I surfaced, he allowed me to get hold of it. I finished up on the concrete floor like a drowned rat, at which point I was told to lie belly down and I was shown the arm and leg movements of the breaststroke.

After the first few lessons, we non-swimmers were classed as "backward swimmers". Before we went to the pool for the first time, I used to hear on the barracks' loud hailer system, "backward swimmers fall in". At that time I used to think, "Fancy being able to swim backwards, I can't even swim forwards."

After 10 months of training, I was drafted to my first ship, the destroyer HMS *Ardent*, which was sailing to Gibraltar to join the Mediterranean Fleet.

In 1935, Mussolini invaded Abyssinia [Ethiopia]. He also stated he was going to clear the British fleet out of the Mediterranean, so we moved from Malta and made our base at Alexandria in Egypt where a large British fleet was moored in anticipation of the Italian threat.

We went to Barcelona in Spain about mid-June 1936. The Spanish War had broken out. Our role was to evacuate any British nationals who wanted to leave. We took on board people of any nation who wanted to leave. These refugees were of all ages including babies. Some had never seen the sea. We took them to Marseilles in France. They had a very rough trip.

On one trip we were attacked and bombed by Italian aircraft in spite of the fact that over our bridge awning we had a white ensign fixed. Their excuse was they mistook us for Spanish Government destroyers. About April 1937, a Spaniard who rowed out to us in a dinghy advised us that we were on a short list for a torpedo attack. The threat was taken seriously and so ended our two years in the Mediterranean Fleet.

On 23 March 1939, I was drafted to a destroyer called HMS *Bedouin* and we were suddenly ordered to proceed at full speed to the aid of the submarine *Thetis*, which had got into trouble during acceptance trials in Liverpool Bay. We reached the *Thetis* at first light the next morning. About 8 or 10ft of her stern was showing above the waterline and her bows were fast in the mud on the bottom.

We lowered a whaler [a lifeboat] and tied up to her tail. Three men, including the captain, surfaced using an escape apparatus. The only way to free the others who were still trapped in the submarine was to cut a hole through the hull of the tail end that was above the waterline.

We proceeded to Cammell Lairds in Birkenhead to take a large steel tube off their yard and put it on board. We lowered it down onto the hull together with underwater welding gear. This tube was long enough to reach the hull and still have the other end clear of water. Unfortunately, when we arrived back on site, we found the tube wasn't long enough because of the tide.

After a given number of hours, the crew were considered dead, overcome by chloride gas fumes from salt water which was entering via one of the forward torpedo tubes. [Chloride gas is given off as a reaction to salt water flooding the batteries.] In 1940, the *Thetis* was raised, towed to the maker's yard, engines stripped and repaired, etc, and was later recommissioned and renamed HMS *Thunderbolt* or *Thistle*. The bodies from *Thetis* were recovered and a burial service was conducted at sea off Holyhead.

On Sunday, 3 September 1939, at 11am, Britain declared war on Germany and Italy. We were stationed in the Orkneys. The Germans were raiding the Atlantic trade routes and many of our merchant ships were sunk. A lot of our time was taken up looking for the lifeboats of survivors reported in various positions in the Atlantic. Some we found, some we didn't. Other times we were hunting submarines.

Early in April 1940, we were in Norwegian waters after Norway had been invaded by Germany. *Bedouin*, with her sister destroyers *Eskimo* and *Cossack*, were ordered to search and capture the prison ship the *Altmark*. It was the *Cossack* that found and boarded her, taking off all the British seamen who had been prisoners. I think we sunk the *Altmark*.

On 13 April 1940, we were ordered to enter Narvik harbour in north Norway and destroy a German destroyer squadron. We managed to get into the harbour in spite of concentrated fire on the entrance from the enemy. By early afternoon, we had sunk all but two of them. These two had taken off to the end of the harbour and entered Rombaks Fjords.

The *Cossack* had received some damage, the *Eskimo* had her bows blown off by a torpedo but we in the *Bedouin* received only a few shrapnel holes in our foremost funnel.

We still had to account for the two German destroyers. We went after them. They were barred by a glacier. We got sight of them and opened up on them with our two forward 4.7-inch turrets.

Both ships were soon ablaze and some of the crew were trying to climb the glacier. We boarded one German destroyer, hauled down the German ensign and replaced it with our own white ensign. Both ships were now deserted except for the dead and one officer who was lying wounded on a stretcher. He was the only prisoner we took.

For the next week or two we remained in the harbour and surrounding fjords, shooting up the railway that was carrying iron ore from Sweden, putting the power station at the end of the harbour out of action to deny the Germans its use.

During this time, we were subjected to numerous bombing raids by the Luftwaffe who, because of the mountainous area, were above us before we were aware of them. Dodging them was difficult due to the lack of sea room.

We had a Norwegian on board who we used to land by whaler at dusk and pick him up again at first light of morning. He deserved recognition for the information that he gathered each night and passed to us on which we were able to act. One morning we went to pick him up but, sad to say, he never appeared and we never saw him again.

Things on board were getting a little difficult; the situation demanded that we were closed up at action stations most of the time and not helped by the fact that in the Arctic Circle at that time of the year there is practically no darkness so we were a good target 24 hours of the day.

Things were getting desperate in the food line and the day came when all we had left was potatoes. A Norwegian trawler entered the harbour and our skipper demanded some of the catch. For a while we lived on fish and chips.

The Polish destroyer *Grom* ["Thunder"] arrived to relieve us. It arrived at about 5.30am and shortly after we were both steaming slowly in line abreast down the harbour while our skipper passed verbal orders to her. Suddenly, over the mountain top there appeared four German bombers. They dropped a stick of bombs which missed us but got the *Grom* fair on her torpedo tubes. There was a terrific explosion and the *Grom* started to sink. We quickly lowered our whalers and started to rescue survivors. The loss of life was very heavy both through bombing and also cold water.

In 1941 or early 1942, I think, we were in Reykjavik, the capital of Iceland, when we were ordered to proceed north to investigate a mysterious radio signal which was being picked up in Britain at 4pm each day.

We proceeded towards the Svalbard Spitsbergen area and ended up among the pack ice. We were looking for a large, armed German trawler. We later learned that the trawler was stationed in that position and permanently provisioned. Every day at 4pm it was sending a weather report to Wilhelmshaven in Germany from which the Germans could work out whether they should send their bombers over Britain that night.

It wasn't easy to spot as, like us, it was well coated in snow and ice. We managed to get aboard the trawler but not before they had disposed of various things over the side, no doubt code books, etc. We took the crew prisoner and tried to tow the vessel back to Iceland but we were forced to slip the tow as we were in danger of getting icebound.

We were on Arctic convoy work for well into 1942. The difficulty of that work can be ascertained from the following excerpt from a report by the Ministry of Defence:

"The Russian Arctic convoys are something entirely new and quite unique in the experience of mankind. The saturation capacity for adaptation is soon reached. Fear, cold, lack of sleep – these are the things that soon break a man. Nowhere are they so intense, so continual as on the Arctic convoys. Can you imagine what it is like up there between Jan Mayen and Bear Islands on a February night when there is 60 degrees of frost and the wind comes screaming off the Polar and Greenland icecaps and slices through the thickest clothing like a scalpel, where the average size ship carries an average of 500 tons of ice on her upper decks, when the bow crashes down into a trough and the spray hits you as solid ice?

"Where you go for days on end with only three hours' sleep out of 24. It's the most exquisite agony in the world, 70 feet waves recorded with no daylight in winter and no dark in summer."

In May 1942, we left the northern waters and Russian convoy work for the last time and made for the UK. I was destined to stay on the ship that had been my home for three and a quarter years. We sailed for Malta about 12 June with a convoy of two tankers, two general cargo and two ammunitions ships.

On the night of the 14th, an enemy destroyer was reported out on the starboard side while we were steaming along the coast of Tunisia. We opened fire, but our searchlight told us that the ship was a British destroyer, *Havoc*. We went into action stations on a submarine, which probably alerted the enemy.

The following morning we were near the Sicilian narrows and barring our way were two eight-inch cruisers, each carrying five triple turrets, and also four large destroyers. We learned that these vessels were the Italian VIIIth Division ships, comprising the heavy cruisers *Eugenio di Savoia* and *Monte Cuccoli*, and the destroyers *Vivaldi*, *Ascari*, *Premuda* and *Malocello*.

We immediately closed for action until we could get close enough to attack with torpedoes. Of course, we were outranged and outgunned. The bridge area was the first to be hit, resulting in deaths among the officers, signalmen and radar crews. One of the multiple .5 crews took a direct hit also. We were being repeatedly hit. It was very much a one-sided affair.

Unbelievably, the Italians kept going, disappearing out of sight, leaving us on fire. Both the ammunition ships were sunk and out of the six ships I believe only one arrived in Malta. After a couple of hours we managed to extinguish the fire, but we were still wallowing in water, unable to get away.

Some of us collected the dead and carried them to the waist [the middle part of the ship] where Commander Scurfield conducted a burial. Collecting the dead was not a pleasant job.

Two Italian cruisers reappeared and again we were a sitting target. We took more hits and lost more lives. I was responsible for the general maintenance of A and B turrets. I climbed the ladder to B deck and found all the crew dead.

Destroyer *Partridge* took us in tow but not for long before we were both under attack. *Partridge* put up a smoke screen between us and slipped tow. We heard later that the *Partridge* managed to get back to Gibraltar.

After the *Partridge* left we were attacked by aircraft in numbers. One fellow, after dropping his bombs, carried on diving and flew low along the ship's side to avoid our small-arms fire. He had a look of terror on his face as he passed only 20ft or so from us.

Chief Buffer yelled, "Torpedo coming in starboard side." Not having much free board [the distance between the deck and the water], I decided that the place to be was up on the forecastle. I had barely got to the top of the ladder when we were struck an almighty blow in the starboard quarter. It was in that area that we had a number of seriously wounded men lying on stretchers on the upper deck. The deck disappeared, taking more lives.

I could see no point in getting wet unnecessarily, so I braced myself against A turret and rolled a tickler [cigarette]. I was joined by two stokers, one of whom could not swim. A number of men were in the water, although I had not heard an order to abandon ship. It is possible they were blown overboard by explosives.

The bomber that did the damage to us was brought down by one or more of our small arms and the pilot was at one stage in the water with us holding [it was said] a small puppy mascot under one arm.

The ship took a further list to port. We manhandled the stoker who couldn't swim and dived into the water. As I dived in, I lost my shoes. I quickly swam away from the ship (I was no longer a backwards swimmer) and I turned to see the stern sinking. The bows were pointing skywards with a crewman clinging to the anchor. Less than a minute later, she disappeared with hardly a ripple. That was the end of the *Bedouin*.

There was only one Carley float to cater for well over 100 men. Some men were in very bad shape with ghastly wounds. It didn't help that we were swimming in oil fuel. The wounded were put on the float. The rest of us took turns in occupying the remainder of it, hanging on the sides or swimming aimlessly around, some clinging to debris.

After a few hours, we were bombed by four Italian aircraft. The bombs dropped a cable or two away [a cable is about 600 feet], but we could still feel the concussion under the water.

A coaster hove into sight. She slowly worked her way through some of our people. At this time, she herself was bombed by her own countrymen. The skipper naturally steamed away. It was a cruel blow, so near to rescue and I believe at this point some of our men "gave up the ghost".

About an hour later, the coaster returned, and lowered a small dinghy, capable of holding two or three people at the most. Those that could swam to the ship. A couple of us spotted a rope hanging over the stern, and with some effort, climbed hand over hand until we reached the deck. I was hauled onto the deck by a couple of seamen. They weren't happy about the oil fuel that we were depositing on their wooden quarterdeck.

We lay on the deck, me naked, my mate half-naked. I still had my money belt on but didn't have it when I came to some time later. The next few hours are a blank. My next recall was lying in a shed on the island of Pantaleria, an Italian convict island.

A few days later we were shipped to Reggio di Calabria across the straits. We were made to sit cross-legged on the ground at a railway station. It was quite fun to whistle to the step of the Germans as they strutted passed us, and even the Italian guards thought it was a heck of a joke until the Germans put their jack boots behind a few of the guards.

Next we were taken to a place known as Concentration Camp No. 52.

For some reason, we ex-*Bedouins* were classed as a bad lot, a reputation we still had when we reached Poland. This camp was about 10 miles or so from Chiavari and again surrounded by hills and was under carabinieri control.

We received Red Cross parcels, one between two men. They were a godsend. One snag was in heating the contents. We were reduced to burning anything that would burn out in the compound or on the ground, especially in the rain.

We were soon carrying rock on our shoulders to make a road, and were able to get a few small sticks into camp but the main supply was from the wooden huts in our barracks. We used the ceiling trusses and home-made knives and a rock for a hammer soon made short work of it. When the Italian linesmen left a pole lying on the ground, we grabbed it and it was sawn up and dispersed.

We made "blowers", which consisted of a piece of board about 12 inches long, two tins, and a piece of Army ground sheet, as home-made food heaters.

Bigger and better blowers were made later, culminating in a fan-type job, when perhaps a half-gallon or so of water could be boiled in a few minutes, provided that fuel was obtainable.

One night during a howling gale, the roof collapsed with the amount of wood we had taken down to burn.

Germans surrounded our camp and took us the 10 miles to

Chiavari. A bus travelling the mountainous area reached a stop about the same time as we did. One of the members of our crew ship, Bill Cantle, said, "See you later, Tommo" and dived into the bus. He wasn't noticed by the guards because of the 5000 men going past. About 18 months later in Poland, I received a letter from home saying, "Mr Cantle called to see us, and wishes to be remembered." Apparently some of the Italian women had hidden Bill under their skirts while he lay on the floor of the bus.

Arriving at Chiavari railway station, we were directed to cattle trucks and taken to Poland.

The first I remember of Poland is lying on a concrete floor. It was some time in early October, which is the beginning of winter in Poland. We were still dressed scantily. There were approximately 30,000 prisoners in this camp. After 24 hours of being stuck in a small building, we were let out into the compound. Men in adjoining compounds came up to the wire for news. One fellow threw me an old Belgian Army coat over the wire.

We made blowers again at this camp. If a "goon" spotted a prisoner using a blower, he would take a flying kick at it and then jump on it and smash it beyond repair, losing our meal and blower. For every blower they disposed of, another was made. They gave up smashing them.

To get out of being sent to work in a mine, I told them I was a Petty Officer and could not be made to work. "But we have you down as a private soldier and so you will work," they said. I told them there were no private soldiers in our Navy. They knew I was lying. In the meantime, the official grave-digging party were one short so I volunteered to do that. The job kept us busy, especially in winter.

We would cut greenery from the surrounding trees and fashioned wreaths with fencing wire. Each grave was laid in line and with a white homemade cross. I lost count of the number of men we buried from all Allied countries.

Every camp had a "man of confidence", in our case it was Sergeant-Major Sheriff. He was a kind of buffer between us and the German authorities. One day Sergeant-Major Sheriff let it be known that a German "plant" was suspected in the camp. He was identified, tracked and killed by our own men and his body thrown into a concrete pool, which was there for fire purposes.

The body was discovered by a guard who raised the alarm. As far as I am aware he was the only non-Allied person that we buried and this was the only time POWs murdered a German and got away with it.

Sometimes on working parties the men would swap dog tags. This would be confusing for the folks at home, because they would write, in their own hand-writing, letters to say they were all right, but sign the letter using the name they had on their dog tag to avoid getting caught out by the Germans who censored the mail.

At times, the men would want to swap back and then find that the man they swapped dog tags with had left camp to go on other working parties, in some cases to Czechoslovakia. Often the men were looking for ways to escape and would swap dog tags again, which would further confuse folks back home.

Among the POWs, there were some very clever people from all walks of life – actors, dancers and lawyers, a lot of them, of course, with various degrees. One man in particular stood out. He was a South African called Olli Squirrel. He acquired bits and pieces of electrical gear and made an electric clock which kept perfect time. Olli disappeared and in spite of numerous inquiries by the International Red Cross, and other organisations, he was never found.

A German guard known as Ukraine Joe would walk through the compound yelling. If you weren't out of your bunk in time, it was known that he would use his revolver. I was there when one victim was carried out dead, although I do not know all the details.

One of the Air Force fellows, while out on a working party, had either acquired or borrowed a small camera and smuggled it into camp. All men had to attend "Appel" [count parade] morning and night. This particular fellow had one hand inside the coat under the lapel area, with the camera lens positioned behind a small hole made in the coat. He photographed Joe as he came by, counting.

I was gratified to learn that the photo was eventually the

downfall of Ukraine Joe. It was the means of him being traced after the war, and he was hanged after being found guilty of war crimes at the trials at Nuremberg.

We had a very good radio in camp. We had smuggled in pieces and then assembled it. Some of the fellows would copy down the BBC news and then visit all the barracks to read the latest news. We set up our own guards to forestall any goons, or ferrets, as we called them, who may have been snooping around.

We were well aware that any war news that was detrimental to the Germans was held back from the public for a period. Armed with the latest news, the following morning at work, we would tell our guard about it. He would dismiss it as propaganda until it would then appear in the national paper, then we would remind him of it.

The guards cottoned on, and there would be concentrated raids any time of the day to find the radio. It was never found. It had been built, then put inside an Army water bottle, hanging on the bed post of a bunk for all to see, and guards would pass close to it many times.

In 1944, the Red Cross parcels stopped coming. We then lived on a cup of ersatz coffee, made from acorns, a slice of black bread about two inches thick and at midday we had a cup of soup – mostly coloured water with the odd piece of cabbage leaf or turnip floating on the top. Once a week, we had about an ounce of margarine, which was a byproduct from coal, and once a month a portion of jam, which was mainly sugar beet.

Getting the soup to the other side of the camp was a mission. Sometimes it would be muddy or snowing. The cauldron had about 40 gallons of soup in it, which would be carried by two of us. We put a pole through the two handles and each man held his end of the pole in front of him with both hands. It was essential that both men kept in step to avoid spillage. As the cauldrons had no lids, a fair amount of rain or snow entered in the winter and dust in the summer.

Early in 1944, naval personnel were moved to a special naval camp near Bremen in North Germany. All were moved, with the exception of me. I do not know why I was not taken with them, perhaps because I was on the cemetery job.

Tragically, just a day or two before the end of the war, the naval people were moved from that camp and as they were travelling on the open roads were attacked by British aircraft. Among others, our Captain, Commander Scurfield was killed, a tragic end to a very good man.

On the 19th to 20th of January 1945, in the middle of winter, we were given notice that the camp would be evacuated in three stages. The Red Army had reached a position not too far from us on the Polish eastern border. At the first light of dawn, we were detailed off by compounds. There was at least 12 inches of snow everywhere, and the temperature was way down to 30 degrees below zero.

Some of the guards had bicycles with them, but what use they would be in 12 inches of snow was hard to figure out. The previous evening, a mate, John, and I had used bed boards to make a sleigh. Having cleared the camp, I noted that our course appeared to be south-west, heading in the direction of Czechoslovakia.

We travelled for 30km before being herded into a paddock on a hill. There was a big barn that some men were lucky enough to be able to sleep in.

After that we remained in the open for several nights while travelling.

Two weeks later, about 200 of us were culled from the rest and were taken off on our own, with a dozen or so guards. That afternoon, we entered a large concentration camp. We knew straightaway what it was as soon as we saw the death's head insignia over the main gate and the words "Arbeit Macht Frei" (Work Makes Free). An officer and a feldwebel gave us a lecture on how we were going to have to work, after which we were told to march.

We were halted in front of a two-storey brick building. There was one six-foot-by-two-foot door, but no other doors or windows. There was no lighting anywhere and the floor appeared to be earth. We were left in there for between 12 and 36 hours. We never found out the reason.

We lined up for work and volunteers were called for various jobs. I volunteered for railway work. We were issued shovels and told to clear the rubble that was the result of an air raid on the place. We had no show of moving smashed trucks, rail lines etc, short of employing a bulldozer. The whole thing was a farce, and I think at this stage the guards were not too interested one way or the other.

John and I decided we would take off at the first opportunity. We worked our way out of sight of the nearest guard, only to reappear again shortly afterwards. We did this a few times until we went through a shed and escaped. We went flat out for about an hour and a half, heading roughly west.

We came across a farm. Two Polish girls saw us and asked us if we wanted Junaks [Polish cigarettes], to which we said, "Yes." As we went to meet them, an old lady appeared with a rake over her shoulder. We said we were workers for the Reich and could she perhaps give us a little bread. As we began eating, a German officer entered the kitchen. He nodded his head at us and kept walking through to another room. We decided to leave as soon as possible.

We found a shed to stay in for the night. This was the coldest night of all. The wind had risen and was blowing right across from Siberia. Sleep was almost impossible.

We set off again at the first light of day. As we were walking, two German soldiers on bicycles appeared from around a bend in the road. The corporal of the two had his rifle off his shoulder and said "Halt." The other fellow, who looked about 16, got into a heck of a tangle trying to get his rifle off, and in the process just about tore his right ear off, lost his balance, and finished up on the ground, with the bike partly on top of him.

We told them we were "English soldaten." The young fellow was told to guard us while the corporal took off on his bicycle. He was back 10 minutes later with another corporal and we were ordered to march ahead. We walked for an hour or so, when we suddenly headed across a paddock to a large stand of trees. We joined up with a number of French POWs.

At 7.30am, we were underway again, but not to the wood-cutting job. We were taken in a different direction. We came to a fork in the road. A contingent of Allied POWs reached the intersection at the same time. I dodged the column and joined up with them and as a precaution took off my Polish hat. We were made to keep walking. These fellows were not in good shape.

We arrived the next day at Stalag 8a, a large Allied camp, in Gorlitz. We were given a bread ration and allocated to huts that were already full. In short, organised chaos.

On 10 February 1945, we headed off again. Being such a large column prevented us from all finding shelter at night. The frostbite was taking its toll and some men were in agony. Others had severe dysentery. Men simply collapsed and crawled to the side of the road to die.

Having reached the Gorlitz area we were in fact entering East Germany. It was obvious that we were being kicked around like an old boot, heading first west then north then south, apparently because of reports coming in of the advances being made by the American, British and French forces. We and millions of civilians were gradually being compressed into an even smaller area.

We were being subjected to attacks by Allied aircraft and one column of Russian POWs received a direct hit, with hardly any survivors. There would have been several hundred in this column.

There was no such thing as first aid and food was a problem too. We collected snails in tins along the way in anticipation that we would cook them after we completed our day's walk.

We reached the city of Dresden, and that day all hell broke loose. It turned out to be the biggest air attack in any city during the war. The next morning, a German we nicknamed the "Black Butcher" decided to take the raid out on us. He crept up the side of the column and let fly with his rifle across the shoulders or head of someone he had taken a dislike to. He seemed to take a delight in doing this when we were going through a town or village where the population could witness it.

At the end of February, we headed for a place called Dobeln, on the way to Leipzig; we came to Zeitz and a couple of weeks later we finished up at Chemnitz, about halfway back to Dresden again.

We had gone in almost a full circle. The next place we came to was Jena, not far south of Leipzig and a week later we entered Gotha near Erfert.

My little Polish diary (which I still have) has no more entries. At that point I must have "given up the ghost".

One day we were taken into a paddock and at the point of rifles and revolvers we were driven down into a gravel quarry. This quarry was about 20 feet deep. The guards lined the perimeter with rifles and a spotlight and had a couple of machine-guns trained down on us. We had instructions to stay put or be shot. Some of our people were up to their ankles in icy water. I am sad to say there were a number of people who did not survive the night.

Just about unconscious, we set off again at first light and it was just a case of following the man in front of you. I don't remember the next week, but one of my boots had completely disintegrated and I was reduced to wrapping a length of sacking around my foot stuffed with straw. I was lucky. Some people had no footwear at all.

Some of our blokes who fell by the wayside were overrun by the Red Army. Of those, some were passed back through the Russian lines and finished up in Odessa on the Black Sea.

We crossed the Harz Mountains and one afternoon we were directed onto a large racecourse. We lay on the ground still under guard but we didn't know the cause of the holdup. We were ordered to move on. At this point, about a hundred of us refused. We were told to get on our feet or be shot. We invited them to fire away, as we were incapable of walking any further. They decided to leave us there. They knew the American Army was only 20 or so miles away.

After an hour or so, a dozen German Army medics arrived and pointed to a town about three miles away and said we would get good medical attention if we walked there. They managed to convince us.

We entered the town of Bad Harzburg, where every roof in this town had a Red Cross painted on it. A dozen or more of us were directed to a fairly large estate where the large house could be seen

Voluntary Aide Irene Stembridge (then Grant) in uniform at No.4 General Hospital in the Pacific in 1943.

Jack Tomlinson receiving his great patriotic war medal from the Russian Ambassador in Wellington.

John Turner (front row, second from right) with fellow members of 1 Platoon, 27th Machine-gun Battalion at Burnham Military Camp in 1939.

Cecil Wright in military dress in April 1940 with church army badges on his hat and uniform.

Frank Gibbison in November 1950 – ready to carry on a family tradition by fighting in the Korean War.

Jack Spiers in a communications trench in "Little Gibraltar" in Korea in the winter of 1952.

"Baz" Nissen (back row, third from left) with other members of 1 Section, 2 Platoon. They were called "The Lonely Ones" because they operated close to the perimeter where no one else wanted to go.

Hini Komene, in full battle array, reading literature found in a Viet Cong village while serving with Victor 2 Company in 1967-68.

The 1970-71 Tour – the sign says it all, "Welcome to Vietnam". [Photo: Hini Komene]

quite clearly through the trees.

We walked down a large corridor and I found myself in a small room with two Dutch female nurses who helped me into a bath.

I dropped the soap behind a gap between the bath and the wall. First, one girl was down on her knees, then the other trying to retrieve it. I got out and did my party piece. The soap was retrieved. It wasn't until later I saw the funny side of it all, me on my hand and knees, all parts swinging in the breeze, trying to get the soap. I imagine it was all in a day's work for them and they'd probably seen it all before.

After a week or so, a fleet of trucks arrived and took us to a place named Derenberg. We were directed to a girls' school. The place was bulging at the seams, so we made off on foot until we reached a large building, which turned out to be an SS dump. There was all sorts of food here. Some Aussies had got there first and were stocking up. John and I loaded a couple of sacks and we came across a middle-aged lady who allowed us to stay in her attic.

Later that night, I popped out for some fresh air. Two Americans stopped and recommended me not to venture outside after a given hour because any time after dark would invite a bullet.

About 2am all hell broke loose. Stationed in the side road directly under our attic was an American tank. The main armament was going flat out as were plenty of small arms.

At first light, we looked out of the window. Big Jimmy, as we called him, was busy cleaning his gun. We asked him what the racket was during the night.

Jimmy said, "Them goddamned Hienies."

We had been told that a mile or two up the road there was quite a concentration of German troops that had been bypassed and we thought it may have been them breaking out. I asked Jimmy if they had captured them?

He said, "Yes, both of them."

Typical Yanks, no such thing as conserving ammunition.

For several days after, POWs were arriving from all directions, on all kinds of transport – horses, bicycles, German Army motor bikes. One crowd was seen coming down the road with a four-wheel dog cart. About three were pulling, three more pushing up behind and six riding inside and all thought it was a hell of a joke.

But the classic piece was a crowd of English and Aussies tearing up the road in an old steam-traction engine. Clouds of smoke were coming out of the tail stack and goodness knows what they were burning for fuel.

Some of the fellows had been with us on the march outside Bad Harzburg and we found out that about an hour or two after we left panic set in with the guards. Our blokes set upon them, took their food and firearms and told them that they were now prisoners.

One piece of news made good listening. The "Black Butcher" was tracked down, he was stripped completely and a couple of our blokes who still had the stamina got stuck into him and sent him on his way, naked.

We were getting to be a problem for the American Army, so they took us in fleets of trucks to an airport called Hilversein and we were then flown by DC3s to Brussels in Belgium.

We were then taken by train to Ostend and next morning we went to the docks, where a cross-channel ferry was berthed.

During my three-month hike from Poland through Germany, most of my personal gear had been discarded along the way, except for a photo of my wife and a leather Russian marine belt given to me by my Russian contact in the cemetery. At the time he had given this to me, I was only six stone. I also held onto my Polish diary.

One of the highlights for me after the war was being chosen to visit Buckingham Palace. Everyone had their hand shaken by King George VI and the Queen and the two princesses. I am not too sure about the British Government at that time. It seemed to me that now the war was over they were not too interested in the people who fought it.

Prior to the war it was the old king and country job and conscientious objectors were disliked and even imprisoned. Looking back, I am not too sure that they were wrong – after all if everyone were of the same mind there wouldn't be wars.

Finally I was discharged. My service papers, which I still have, showed an RR (recommended to re-engage) rating for each of my 12 years' service. The Naval Records people must have picked that one up because a couple of months later I had a letter from them asking me to re-engage for a further term.

I didn't even reply.

Bullets among the Buttercups
John Turner

For John Turner (also known as Jack), the war is now a distant memory. He had a slightly romantic view of it at the beginning, but war itself has a way of coldly replacing the illusion with the reality. However, his story did almost have a Boy's Own *ending.*

I was born in September 1915. My father, Sir Harvey Turner, was a leading fruit merchant in New Zealand and one of the founders and the driving force of the well-known wholesale produce merchant Turners and Growers. The house I live in now was built by my grandfather on a different part of the site where it is now. After building it, he moved it down the hill to its present location.

A few months before the Second World War commenced, in September 1939, my cousin Bert and I were playing tennis at 40 Summit Drive, Auckland. We were talking together after our game and both agreed that it seemed inevitable that there would be another world war. We decided to join the territorial forces, voluntary part-time soldiers, and I became a member of the Pakuranga Mounties.

As soon as war was declared, the leader of the Pakuranga Mounties organised his men to be the first to volunteer for service in Auckland. Accordingly, when the doors opened at the Army offices in Rutland Street, about 20 of us Pakuranga Mounties were first in the queue. We had been there most of the night.

I had a horse at the time. My uncle had been in the First World War cavalry at Gallipoli and had been killed there. I thought I might be able to carry on the tradition and in fact I think I was about number 12 subsequently to receive a notice to attend the military camp at Hopuhopu to join the divisional cavalry (armoured) but a few days later I received another notice to attend Burnham Camp, south of Christchurch, to join the 27th Machine-gun Battalion.

I dutifully went to Burnham towards the end of September as part of the first echelon. We sailed from Lyttelton on 3 January 1940, on the *Sobieski*, a Polish ship taken over by the British. My cousin Bert had joined the medical corps and sailed on the *Dunera*.

We stopped at Fremantle where we had a few hours' leave and at Colombo, Sri Lanka. Then we landed at Egypt at about the end of January 1940. We went to the British military camp at Maadi, near Cairo, where we had further training including guarding the airports at Heliopolis and Helwan. We spent some time in the desert at Bagush beside the Mediterranean.

I started as a private and became a lance corporal, then a corporal, lance sergeant and finally sergeant. My regimental number was 7055. I spent a week in Palestine, Israel, on leave in early 1940. We also had weekend leave sometimes and visited the pyramids in Luxor. In February or March 1941, we sailed from Alexandra for Greece on a British cruiser, the *Gloster*. From Athens we travelled by Army trucks to the north of Greece, camping near the borders of Albania and Yugoslavia.

On 21 April 1941, I sent a letter from Greece to my family. Here is some of it:

> "I'm sitting under a green olive tree which is just about coming out in fruit buds. The ground has been ploughed not so long ago, but is now a mass of colour for wild flowers, mostly vivid red poppies. This is a great country for wild flowers, millions of violets, little daisies, big daisies,

buttercups, blue cornflowers and many others. I picked a few violets the other day in a grove of trees, small but sweet.

On Thursday, we heard the first sounds of artillery fire and on Easter Sunday Morning had our first little bit of action ourselves. I hope you're not worrying, we're okay so far...."

On Easter Sunday, 1941, we had taken positions facing the main road leading out of Yugoslavia into Greece. We had the task of stopping the German Army from entering Greece from Yugoslavia. In due course, the German Army trucks and tanks appeared coming down the road and we held them up for about half an hour until we ran out of ammunition.

We started to run back to where our trucks were. On the way back, the Germans were chasing us and firing at us. A bullet hit my steel helmet and knocked me down. My friend rushed over to look at me. I wasn't hurt, but there was a big dent in the steel helmet. I stood up again, I ran back to the truck. I got out my *Bible* from the truck and read the 23rd Psalm:

"The Lord is my Shepherd, I shall not want...." I thought it was fitting because I had come so close to death.

This was the beginning of the British forces' retreat, down through Greece, then on to Crete and eventually back to Egypt.

After the inevitable surrender of the Army, which had had little or no air support or reinforcements, the order came, "every man for himself". At that stage, my gunner, who had had an injury to his knee, and I sheltered in a cliff cave during the day, often being peppered by the rear gunners of the German planes as they swept low over larger targets. At night, we would venture to the beach for ablutions but soon the Germans overran our positions and we were captured.

Once back in Greece, we were herded like cattle into train wagons (standing room only and no food or toilet facilities for days on end), heading for Stalag 8B and Germany, where I volunteered for a work party in a sugar-beet factory. The owner was a decent old German gentleman called Herr Muller who tried to make life not too unpleasant.

One night before final lock-up time I escaped with an Australian friend to a nearby potato patch and lay there waiting for a train to come past. When the train did arrive, we couldn't get up because people were watching.

Finally we were able to move on but unfortunately after about five days we were recaptured and put in solitary confinement for 10 days, before being sent back to the factory, thanks to Herr Muller's intervention.

It was only later that I discovered my father, who was a very remarkable man, was at one time planning to "spring" me from my captivity. My father missed out on the First World War. By the time he had finished his training, the war had ended.

He had offered his service again even before the Second World War broke out. As a result, he later received a cable from General Freyberg which read:

SEND HARVEY TURNER TO BE IN CHARGE OF THE NEW ZEALAND FORCES CLUB AND LOCAL BUYING STOP RANK LIEUTENANT WITH POSSIBLE PROMOTION LATER.

My father felt that the rank of captain would be better suited to carrying out the position, though he would accept a lieutenant's pay. He also said he would pay his own airfare. The rank was confirmed and the Government said they would pay the airfare. A week later my father flew to Cairo in a flying boat.

As my father recorded in his autobiography, *The Country Boy*, he told his plan to get me out to an officer who was dining in the Forces Club. The officer immediately replied, "Count me in." That officer was Charlie Upham. My father was unaware at the time that Upham had already been recommended for the VC and would later earn a second one, the only man to do so during the Second World War.

In the end nothing eventuated, but can you imagine being rescued by New Zealand's most highly decorated soldier? And if anyone could have pulled it off, it would have been Charlie Upham.

Instead, I saw out the war as a POW and then travelled from France to England and finally back to New Zealand where I rejoined the family business, taking over the position of chairman from my father in 1969.

The Last Rites
Cecil Wright

The final Second World War story in this book is of Cecil Wright, who was a padre and so never fought as a combatant. His job was to uplift the living and to bury the dead.

I was born in 1913. My parents were farming people in the Hikurangi–Whangarei districts. I was home-taught until we moved to Otaika near a school. In 1928, at the age of 15, I gained my proficiency and left school to work on the farm with my parents and sister until I was 26. Then I left to work with the Church Army, a Church of England lay society.

We were given 10 shillings a week and our keep. In 1939, I was working in the Plimmerton parish when World War Two broke out and I volunteered. Even though I was born in New Zealand, we thought of ourselves as British. My grandparents came from England. So I'm British–European really. Other New Zealanders at the time had the same point of view. We were in the British forces. We belonged to the Allies.

I didn't volunteer to fight. It was the accepted thing that we were of the chaplain's department and the chaplain's department and the medics were non-combatants. I worked with the RAP [Regimental Aide Post], that is the medics, looking after the wounded.

In May 1940, I embarked at Wellington for overseas. After spending several months training at Aldershot, I was transferred from the 21st Infantry Battalion to the 7th Field Company, NZ Engineers.

In January 1941, I embarked at Liverpool and we steamed in convoy to the Middle East via Cape Town. We landed at Port Taufig on 1 February, then travelled by train to Helwan Military Camp, north of Cairo.

On 1 April, we left Helwan bound for Greece, arriving at the port of Piraeus on 3 April with the intention that we would support the Greek, British, Australian and New Zealand troops already at the battle line. The Australians and the British tried to hold off the Italians but when the Germans came they put in 12 divisions. I think we had two.

And when they arrived with all their military equipment and tanks they forced us all back. We were driven back to the coast and there the Navy was able to send ships and lighters ashore to evacuate our boys from whatever beaches they could get at. We destroyed all of the equipment and any trucks we had. They would drain the oil and run the engine until it seized and push the truck over a cliff. It was very soul-destroying, but it had to be done. We left Greece with only what we stood up in and steamed to Crete.

We were sent to Hill 107, which was the main hill overlooking the Maleme airstrip. There the Germans suffered heavy losses through their paratroopers just jumping out in the daylight.

Paratroopers are supposed to land at night, which was really unfair because for any Allied soldier with a rifle it was an opportunity to destroy the person before he arrived on the ground. There was not much sense letting them getting established on the ground for combat was there? Those of our boys in the olive trees who did have a rifle ... it was a kind of slaughter for them.

It is hard to watch people dying but that's war. Quite a few of the German boys coming down didn't die straight away and that was agony to see poor fellas dying.

Hitler didn't use his paratroops again. He learned a lesson. But of course the British did. And they sent theirs in at Arnhem, didn't they? And there again it was unfortunate ... they should have been more cunning.

After the paratroopers had come down, the battle raged for days. By night we couldn't rest because you weren't sure where the enemy was and then as soon as daylight arrived there were more strafing and bombings so there was no let-up. It was a repeat of Greece. To retreat and counter-attack and retreat. All the way to Sfakia, marching over the mountains, but it wasn't really a march, it was a trek and those Cretan hills are very steep.

The Germans had cut off our supplies from Suda Bay by bombing. We were short of rations and water from about the 23/24th and had had nothing to eat or drink for days. At that stage, all I had was just the uniform I stood up in and my two side packs, which contained shaving gear.

The exhaustion from battle was really terrific at that time. There was nothing like that battle tension to wear one down and some cracked.

On 31 May, the last ship left Sfakia. It's amazing how the bush telegraph works. One tells another and it came through that there'd be no more ships. At about 11.30 on 31 May, I heard an aircraft. It was the Sunderland aircraft that came in and took General Freyberg and his staff off the island.

On our way to Sfakia, we longed for a drink. Quite often we'd come across a well that was dry because there'd been so many people at it before. We trekked to just above Sfakia, near the cave that General Freyberg and his staff had occupied prior to his flight out. And near that cave was a well that had water, sufficient water for our needs.

Fortunately, I had a small tin and some nylon cord that I had saved from a German parachute. And I let down my tin and brought water to drink. And one was amazed how quickly the sweat appeared on one's wrists – almost instantly after swallowing the water.

When the German infantry caught up with us they all came down the ravine yelling and shouting and shooting. The word came around that we were to surrender and pile arms. I remember seeing the major of the artillery very unhappy about it … having to submit to their orders, he was thinking, "Fancy us having to surrender … surely not British."

Then the Jerries herded us all in together near this village and then set us off back up the hill. There was no refusing because you got a rifle butt in your backside – or a bullet.

There were so many of us who wanted a drink and I was able to let my tin down a well again. It was about 20 feet down to the water level and then I would haul it up. The guard hurried us up and threatened us with shooting because we were getting behind the column.

We trekked back over those hills under armed guard. For two or three days they kept us in a tent that used to be used by the Allies as a hospital at Galatas. And then as German troop carriers were coming in from Greece to Maleme, they would load us back on the empty ones to Athens.

From there we were taken to Lubeck in Germany and there we had our first wash, which was rather good. They used to shower us because the Germans were afraid of lice and tetanus.

I was given my dog tag [POW identification number] which was OFLAG XC 3331. OFLAG meant officers' camp. All the officers went to oflags. All the ORs, that is other ranks, went to stalags. XC meant Camp 10C.

The dog tag had perforations through the middle of it so that if someone died then it could be broken off and half of it was left with the body and the other was sent to the Red Cross, which sent it on to the person's next-of-kin.

The Jerries were rather strange but they appreciated a soldier. So much so that even if they'd shot one of our boys trying to escape, they would give him a decent burial.

At another camp, one of our boys died in camp and we all went to his funeral and the Jerries provided the coffin. It was very crude. Two kind of black parts that met like a V. Our boys carried it and he was buried in a German cemetery, under guard of course. Two British chaplains took the service.

On the battlefield, we just buried them. I did bury one of our officers and then there was a lull in the fighting and we transferred him to a Cretan cemetery.

In the POW camp, my job continued pretty much as normal, looking after the boys and keeping up their morale. One's own personal courage was important in all cases. The boys expected us to be able to cope and, of course, if we didn't cope well that was demoralising to them.

It was the same with the officers. The boys always expected the officers to be superior to all the elements.

I was mentioned in despatches for my courage and fortitude and usefulness in the battle area with the wounded and with prisoners of war.

I was held in captivity until the end of the war when on 26 April 1945 the British Forces coming across from Normandy overtook our camps and released us. After some months' parish work in England, I returned to New Zealand in late October 1945.

After the war I worked in numerous parishes. I have never actually retired ... to me the word means "re-tyre" as in "retread" – like a tyre. Even since receiving my pension and leaving full-time parish work, I've taken on responsibility in 20 parishes since then. I'll still take funerals anywhere in the Auckland province for RSA boys.

Got to Be a Kiwi
Frank Gibbison

A century of military tradition runs through Frank Gibbison's family. It looked like he was set to be a farmer, but he found the country life too quiet.

I was born on a family farm in Kauroa, just out of Raglan, in 1926. My people have been there since the 1850s. I was number four in a family of nine. My father served at Gallipoli and was badly wounded. My great-grandfather was involved in the Maori Wars in the 1860s. I turned 19 towards the end of the Second World War and wondered if I had missed out on something exciting. My brother was in the Air Force and he was killed.

In 1947, New Zealand maintained troops in Japan with the Occupation Forces and I thought I'd get out of New Zealand, and so I joined and had a year there and then was discharged.

Two years later, when the Korean War came up, I thought about it for a day or two and decided, "Yes, I would like to be involved with that." So I went over to Hamilton, about 30 miles away, and put my name in. I was accepted … me and many others. They wanted about 1500 guys and in a couple of weeks they had 6000 volunteers.

I went into Papakura Camp, where I had trained before going

to Japan. This time I was selected to go to Trentham for officer training. We did three or four weeks of basic instruction, administrative and weapon training then we were sent to Waiouru to the School of Artillery to learn artillery work.

At the end of November, those of us who passed the training were commissioned as second lieutenants. I was posted to 163 Battery of 16th Field Regiment, just a couple of weeks before we sailed for Korea on 10 December 1950. We went via Brisbane and Manila. From being stinking hot in December, a few days later we arrived in Pusan in Korea. I've never been so damn cold in all my life! It was really freezing.

From Pusan, we moved to a place called Miryang, We got a bit of a rude awakening the day we arrived in Miryang. It wasn't a very long trip but a couple of vehicles had broken down along the way and been delayed. Our battery sergeant major and the vehicle mechanic had gone back to find the vehicles and bring them up. They didn't find the vehicles. Before they got there, they were picked up by guerrillas and they were both murdered. It made me realise we really were in a war situation.

We then moved to join the 27th British Commonwealth Infantry Brigade in Taegu area. The fighting was very mobile at this stage. This was just after the Chinese had entered the war after General MacArthur's landing at In'chon and we wondered if there was going to be enough of Korea left for us to land on. They had stabilised it and at the time we went in they were just starting to push back north again. We were virtually on the move every day, sometimes twice a day.

One of the things that made an impression on us at that point was that there had been an American company-sized patrol that had been out in front of their own lines and either the Chinese or North Koreans had hit them at night. They had wiped out the whole lot of them, about 100 men. As one of the young officers of the battery, I was told to round up any spare people of our troops and march them through where these guys had been killed as an object lesson in "Do not go to sleep on night picket."

They had been shot in their sleeping bags or half out of their sleeping bags. By the time we got there, these guys were frozen stiff, and they were just stacking them up on a truck to take them out. I took a look at one bloke who was lying there with no pants on, dead as a mackerel, and I said, "There's one thing for sure, I'm not taking my pants off to go to bed."

That was the first time we saw real results of warfare.

By early April we were right up in the Kapyong Valley, very close to the 38th parallel. At that stage they had slowed things down and it was decided that 27 Brigade would come out of the line for a rest and their position was taken over by the 6th Republic of Korea Division.

We were coming up to Anzac Day and the plan was that our unit, the 16th Field Regiment, would also be withdrawn from the line, go back to this rest position and have a big slap-up Anzac Day celebration. This was to include Turks and Australians as well. I was one of a group that was sent back to prepare the rest position.

The next morning, we'd just got out of bed when a truck from the battery came screaming in and they said, "You've got to report back to your unit as fast as...."

We went back and found that the regiment had been withdrawn 15 or 20km because the Chinese had put in a massive attack during the night. The South Koreans had decided they knew better places to be and they'd gone and the regiment was left out on its own.

We joined up with the regiment and the decision was made that the guns would go back up the valley, virtually to where they had been the previous night because the Chinese had not actually come through during this time because they went on foot.

During the afternoon, the regiment went back up the valley and the Middlesex Battalion, which had in fact been withdrawn and was almost on its way back to Hong Kong, had come back in to provide local defence for our guns.

It was quite a strange situation when we went back up this valley. We knew the Chinese were coming, but we had not much in the way of observation people to see what was going on. We were sitting there with our guns ready to fire; it was chilly, it was dead quiet and everybody was tensing up.

Then the next thing these Koreans that had been rounded up from the previous night's departure went again. There must have been thousands of them running down the road.

I was sitting there and I got the tremors a little bit. One of the guys at the command post said to me, "What's the matter with you, sir, are you cold or scared?"

I said, "Actually, I'm bloody scared."

It relaxed everybody and they laughed their heads off.

We banged away at the Chinese until it was decided to withdraw towards midnight. The Middlesex Battalion came down and got wherever they could on our vehicles and we withdrew down the valley to where we had been that morning.

Just before this one of our gunners, Jack Crotty, had been put on a misbehaviour charge – he'd got a bit drunk and done something stupid. I had to go and stand alongside him as his immediate commander. The commanding officer had sentenced him to field punishment, which meant he had to go to the field punishment centre. In the meantime, he was under my authority on open arrest.

Then I got sent off on rest position and handed him over to somebody else and didn't think any more about him. The night of the withdrawal, I was the duty officer in the battery command post. One of the troops was running short of ammunition and I was trying to organise something for them when Jack Crotty came up to me and said, "Sir, what am I supposed to do?"

The Chinese were starting to come pretty close to our positions so I said, "Bloody hell, get your rifle and get out there on the perimeter ... local defence."

He said, "Sir, I'm under open arrest, I'm not allowed to have a rifle."

I said, "Well, that order has just been cancelled. Go and see the battery sergeant-major, get a rifle off him and go where he tells you. Get!"

About an hour later, the adjutant at Regimental Head Quarters called on the radio and said, "Is there any close enemy activity in your vicinity?"

I went outside to have a look and there was tracer going over the top of us in all directions. It was right old fun and games.

I went back in and told the adjutant and he ordered us to move to a new position. We got in there at about 4am and I was totally buggered. The command post officer was there waiting for me so I handed over everything and he said, "Right, go and get some sleep."

I got into my sleeping bag. I wasn't about to be left behind so I rolled it out underneath the command post truck. I remember being mad as hell because I couldn't get into my sleeping bag with my boots on. I had to take my boots off, but that was all! I crashed out regardless of a couple of batteries of guns close by firing all night.

About three hours later, I was woken up with the news that one of the guys that had trained with me on the officer training course had been killed the night before, observing fire for the Australians.

The next thing an Australian jeep pulls up and Crotty falls out from the back of it.

They said, "Is he yours?"

I said, "Yeah. Where did you find him?"

The Aussie said, "Up the road, in that position where you were last night."

It turned out that Crotty had decided that he was under arrest and he wasn't going to get involved with any of this local defence stuff. He had taken his sleeping bag and gone over a little bank into another little paddy field and curled down there and gone to sleep. He hadn't realised we had gone.

During our withdrawal we'd had to cross over a narrow little defile and an American unit coming a bit behind us had run into a roadblock there and had been chopped up by the Chinese. So at daylight next morning the Australians had gone in to make sure it was clear for the next people coming through.

They found Gunner Crotty just getting out of his sleeping bag. They told me, "We saw this guy in the paddy field and I was just about to shoot him when my mate said, "Hey, hang on a minute, no Chinese is stupid enough to be out there on his own ... that's got to be a Kiwi."

We were fully occupied all of the next day, firing in support of the infantry people. We wrecked a few guns that day by keeping firing without allowing the guns time to cool. The paint was stripping off the barrels and the insides of the bores were in pretty bad shape. The ammunition was normally brought in by the supply trucks and dumped and carried up by our own trucks, but there was no time for that. The supply people were bringing it direct from the port on to the gun positions.

The brigade stopped the Chinese attack at that point but we still had to withdraw to consolidate. The regiment covered the action of the rear guard all the way down the Pukhan River.

Not long after that I was re-posted as intelligence officer for the regiment. One of the operations at that time was called Operation Commando, a limited objective offensive to push the enemy lines back a bit to give clearance to our main supply route. A major fire plan was developed to support these advances by the infantry. I was given three copies of this fire plan and sent off as intelligence officer to personally deliver one copy to each of our three battery commanders, who were located with the Australian and British battalions which were to start the attack the next morning. Each of these battalions was harboured overnight in a position held by a Canadian battalion.

I got away late in the afternoon, left the Jeep with the driver and started up the hill. It was almost dark and there was nobody about. There was a long track winding up the hill. The Chinese were doing a bit of harassing and every now and again and one of their shells would whistle over. None of them came close to me but it was still a bit unsettling.

Halfway up the hill, just about on dark, a voice said, "Halt!" and asked for the password. I panicked a bit and said, "I've forgotten what the password is, but I'm a Kiwi."

The voice said, "You're all right, mate, your accent saved ya."

He was an Australian lineman who'd been out fixing a wire cut by a shell burst. We went up through the trees, to the battalion command post and I gave a copy of the fire plan to the battery commander. I asked him where the next battery commander was.

He said, "I'll be seeing him in 20 minutes, I'll hand it to him."

I said, "Sir, I've got orders to hand it to him personally."

We had a discussion, but majors can always beat second lieutenants, so he took the fire plan and I asked where the third battery commander was. He told me he was on the next hill but then added, "We'd better be careful about this because that battalion is harboured in with the Vandoos [a corruption of vingt-deux, the Royal 22nd Regiment, French Canadians] and they're mad as bloody snakes."

They arranged for a Vandoo guide to take me over. Eventually, a horrible looking little man appeared, jabbering away in French and not admitting to speaking any English.

The Vandoos had been on this position for some time and they had put a double apron of barbed wire all around it. He looked at it and said something in French indicating that we should go through it.

I said, "You go first," which wasn't smart as it turned out.

He carefully climbed through the wire and I followed straight after, putting my feet where his feet had been. He got clear of the wire, I was halfway through and he started off through the trees and suddenly there was a "ping".

He had hit a trip wire and a little fuse started sizzling about two metres to my left. I was about two feet above the ground, hung up in barbed wire … I just lay there thinking, "Please God, don't let it be a grenade or a mortar bomb on that end of that trip wire."

It wasn't. It was a parachute flare.

It went straight up in the air and ignited and there was me spread-eagled on the barbed wire and about 50,000 Vandoos came running out, waving rifles, shouting and screaming and I thought, "Oh no, I'm going to get riddled by these guys."

But the guide managed to persuade them that they didn't need to shoot me.

As intelligence officer I used to do a bit of liaising with the neighbouring units and formations. One day, I was going up a very narrow track alongside which the Americans were using "Long Tom" guns with very long barrels. They could throw a 100lb shell about 25km. The two of them were about 50 yards apart right beside the road and as I drove under the muzzles they fired the pair of them. My ears started ringing that day and they've been ringing ever since.

After going back to a gun battery, I was in the Observation Post one evening when the telephone rang. The signaller answered it. He was saying "Oh yeah, yeah, right, yeah, right I'll tell them."

We asked him what that was about and he said, "Oh they just rang up to say old George has kicked the bucket."

That was the death of George VI. It got a bit more formal the next day. We fired a royal salute of live shell on the Chinese positions to give him a send-off.

I arrived home from Korea on 18 December 1952. I took my discharge from the Army then but I joined the Territorials and while I was there I was promoted to captain. I stayed on the reserve of officers in the Territorials until 1969.

That year I was offered a posting as a United Nations observer in Kashmir and was promoted to major. After that I didn't want to go back to the farm, dagging sheep and getting paid peanuts, and I was offered a job as a sub-unit commander in Army Training Group, Waiouru. I stayed there until 1976 and then retired.

On the Hook
Jack Spiers

Jack Spiers was in the New Zealand Army for 28 years, eventually attaining the rank of major and seeing service as a UN observer. His father before him was one of the few who fought in both world wars. Jack was one of only a handful of NZ regular infantry soldiers to fight in the Korean War.

I was born in Dunedin in 1931. My father was a bank clerk, my mother was an English war bride. My father had a long soldiering background in the Territorials. He fought as an officer in the First World War and won an MC [Military Cross]. He went away with the original 2NZEF with the 20th Battalion in the Second World War. He had his 50th birthday in the desert and he was obviously far too old as an infantry soldier so he came home in about 1942.

So I had that military background and I was always keen to be a soldier. I was in the school cadets at Christian Brothers High School in Dunedin and when I left school I joined the Army as a private soldier. I did my recruit course in Burnham in 1949. I did an instructor's course and various specialist courses and I was very keen to get overseas. The Korean War had started in 1950 but I was under 21 at that stage. As an infantryman, I didn't want to go over with other corps, I wanted to be in my own corps but New Zealand had no infantry in Korea.

After many written applications (and perhaps with some influence from some of the senior officers who had known my father), I managed to get transferred to K Force in 1952, immediately after my 21st birthday.

I arrived in Japan in September 1952. There they endeavoured to get me into the artillery but I stood on my dig and said, "No, I am over here to get experience in infantry."

After a week or so, I was transferred over to the Australian Holding Unit in Hiro. From there I joined the 3rd Battalion, Royal Australian Regiment (3RAR). I was promoted to sergeant and made the fire controller for the mortar platoon.

There were a lot of soldiers in that battalion of Second World War vintage. Unlike other battalions in the Commonwealth Division, the Third Battalion remained there throughout and was reinforced by individuals. It was with some apprehension that I joined the battalion as a very young inexperienced guy at the age of just 21.

In all, there were seven of us NZ regular infantrymen who served with 3RAR (and one with 1RAR) – six officers and two NCOs. We had a 50 per cent casualty rate – one killed and three wounded. It was pretty tough going in the infantry. In 3RARs three years there we had something like 900 casualties.

Although at that stage it was static, it was an infantryman's war.

In winter the conditions were very bad. It was probably down to about 38 degrees below zero. As front-line infantry we had very little warmth. You had to be very careful with your weapons, keeping them warm because unless you had special oil on your weapons the mechanism would freeze. You daren't touch metal with your bare hands because the skin would adhere to the metal. Any moisture on your face would freeze.

Sometimes in a platoon or a company's headquarters bunker, they might have a fuel stove. I never had any heat in my dugout right throughout the war. It was extremely difficult to keep warm, I used to run up and down the trench line at night to keep the circulation going but my feet were always numb. You had to prise fingers loose from the field telephone after sending fire orders and then, by painful endeavour, restore the circulation.

Forward infantry companies were forbidden to use sleeping bags or remove boots in case of a surprise enemy attack. The Black Watch had allegedly been caught napping during a previous battle.

At night when the Korean porters brought up supplies I used to nick the cardboard container from the ration packs and set a fire about six inches in diameter, but not light it. I'd endeavour to wait for as long as possible until things were quiet, until about 4am. Then I would go to my dugout and light this little prize and warm my hands. To me that was a piece of heaven.

The food wasn't great. We were on British rations, which were less than what Australians or New Zealanders would expect. We did get extra rations, but it was still bloody awful. I have never allowed a tin of bully beef in my house since then.

The war for the infantryman was very rugged. Out of our battalion of about 800 to 900 men, every night 100 would be out on patrol; standing patrols, recce patrols or fighting patrols. This was why our battalion performed so well – they dominated no-man's land.

The infantryman patrolled at night or he "stood to" and then he worked during the day. I suppose we would go into the line for probably four to five weeks perhaps and you might average four or five hours' sleep during a 24-hour period.

I've seen many other armies on operations, training or other circumstances and I would say there is none in the world that measures up to the standards set in training by the New Zealand Army. They are one of the few (or were one of the few) armies in the world that had an instructor's course, which developed tremendous knowledge and ability among the junior soldiers and NCOs.

As a junior NCO, when I arrived in Korea, I had completed an instructor's course, a minor tactics course (for junior officers and NCOs), an anti-tank instructor's course, and a 3-inch mortar instructor's course. This was a fantastic background for a junior NCO to have. I'm not undermining the ability of the Australian soldier in battle, he's bloody good and I was very proud to serve with them, but nobody else in 3RAR had that sort of training.

Our battalion in the main was supported by New Zealand artillery, 16th Field Regiment and we knew they would always be there. In return, the Kiwis knew the Australian battalion in front of them would always stand fast. There was that bond. It wasn't the same with the Korean and the American divisions.

Once on Hill 355 we were relieved by the Americans and when we went back into the line after about a month we couldn't believe it. We got a hell of a hiding for a start because the Americans had allowed the Chinaman to dominate no-man's land. They'd allowed the Chinaman to patrol right up to our wire and minefields and we had a hard job regaining the initiative.

In battle you must dominate. You must retain the initiative and this is what the Commonwealth and the Australian battalions in particular were noted for.

The command structures and discipline were also big factors. The Americans tended to drop their command structure one level below if anything happened. For example if the enemy attacked an American platoon, you would find that the company commander would come down and dominate the platoon strategy tactics and the battalion commander would come down to the company level, which was bloody stupid because if you've got a commander at that level, you let him fight his battle.

The American Marines were good, nearly up to a par with the Commonwealth forces. Initially the ROK [Republic of Korea] Battalions were ill trained and were terrible. They used to say you thought it was the Chinese tracers retreating but it was the cigars of the soldiers retreating.

Because we dominated the air, the Chinaman had a big problem getting his supplies up to the front line, so he was loath to waste any ammunition. If he started a firefight [heavy shelling or mortaring] you knew it was going to be "all on". They would advance very close to their own barrage and sometimes right in it.

We were attacked one night on Hill 355 at about last light and it was probably the heaviest shelling I'd ever seen or experienced. There were shells and mortars falling on us around about once every five seconds.

I fired my DF [defensive fire] tasks and this and the Kiwi artillery fire must have broken up their attack because they didn't get into our wire. I think we killed a lot of them outside the wire. It eased off around about 10 or 11pm that night, but continued sporadically until about 3 or 4am in the morning. I estimated about 5,000 shells landed on the company area that night.

Last year, I went across to Canberra and looked up the battalion war diary. I didn't know the exact date but I went through the war diary of about that time to find out what that event was all about but amazingly it doesn't even get a bloody mention. Things must have been so hot that no one had time to enter it in the diary.

At the Commonwealth position at the extreme left flank was a place called The Hook, which was a strategic spot in that it dominated the surrounding ground, so whoever held The Hook commanded that area. The Chinaman was dug in only about 50 yards away. The Hook was a scene of about three or four big battles.

In the last Battle of the Hook, just before the Armistice, we were immediately behind the front positions and there was a tremendous battle that night. The Chinese were trying to take The Hook and they probably lost about 5000 men.

In that battle, my first call for "fire" was about 50 rounds rapid to the mortar platoon. There was so much artillery and mortars landing, I couldn't even tell which were mine.

The war ended in July 1953. As a 21-year-old I grew up very quickly in Korea and I realised that war wasn't very romantic at all. In later years I became very concerned about the futility of war. It is a terrible thing and I saw lots of my Australian friends killed and wounded and it makes you wonder, "Was it worth it?"

I think all of our endeavours should be towards peace. War is just so stupid ... absolutely stupid. However we must remain prepared.

I often wonder now that I've got older about the number of Chinamen who were killed. I think, "What were their thoughts that were lost? What thoughts did they have for the future? How many of those killed had people at home who grieved for them? What were their thoughts?"

Grey Ghosts
Baz Nissen

Despite having celebrated his 60th birthday, Baz Nissen still retains the physical and mental alertness of a soldier. He carries no excess weight, he assesses situations quickly and acts or responds immediately with precise efficiency.

My intention wasn't to be a professional soldier. I only signed up for three years when I joined up with the Army.

It was the time of the Malayan emergency and the guy that was in charge of the territorial unit I belonged to in Hawkes Bay knew that I was getting married and he suggested I join the regular force and get a trip to Malaya. We got married 12 months earlier than we intended and we were on our way to Malaya in 1961.

I was in Malaya when the first company went from Malaya to Vietnam. After serving in Malaya and Borneo, I came back to New Zealand because the maximum overseas posting was two years. I was in New Zealand for 12 months and went overseas again. I went to Singapore, then Vietnam with Victor 5 Company.

Initially the French were there in the very early stages. We found French weapons left in caves. Bamboo clumps had grown through them, they had been left where they were sitting. My belief from the things that I saw while we were there was that the French weren't properly prepared.

We were trained for jungle warfare before we went in while 80 per cent of the American soldiers that went to Vietnam were conscripted off the streets. To a certain degree, the Australians used territorial soldiers who were better trained than the Americans, but I don't think as thoroughly prepared as we were for the type of operations we were doing. The New Zealanders very quickly established a reputation of being very professional soldiers, which wasn't entirely true, it was just that we had trained for that situation.

We were called the "grey ghosts" because no one knew where we were. The "non-professional" soldiers couldn't communicate without making a hell of a lot of noise and everybody knew where they were all the time. Later, when I was offered promotion and it meant transferring out of the section I refused because in my existing section we only had to look at each other to know what we were going to do.

We moved around in a platoon. There's 30 in a platoon with three sections of eight men. Except in mine – I had 10 because I had two machine-guns. There are two men to a machine-gun – one to fire and one to feed the ammunition belt.

The platoon was made up of 24 soldiers and then there was the platoon headquarters (commander, sergeant, signaller, medic, etc).

What we were trained to do was to search and destroy, to patrol by day and try and locate the Viet Cong. By night we would ambush.

They built bunker systems, they lived underground but they had bunkers above ground as well, so they could fire from them. When we found a bunker system we would pull back, get the air support in and blow the bunkers in. Or we would put charges on top of the bunkers and blow them in. On one occasion, we found a whole hospital complex dug underground so we didn't blow that in, we cleared it. The Americans and Australians had what they called tunnel rats who cleared the bunker systems.

In the mornings, a typical day consisted of getting up before first light and pulling down all of your shelter. You put everything in your pack except your weapon and ammunition and you sat there until it was daylight.

The moment it was daylight and there was no activity you started patrolling because your position may have been picked up during the night. You patrolled, depending on how hard the going was, for 500 or 1000 metres, then stopped in what you believed would be a safe area, fell back from the forward edge, put sentries out and had a cook up at about 10 o'clock.

So you'd do about four hours' work before you'd have breakfast. You'd rest up for an hour, then just start patrolling again and continue patrolling until you had another meal at about 4 o'clock.

After the afternoon meal, we'd walk for another 500 to 600 metres and set up an ambush base because half an hour before sunset and the first half-hour of light in the morning was the most likely time of attack. The South Vietnamese quite honestly were bloody hopeless when it came to ambushing, and the North weren't much better.

By last light, everybody had their rain shelters up and we'd arm the claymore mines. They were filled with an explosive and they put thousands and thousands of ball bearings in front of the explosive. It's a very effective weapon. The North Vietnamese would sometimes crawl in and try and turn them around because they were directional weapons.

We always used what we call a "triangular harbour". The point of your triangle, the initiation point, would be where your ambush was. You would have a section on each leg of the triangle and the headquarters in the middle. During the night, these guys would interchange on that initiation point. They would be on the initiation point for an hour and sleep the rest of the time.

Weapons were facing out within the triangle, so no one could get into where we were. Each gun-pit was only about six or eight feet apart, so you were in eyeball contact with each guy around your perimeter.

If there was contact during the night and you blew your ambush, we used to move. It might be only 30 yards but we used to move. Once the ambush had been detonated, the whole platoon would be on stand-to so that any further action could be dealt with.

If the group was larger than expected, we'd get in an aircraft to light up the area. We didn't fire weapons in the dark because the moment you fired they knew where you were. A plane was used to light up the area and then we called the artillery fire in so your map-reading had to be spot on. We had what we called "mortar-fire controllers" within the company. The guys that were mortar-fire controllers were really spot on with map-reading. The guy that we had, I would get him to call rounds to within 10 metres of where I was. I had that much confidence in him.

On patrol, you had to be careful where you walked because of the mines and the booby traps that the North Vietnamese had set up. Fifty per cent of our injuries to our guys were caused by booby traps and mines. The booby traps could be a grenade in a piece of bamboo with a trip wire on it, primitive stuff but very effective. They also dug pits, with sharp bamboo stakes at the bottom of it, and covered it. Trip into there and you wouldn't be climbing out of it.

We managed to avoid booby traps by noticing trip wires and branches that were bent out of place. You got to the stage, having been in that situation for 30 days at a time, that you could see if a guy had rested his rifle up against a tree, just because it was different. It stood out like a proverbial sore thumb.

We never used soap or toothpaste or anything like that because as soon as there is a different smell you can pick it up. That's how we picked most of the bunker systems up, because they had been cooking or they were still sleeping. You could smell body odour that was different to ours and we stunk to high heaven being out there for 30 days at a time … you can imagine it … but you could still smell something different.

After 30 days it became a real strain. You had your whole life on your back. Your home, your sustenance, your meals, your water, ammunition, everything was on your back. We got resupplied every seven days. So by every seventh day the pack was pretty light, but it didn't last very long. You'd pull back into an area that had already been cleared, and the choppers would come in and give you more.

It was real jungle warfare. While there is a certain amount of physical strain, it's more mental strain in jungle warfare. You can't see anything, the enemy could be behind the next tree, you'd never know.

I lost one of my own guys due to the mental strain. He didn't go nuts or anything, he just couldn't hack it any more and he was sent back to New Zealand. Some guys just signed up for three years. Career soldiers like myself referred to them as "short timers". They just left and tried to forget it all, but they didn't have the opportunity like guys like myself and hundreds of others that stayed on with the military life – we got it out of our system.

We had 30 days on patrol, then three days' break and sometimes a week break midway through your term. For some it was hard to go back after a week. Even after three days it was hard to go back, because in those three days you'd come out one day, de-kit, have a good feed, a few beers and then go to a place called Vung Tau, which was the Australians' rest and recuperation centre.

It was just like being back at Singapore. You could go down to the beach but because it was only three days, blokes would go into the bars in town and get smashed out of their brains for two days and lose it all. Then you'd go back to base and the next day you're kitted up and the following day you went back out on operation or you went out on patrols which were around the immediate vicinity of the home base looking for any activity that might have taken place.

The toughest scrape I got in was the first one. We lost two guys, and one of our section commanders got killed. We lost four guys in the 12 months that I was there and had a number injured.

The death of friends and killing of others was seen as part of the job. I'm not saying that it doesn't have any effect on you but you accept it as part of the job. You've got to. Those that served in Vietnam were trained in applied selective memory.

Imagine putting yourself in one of those soldiers' places, in the middle of the bush, where behind any one of the 30 trees that's around you, there could be an enemy soldier. What are you going to think about? Are you going to think about your friend that's just been shot? Or are you going to think about yourself to stop some bugger behind those trees shooting you?

You have to think about yourself. That's applied selective memory. You have got to do it to survive.

Some of our men were asked to go and see the movie *Platoon* when it came out. In the movie you see some of the American soldiers walking around with rifles slung over their shoulders. Now in a jungle situation how the hell are you going to get your rifle off your shoulder and fire a shot? Everything is instantaneous.

If a New Zealand soldier was on patrol in the jungle in Vietnam with his rifle slung over his shoulder, he'd be disciplined. He's totally bloody useless, because by the time he got his rifle off his shoulder and put it round, he'd be dead, it's as simple as that.

In Vietnam, one of the officers and myself were shifted down to a South Vietnamese company that were taken out on operation to show them our way of doing things. The first night we were out, I took two platoons of the company down to an ambush position and during the night we were hit by the Viet Cong.

I knew there was equipment in the area, I had picked up two machine-guns and three radio sets and was in the middle of what I thought was our ambush area. As I moved around it, it became quite apparent that there was nobody else there. I was alone. There was rifle fire going on so I called a helicopter in to winch this gear out rather than let the Viet Cong have it.

Of course he came over the top and immediately switched his light on, which didn't do me any good. After exchanging a few "pleasantries", he turned his light off and put the jungle penetrator down. I hooked the gear on it and he winched it up. He put the penetrator back down, I climbed onto it and got winched out. He flew me back to where the main body was supposed to have been and put me down again.

They weren't there, but of course by that time I was out of the danger area and made my way back. What had happened was the

South Vietnamese had blown the ambush and had gone back to main base and then went back to their camp – the whole bloody lot of them. For that the Vietnamese awarded me the Vietnam Gallantry Medal, which is the highest award the Vietnamese Army makes.

I enjoyed the service life. I re-engaged to five, then to eight, then to 12 years and stayed until the age of 48.

These days a lot of people say to me "For God's sake, relax," but you don't because having spent 27 or more years in a situation where you are continually aware of the need to look after yourself, or you are teaching others how to look after themselves, it becomes a natural instinct to always be alert.

A Man with Guts
Hini (Jim) Komene

Hini Komene spent most of his life as an anonymous soldier until 1998 when Brigadier Roger Mortlock, earmarked as the next Army Chief of General Staff, publicly admitted that he had covered up a friendly fire incident in Vietnam. Hini bravely stepped into the glare of national publicity and admitted that he was the one who had accidentally caused the death of a fellow soldier – an unfortunate tragedy in the lottery of war.

I was born at Kaikohe in North Auckland. My tribal affiliation is Nga Puhi. At that time, growing up in Maori communities, we had a tendency to go from one family to another family. We'd go and stay with an aunty or go and stay with our grandparents or something like that. Eventually my mum and dad finally settled down and they bought a home and we grew up there.

I left school and my father decided I had to go to work so he helped me find a couple of jobs. When I was doing one of these jobs I just happened to be walking through the main street of Kaikohe and they had this big Army display. Everybody was going in and out and as I was passing this tent, the guy said "Hey, come over here."

He asked me a couple of questions and explained to me where

I would go and how I would go, if I joined the armed forces. My intention at the time was to join the Air Force. There was something about planes that I liked and I could see myself hopping on a plane and flying out of Kaikohe.

What really attracted me to the military, I guess like any young person at that time, was all I was interested in was how much money I was going to make. The guy showed me the pay scales but what I didn't realise at the time was that I was looking at the higher pay scale. So I filled in the papers and sent them off.

A couple of weeks later I got a letter saying I was required for a medical. The letter said, "Here's your bus ticket and we'll see you down at the medical station." So I hopped on a bus and away I went. That was in 1963.

I was posted to Malaysia in November 1965 on active service with the NZ Infantry Battalion.

In 1966, the battalion was posted to Borneo and in November 1967 we were posted to Vietnam as Victor Two Company. I was with 2 Royal Australian New Zealand Battalion or the "Anzac Battalion".

I was a machine-gunner. Mainly our role was to do patrols and maintain some form of security and some form of protection for the local population against the Viet Cong. It was on those types of patrols that we grew together as a company.

There were times when we were called upon to search the local villages, because the intelligence reports had informed us that there was Viet Cong movement in the villages. Often the Viet Cong had family in the villages. We would try to catch the Viet Cong as they were going out or coming into the village.

It was difficult to tell who was a Viet Cong and who was a local, because they all looked the same. They wore straw hats, black pyjamas, and Ho Chi Minh sandals. This was everyday dress for the local community and families.

So our task was difficult in being able to recognise the Viet Cong and I would say many of them slipped through our roadblocks. Sometimes we would stop people at roadblocks and search through their equipment (some would come through on little motor bikes or ox carts) and they would become aggressive. They would start yelling and screaming, so we knew we had a suspect. They knew sooner or later that we were going to find a weapon or something that was supposed to be for the Viet Cong.

For most of our roadblocks we had the local police – they used to call them the "White Mice" – and we'd hand the person over to them.

I remember one particular operation during the major Tet offensive when we were lying in ambush and there was all this movement going on at this particular part of the track we were on. Our platoon commander had initiated the ambush by setting off the claymores. Once the claymores were set up, that's when my No. 2 on the gun and I had the responsibility of spraying [shooting] the actual track where the Viet Cong had been moving through in the night.

I was holding the machine-gun and shooting and firing away and I said to my mate, "Duncan, look just keep feeding the belts into the machine-gun, make sure it doesn't get jammed in the gun."

So away we went and then all of a sudden my gun stopped and I looked down and my mate was out. I thought he had been shot.

I punched him and said, "Duncan, Duncan, get up, get up." He shook his head.

I was so happy that he shook his head – that at least told me he hadn't been shot. I said, "What happened?"

He said, "I don't know" but when he had fully come to he said, "Didn't you see those two tracers?"

I said "What tracers?"

He said, "They came in between you and me."

After that particular operation we continued on operating in platoon groups. We knew we had wounded some of them and followed blood trails. The markings were still fresh on the ground.

We swept through the whole area as a company and in the evening we ran into a Viet Cong sentry post. The sentries opened up on our company and one of our radio operators was killed.

We knew that we had hit something big and our commander at the time decided we should go into a defensive position. So we harboured up and each of the platoons set up their own defensive systems ... the claymores, the machine-guns, the trip flares, so we could form some protection around our company perimeter.

In the early hours of the morning at about 2 to 3am, everybody was stood to and you could hear all this rustling and noise. Our platoon commander went forward and sprung the ambush and then it was all on for young and old.

We knew that there was a big Viet Cong unit that was out there trying to take us out. We hung in there and stuck together. The battle lasted until daylight and the whole time we were being shot at by anti-tank rockets, what they call the RPGs. They used those weapons against tanks ... they were using them against us.

When you are in the middle of the battle it's total noise, people screaming, Viet Cong screaming ... some of our wounded guys, they were yelling out "Medic, come over here."

While this was going on, we had the support of helicopter gunships and of our artillery and mortars in the area. Normally when you bring in artillery fire, the closest and safest they can get to your position is 1000 metres off your perimeter because of the shrapnel and the blasts. But that morning we brought it down to within 50 metres of our perimeter and not only the Vietnamese were copping the shrapnel but we were too.

In the morning when we did our clearing patrols, we found a string that they had been setting up around our harbour positions. They were going to hold onto it and move into position.

When you are on operation you sleep with one eye open. Even in the middle of the night you can still see, even though it's pitch black out there. You can visualise in you own mind even though you are staring into the darkness that there is movement out there, you can feel it within yourself. It keeps everybody on their toes, although some guys can sleep through the whole thing, but for me and others in the company, that's how we express ourselves, "You must sleep with one eye open, because if you shut both eyes, you won't be able to open them again."

Once we cleaned up after this operation, we had a high enemy body count. It came to about 30 plus out of about 120.

My first tour in Vietnam ended in May 1968. I had gone home

and then went back to Vietnam again in 1970. That was when I had my incident.

On the day of the incident we received intelligence reports that we were in an area where there was Viet Cong movement. We split up as a platoon and operated as half-platoon patrols. I was in the first half with our platoon commander.

As we were following up the intelligence reports, we came across this stream. It was a stream you could normally cross over and just get your ankles wet, but because of the wet season it was up over our heads. We had to cross it, so I said to our platoon commander, "This is where we'll cross it and I'll go first."

I stripped off and jumped in and as soon as I got across to the other side, the rest of the patrol followed. On the other side of the stream as one of the guys was coming through, he handed me the machine-gun.

I reached for it and as I did my finger went through the trigger guard and onto the trigger, firing off an 8–10 round burst. There was no way I could stop it. The rest of the guys were coming through the stream. It all happened so quickly.

As mentioned on the *Holmes* television programme, the incident was recorded and relayed back to the appropriate authorities. Through the signal operator, the platoon commander sent back the information as a contact report as opposed to an incident report. There are two major differences. On a contact report you've made contact with the enemy; an incident report means an accident or anything else that pertains to friendly forces.

The platoon commander was the one who sent back the report as a contact report. I was never told why, it may have been to protect me, I don't know. People have their own thoughts on that.

The platoon commander knew about it. Then it went higher and whatever they decided at their level, at command level, was their responsibility and it was out of my hands. When a military decision is made, it's made. That's how I felt at the time.

When you understand the military command chain, all that information is relayed all the way back to the Government. I believe that was done and because the Government didn't knock on my door and say, "Mr Komene, we need to see you...." None of that occurred. I believed that the report had been settled as it had happened – an incident report.

The Government officially acknowledged and welcomed home all war Vietnam veterans in 1998 [the war had finished way back in the 1970s]. They sent out invitations to all Vietnam veterans and their families to rally together down in Wellington, Queen's Birthday Weekend, 1998.

I went down there very open-minded about the incident that had happened in Vietnam. Nobody talked about it, but I felt the company members wanted to say something about it. Over the years they had known about it, but I guess they didn't know how to approach me about it, even though we had been best of mates since our Vietnam days. We'd meet every so often, shake hands, have a natter, catch up ... but I know deep down within their own hearts they want to say, "Jim, something needs to be done about this."

So I went down there and everybody was happy and everybody said, "It's nice to see you ... " and everything else, but as I hopped on the plane to leave I said to my wife, "You know, it hasn't gone to sleep."

When I was spoken to on *Holmes*, I knew that this was my opportunity to say something nationwide and hopefully put it to sleep.

The whole nation heard my story. After that my phone was red hot, people ringing in, and it was all complimentary. They never had any bad things to say about it. I even had old Second World War veterans ringing me up and saying I had guts. They told me, "We had incidents like that but we didn't know what to do about it."

I hope and pray the ghost of Vietnam has gone to sleep.

Epilogue
Journey's End

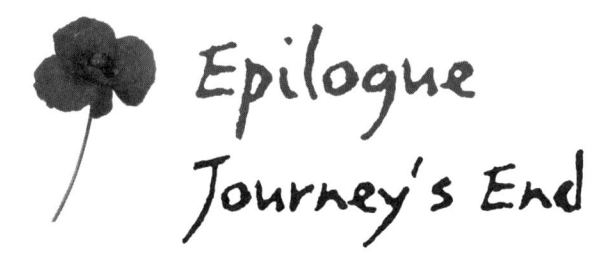

It has been my honour to help these people to tell their stories. They did their duty and for that the very least we can do is to offer our gratitude. That is best summed up by the foreword to the memoirs of Michael Hanan that was typed by his daughter. It read:

> Dad,
> The typing of this book has been a privilege for me. I have learned a lot about a young man called for war in the prime of his life. A man prepared to give of that life for others. His torment of being torn between the love for his family and his loyalty towards his men. This has been a lesson in humility for me and I feel a great sense of pride in the way you so courageously and unselfishly gave of yourself during those war years.
>
> *Jill*

As we embark on the new millennium, let us not forget the catastrophes of the previous one so that the black beast of war does not rise again.

Prior to the war, it was the old king and country job and conscientious objectors were disliked and even imprisoned. Looking back, I am not too sure that they were wrong. After all, if everyone was of the same mind there wouldn't be wars.
Jack Tomlinson

I wouldn't advise my son to go to war.
Maurice O'Connor

The whole world is one country.
Arch Scott

Appendix
War Service

Gibbison, Francis (Frank) Hume
Force: New Zealand Army, Artillery
Rank: Major
Serial no: 203 678
Joined up: 1947
Active service: Japan, Korea, Kashmir (United Nations observer)
Discharged: 1976
Medals:
- British Commonwealth Korea Medal (1950-53)
- United Nations Medal with Korea Clasp (1950-57)
- United Nations Medal (observer in Kashmir)
- New Zealand Service Medal (1946-1949)

(Awarded in 1996 for service in the Occupation Forces)

Hanan, Michael Kempthorne
Force: New Zealand Army, Infantry
Rank: Lieutenant
Serial no: 8771
Joined up: 5 January 1940
Active service: Greece, Crete, Desert Campaign, Italy
Discharged: 2 January 1945
Medals:
- Mentioned in despatches
- 1939-45 Star
- Africa Star
- 8th Army Clasp
- Italy Star

- Defence Medal
- War Medal 1939-45
- NZ War Service Medal
- Greek Medal

Henderson, Jim Herbert MBE
Force: New Zealand Army, 29 Battery Artillery
Rank: Gunner
Serial no: 24563
Joined up: 1 December 1939
Active service: 1941 Egypt, 1 December 1941 wounded at the battle of Sidi Rezegh, POW, 2 June 1943 repatriated
Discharged: 1945
Medals:
- Africa Star
- Defence Medal
- War Medal 1939-45

Hitchcock, Frank Norman
Force: Fleet Air Arm, RAF and RNZAF
Rank: Warrant Officer
Serial no: NZ4310172
Joined up: 1940
Service: 1940-1943 training England and Canada, 489 Squadron, shot down 29 August 1944, POW, released April 1945
Discharged: 1946
Medals:
- Atlantic Star
- Defence Medal
- War Medal 1939-45
- NZ War Service Medal
- Goldfish Club (saved life by the use of a dinghy)

Komene, Hini (Jim)
Force: NZ Army, Infantry
Rank: Staff Sergeant

Serial no: B 40734
Joined up: January 1964
Active service: Malaya, Borneo, Vietnam, Singapore
Discharged: 1988
Medals:
- Vietnam
- Borneo
- Long service and good conduct

McColl, Murray Ian Douglas
Force: NZ Army, 27th Machine Gun Battalion
Rank: Gunner
Serial no: 6504
Joined up: 1940
Active service: 1941 Greece, Crete, 24 May wounded, POW, November 1943 repatriated
Discharged: 1944
Medals: "Not applicable. I got three or four, my son has them. I got the 'barbed wire' medal."

McLagan, Murray Dawson
Force: NZ Army, Artillery, First Echelon
Rank: Gunner
Serial no: 2007
Joined up: 1939
Active service: 1940 Egypt, 1941 Crete, Greece, POW, escaped 16 July 1941 from POW camp, 8 May 1943 escaped to Egypt, Ruapehu Furlough to NZ, Italy, Fifth Reinforcements in 1945
Discharged: August 1945
Medals:
- Mentioned in despatches
- 1939-45 Star
- Defence Medal
- War Medal 1939-45
- NZ War Service Medal
- Africa Star
- Italy Star

Martin, Stanley Leonard
Force: NZ Army, Medical Corps 4th Field Ambulance
Rank: Private
Serial no: 8665
Start of service: 4 October 1939
Active service: 1941 Greece, POW 26 April 1941, escaped May 1945
Discharged: 1 October 1945
Medals:
- 1939-45 Star
- Africa Star
- War Medal 1939-45
- NZ War Service Medal

May, Herbert Kelly
Force: NZ Army, 27th Machine Gun Battalion
Rank: Private
Serial no: 8728
Joined up: 1939
Active service: 1940 Egypt, 1941 Greece, Crete, POW May 1941, 29 April 1945 liberated
Discharged: 1945
Medals:
- 1939-45 Star
- War Medal 1939-45
- NZ War Service Medal
- Africa Star

Miles, Cyril David
Force: Royal Navy, Royal Marines
Rank: Royal Marine
Number: PLYX4018
Joined up: 1937
Active service: HMS *Exeter*, sunk 1 March 1942, POW No 364, released 1945

Appendix

Discharged: 1945
Medals:
- Pacific Star
- Burma Clasp
- 1939-45 Star
- General Service Medal

Moncur, Patrick Ernest
Force: NZ Army, Infantry
Rank: Lance Corporal
Number: 48003
Start of service: 1940
Active service: 1941 Egypt, 15 July 1942 captured at the battle of Ruweisat Ridge, POW, escaped, fought with Italian partisans, escaped to Italy, fought with American Army in France, repatriated 8 January 1945
Discharged: 2 July 1945
Medals:
- 1939-45 Star
- War Medal 1939-45
- NZ War Service Medal
- Africa Star

Newlands, Ian Douglas
Force: RNZAF
Rank: Sergeant Pilot
Number: NZ404927
Joined up: 1 December 1940
Active service: 43 Squadron RAF Great Britain, 232 Squadron Great Britain, Africa, HMS *Indomitable,* Singapore, Sumatra and Java, Far East POW 8 March 1942–11 September 1945, FEPOW Hakodate 868
Discharged: 6 March 1946
Medals:
- Atlantic Star
- Pacific

- Africa
- War Medal 1939-45
- Defence Medal

Nissen, Basil Maurice John
Force: NZ Army, Infantry
Rank: Warrant Officer
Serial no: A 570354
Joined up: 1961
Active service: Malaya, Borneo, Vietnam
Discharged: 1988
Medals:
- Long Service and Good Conduct
- Malaya
- Borneo
- Vietnam
- Vietnam – Gallantry

O'Connor, Maurice Edward Odlin
Force: NZ Army, Artillery
Rank: Gunner
Serial no: 21089
Start of service: 1940 (aged 17)
Active service: 1941 Greece, Crete, Desert, POW, escaped through enemy lines
Discharged: 1944
Medals:
- 1939-45 Star
- Africa Star
- Defence Medal
- War Medal 1939-45
- NZ War Service Medal
- Greek Medal

Russell, Robert Patrick
Force: NZ Army, 24th Battalion

Rank: Private
Serial no: 12269
Joined up: April 1940
Active service: Desert campaign Egypt, POW, escaped 8 September 1943
Discharged: 1944
Medals:
- 1939-45 Star
- Africa Star
- Defence Medal
- War Medal 1939-45
- NZ War Service Medal

Scott, Arthur Wallace
Force: NZ Army, 24th Battalion
Rank: Private
Serial no: 62457
Joined up: January 1941
Active service: Desert campaign, POW 22 July 1942, escaped in Italy 11 September 1942, escaped back to Allied lines 13 April 1945, temporary Military Governor of Portogruaro
Discharged: April 1946
Medals:
- 1939-45 Star
- Africa Star
- Italy Star
- Defence Medal
- War Medal 1939-45
- NZ War Service Medal

Made Honorary Italian, 25 April 1995

Smith, Allan Henderson
Force: RNZAF
Rank: Squadron Leader
Serial no: NZ411947
Joined up: March 1941
Active service: March 1942–January 1944 486 NZ Squadron,

January–July 1944 Test Pilot Gloster Aircraft Co, July 1944–December 1944 197 Typhoon Squadron, POW No. 9207 January 1945–May 1945, transferred to reserve 13 December 1945

Medals:
- DFC and Bar
- UK Defence Medal
- NZ Defence Medal
- NZ War Service Medal
- 1939-45 Star
- Air Crew Europe Star
- France and Germany Bar
- Mentioned in despatches

Snelgar, Frank Victor
Force: NZ Army
Rank: Corporal
Serial no: 12127
Joined up: May 1940
Active service: Egypt, Greece, Crete, POW 21 May 1941, escaped 8 June 1941, recaptured 1941, POW, released May 1945
Discharged: 1946
Medals:
- 1939-45 Star
- Defence Medal
- War Medal 1939-45
- NZ War Service Medal

Spiers, John (Jack) Mason
Force: New Zealand Army, attached to 3rd Battalion Royal Australian Regiment (in Korea)
Rank: Major
Serial no: 33391
Joined up: 1949
Active service: Korea, Malaya, Brunei, Borneo, India and Pakistan with the United Nations

Discharged: May 1977
Medals:
- Korea Medal (British)
- Mentioned in despatches
- UN Medal Korea
- NZ General Service Medal Malaya
- British General Service Medal Borneo
- UN Medal Military Observer Group India, Pakistan
- Republic of Korea War Veterans Medal

Stembridge, Irene Gertrude Lloyd (nee Grant)
Red Cross
Voluntary Aide
Service number: 824141
Service: No. 4 General Hospital Pacific (New Caledonia), No. 3 General Hospital Bari (Italy), Clearing Station Florence (Italy), No. 6 General Hospital Florence (Italy)
Awards:
- RSA Merit Award and Certificate

Tomlinson, Jack Vincent
Force: Royal Navy
Rank: Able Seaman
Serial no: 15746
Start of service: December 1935
Active service: HMS *Ardent*, June 1936-April 1937 Spanish Civil War (non-combatant – relief ship), HMS *Firedrake*, 23 March 1939, HMS *Bedouin*, HMS *Bedouin* sunk June 1942, POW 29346
Discharged: 1946
Medals:
- George Cross Island Medal (Malta)
- Great Patriotic War 1941-45 (Russian)
- Defence Medal
- War Service Medal 1939-45
- Italian Medal
- Atlantic Star
- North African Star

Turner, John (Jack) Penman
Force: NZ Army, 27th Machine Gun Battalion
Rank: Sergeant
Serial no: 7055
Joined up: September 1939
Active service: Greece, Crete, captured June 1941, POW, liberated by the Americans April 1945
Discharged: 1945
Medals:
- 1939-45 Star
- Africa Star
- War Medal 1939-45
- NZ War Service Medal

Wright, Cecil Leonard QSM
Force: NZ Army
Rank: Padre
Serial no: 23697
Joined up: 12 March 1940
Active service: 21st Infantry Battalion, 7th Field Company NZ Engineers, 1941 Egypt, Greece, Crete, POW, released 26 April 1945
Discharged: 31 January 1946
Medals:
- Mentioned in despatches
- 1939-45 Star
- North Africa Star
- Defence Medal
- General Service Medal
- New Zealand Service Medal